D0072989

Mozart
on the Stage

Presenting a fresh approach to Mozart's achievements as a composer for the stage, John A. Rice outlines the composer's place in the operatic culture of his time. The book tells the story of how Mozart's operas came into existence, following the processes that Mozart went through as he brought his operas from commission to performance. Chapters trace the fascinating series of interactions that took place between Mozart and librettists, singers, stage designers, orchestras, and audiences. In linking the operas by topic, Rice emphasizes what Mozart's operas have in common, regardless of when he wrote them and the genres to which they belong. The book demonstrates how Mozart's entire operatic oeuvre is the product of a single extraordinary mind and a single pan-European operatic culture.

JOHN A. RICE has taught music history at the University of Washington, Colby College, the University of Houston, the University of Texas, and the University of Alabama (where, in 2005, he occupied the Endowed Chair in Music). He is the author of W. A. Mozart: La clemenza di Tito (1991), Antonio Salieri and Viennese Opera (1998, winner of the American Musicological Society's Kinkeldey Award), Empress Marie Therese and Music at the Viennese Court, 1792–1807 (2003), and The Temple of Night at Schönau: Architecture, Music, and Theater in a Late Eighteenth-Century Viennese Garden (2006).

Sig.ra Andriana Ferrarese, Principal Singer
at the King's Theater.

Tho' sweeter notes than Philomela's Lay,
Melt on her Lips, and snatch the sense away;
Yet 'midst these sounds, new Pleasures are in store,
We now the Singer th'Actress now adore. LR

Adriana Ferrarese, who portrayed Susanna in the 1789 revival of *Le nozze di Figaro* and created the role of Fiordiligi in *Così fan tutte*. This portrait pays tribute to her performances in London in 1785–86, where she sang in both serious and comic opera, winning applause (as the poem attests) for her acting as well as her voice. Engraving by Allanesi. New York Public Library, Muller Collection.

Mozart
on the Stage

JOHN A. RICE

CAMBRIDGE
UNIVERSITY PRESS

CAMBRIDGE UNIVERSITY PRESS
Cambridge, New York, Melbourne, Madrid, Cape Town, Singapore, São Paulo, Delhi

Cambridge University Press
The Edinburgh Building, Cambridge CB2 8RU, UK

Published in the United States of America by Cambridge University Press, New York

www.cambridge.org
Information on this title: www.cambridge.org/9780521016612

First published 2009

Printed in the United Kingdom at the University Press, Cambridge

A catalogue record for this publication is available from the British Library

Library of Congress Cataloguing in Publication data
Rice, John A.
Mozart on the stage / John A. Rice.
     p.   cm.
Includes bibliographical references and index.
ISBN 978-0-521-81634-2 (hardback) – ISBN 978-0-521-01661-2 (pbk.)
1. Mozart, Wolfgang Amadeus, 1756–1791. Operas.   2. Mozart, Wolfgang Amadeus,
1756–1791 – Criticism and interpretation.   3. Opera – 18th century.   4. Opera –
Production and direction – History – 18th century.   5. Opera – Stage-setting and
scenery – History – 18th century.   I. Title.
ML410.M9R538   2008
782.1092 – dc22   2008033466

ISBN 978-0-521-81634-2 hardback
ISBN 978-0-521-01661-2 paperback

For Daniel Heartz
on his eightieth birthday

CONTENTS

ABBREVIATIONS

Anderson   *The Letters of Mozart and His Family*, trans. and ed. Emily Anderson, 3rd edn., New York, 1985

Deutsch   *Mozart: A Documentary Biography*, ed. Otto Erich Deutsch, trans. Eric Blom, Peter Branscombe, and Jeremy Noble, 2nd edn., London, 1966

Eisen   *New Mozart Documents: A Supplement to O. E. Deutsch's Documentary Biography*, Stanford, CA, 1991

MBA   *Mozart: Briefe und Aufzeichnungen*, ed. Wilhelm A. Bauer, Otto Erich Deutsch, and Joseph Heinz Eibl, expanded edn., 8 vols., ed. Ulrich Konrad, Kassel, 2005

MDL   *Mozart: Die Dokumente seines Lebens*, ed. Otto Erich Deutsch, Kassel, 1961

MDL, AC   *Mozart: Die Dokumente seines Lebens*, Addenda und Corrigenda, ed. Joseph Heinz Eibl, Kassel, 1978

MDL, ANF   *Mozart: Die Dokumente seines Lebens*, Addenda, Neue Folge, ed. Cliff Eisen, Kassel, 1997

What possible justification can there be, in the aftermath of Mozart's two-hundred-and-fiftieth birthday in 2006, for adding to the large number of books, many of them first rate, that have been written about his operas?

Most books on the subject, including Edward J. Dent's *Mozart's Operas* and János Liebner's *Mozart on the Stage*, follow a chronological plan, with one or more chapters devoted to each opera. Charles Osborne's *The Complete Operas of Mozart* and William Mann's *The Operas of Mozart* subject each opera to a scene-by-scene description and analysis of its music and plot. Rudolph Angermüller's *Mozart's Operas* is a richly illustrated, chronologically ordered survey.

Carolyn Gianturco, in *Mozart's Early Operas*, uniquely limited herself to the works written before *Idomeneo* (1781); many other books focus on the later operas, beginning with *Idomeneo* or, more rarely, with *La finta giardiniera* (1775). Daniel Heartz's *Mozart's Operas* begins with *Idomeneo*, Stefan Kunze's *Mozarts Opern* relegates the operas written before *Idomeneo* to a single opening chaper, while Nicolas Till's *Mozart and the Enlightenment: Truth, Virtue and Beauty in Mozart's Operas* presents a chronological discussion of the operas from *La finta giardiniera* onward, interspersed with biographical and contextual essays.

Another approach favored by writers on Mozart's operas has been to direct their attention to some but not all of the operas written after *Die Entführung aus dem Serail* (1782). In *Mozart the Dramatist*, Brigid Brophy was largely concerned with *Figaro*, *Don Giovanni*, and *Die Zauberflöte*, while Andrew Steptoe, in *The Mozart–Da Ponte Operas*, discussed the three last opere buffe and their cultural context. Wye Jamison Allanbrook's *Rhythmic Gesture in Mozart: Le nozze di Figaro and Don Giovanni* subjects two of the late operas to a stimulating critical examination.

All the operas from *Idomeneo* on are the subject of individual books. Monographs on *Don Giovanni* and *Die Zauberflöte* alone could fill whole shelves.

The anniversary year saw the publication of several fine books on Mozart's operas. David Cairns, in *Mozart and His Operas*, followed Stefan Kunze in presenting, in chronological order, chapters on all the major operas from *Idomeneo* on after an introductory chapter that quickly covers the operas written before *Idomeneo*. Jessica Waldoff's *Recognition in Mozart's Operas* examines closely a theme of central importance to Mozart and his librettists as they treated it in several operas, from *La finta giardiniera* to *Die Zauberflöte* and *La clemenza di Tito* (mostly in the order in which they were written). Kristi Brown-Montesano's *Understanding the Women of Mozart's Operas* explores the female characters in four of the late operas (*Don Giovanni* followed by *Die Zauberflöte*; *Figaro* followed by *Così fan tutte*), using a broadly chronological framework.

I do not call into question the value of any of these books, or suggest that this one will make any of them less useful. On the contrary: it is the effectiveness with which they have covered their chosen ground that has made this book possible. My predecessors have given me both the freedom and the obligation to do something different.

Only twenty-seven years separated Mozart's momentous encounter, at the age of eight, with opera seria in London and his death in Vienna in 1791. Only twenty-one years separated the first performances of *Mitridate* in Milan (1770) and of *Die Zauberflöte* and *La clemenza di Tito* in Vienna and Prague (1791). The brevity of Mozart's life means that the operatic culture that he entered as a child in the 1760s resembled in many ways the one to which he contributed the masterpieces of his final decade.

Mozart was not only tragically short lived but amazingly precocious. While we might justifiably ignore the teenage works of great operatic composers whose musical development took place at a more normal rate, the experience and skill that the teenage Mozart brought to the composition of his early operas should discourage us from dismissing them as juvenilia. As opera lovers we might legitimately prefer *Tito* to *Lucio Silla* (1772). But as historians and readers of history we should find the earlier work and its context as interesting and as revealing of Mozart's approach to operatic composition as the later one.

The letters of Mozart and his father constitute one of the greatest sources of information about eighteenth-century operatic aesthetics and practices. Many of these letters deal with the early operas. They tell us much more about the composition of *Mitridate*, *Ascanio in Alba*, and *Lucio Silla* than we know about the composition of *Don Giovanni*, *Così fan tutte*, and *Die Zauberflöte*. Only by paying close attention to the early operas can we make full use of what the letters say about Mozart's operatic ideas and working methods.

It is with these thoughts in mind that I propose what anthropologists might call a "synchronic" study of Mozart as a composer of operas: a book organized not chronologically or by individual operas, but by topics as relevant to the early operas as to the late ones. In doing so I hope to emphasize what Mozart's operas have in common, regardless of when he wrote them and the genres to which they belong. I intend to play down some of the more obvious differences between opera seria, opera buffa, and Singspiel, in order to show how Mozart's entire operatic oeuvre is the product of a single extraordinary mind and a single pan-European operatic culture.

Having rejected an approach based on the chronology of Mozart's life, I have adopted another kind of temporal organization, following the process that many eighteenth-century composers went through as they brought operas from commission to performance. This book shows how Mozart – whether he was thirteen or thirty, in Milan or Vienna, writing a Singspiel or an opera buffa – put an opera together in a series of interactions with a libretto (and sometimes – but not always – a poet who wrote or revised the libretto), singers, a stage designer, an orchestra, and an audience.

The chronological framework suggested by the titles of the following chapters is simpler and more rigid than the actual calendar of activities that Mozart faced when he wrote an opera. Many of those activities overlapped. Most if not all of the operas that he wrote from *Idomeneo* on benefitted from close collaboration between him and a librettist, which in some cases took place at more or less the same time as composition. The librettist's work, moreover, was not finished when he completed the text; he often played an important role in staging. In composing arias Mozart normally worked directly with the singers who were to perform them; that collaboration often involved a combination of composition, rehearsal, and revision. Later rehearsals, especially those involving the orchestra, were often attended by members of the court and nobility. Mozart hoped these influential audiences, impressed by what they saw and heard, would spread positive news about the opera that would enhance its effect before the general public. Rehearsals, serving as the eighteenth-century equivalent of theatrical previews, are thus part of the history of an opera's reception. I have tried to do justice to the complexity of the interaction of people and activities that produced Mozart's operas, while at the same time showing how these activities followed a roughly chronological pattern.

This book had its origins in a suggestion made to me in 2000 by Victoria Cooper, Music Editor at Cambridge University Press, to whom I am most grateful for her patience and her continued interest. It includes material that I presented first in the form of lectures given, for the most part, between 2002 and 2006, and I thank those who made those lectures possible. Margaret Butler, formerly of the University of Alabama, invited me to occupy that university's Endowed Chair in Music during November 2005; Christine Getz and Roberta Marvin arranged for me to address the Opera Studies Group at the University of Iowa; and David Buch asked me to give two colloquia at the University of Northern Iowa. To them and to their colleagues and students, with whom I enjoyed many stimulating conversations, I am most grateful.

I read earlier versions of the first chapter at the conference "Der junge Mozart," given by the Internationale Stiftung Mozarteum in Salzburg in December 2005, and at a session devoted to Mozart during the annual meeting of the American Philosophical Society in San Francisco during November 2006. I thank Christoph Wolff, who helped to organize both meetings, for inviting me to take part in them. The discussion of Antonio Baglioni, who created the roles of Don Ottavio and Tito, is based on a talk I gave in Prague in October 2006, at a conference memorably framed by performances of *Don Giovanni* and *La clemenza di Tito* in the theater for which they were written. I am grateful to Milada Jonášová for organizing that conference and for asking me to participate in it.

This book has benefitted from discussion and correspondence with many colleagues other than those I have mentioned already. Mario Armellini, Evan Baker, Karl Böhmer, Daniel Brandenburg, Bruce Alan Brown, Paul Corneilson, Sergio Durante, Dexter Edge, Daniel Heartz, Dorothea Link, Michael Lorenz, and Michel Noiray have generously given me information and advice. Final and special thanks go to Margaret Butler, Daniel Heartz, and Simon Keefe for reading and correcting the manuscript and giving me many suggestions for improving it, and to Bruce Alan Brown for reading the proofs.

   In the many quotations throughout this book from the letters of Mozart and his father and from documents related to Mozart I have translated some passages from the originals myself. Others I have borrowed from Emily Anderson's elegant, lively, and idiomatic translations of the letters – familiar to all English-speaking students of Mozart – and from the translations of the documents by Eric Blom, Peter Branscombe, Cliff Eisen, and Jeremy Noble. I have always checked these translations against the originals, as published in *Mozart: Briefe und Aufzeichnungen* and *Mozart: Die Dokumente seines Lebens*, and have made changes whenever I thought it might be possible to render the meaning more accurately.

ROCHESTER, MINNESOTA

March 2008

CHAPTER 1

Mozart in the theater

The word "miraculous" comes easily to those who think about Mozart's operas. In no genre did he more obviously surpass even the most talented of his compositional contemporaries. Since his training, the operas of other composers, and the musical life that surrounded him in Salzburg, Vienna, and other cities cannot fully account for the perfection of his later operas, we may be tempted to call them miraculous and leave it at that. Yet there is something about Mozart's relations with the theater that may help to explain some of what he achieved as a composer of opera. Throughout his life he was preoccupied with the theater, not only as a composer but as a member of the audience.

Spoken drama as well as opera fascinated Mozart. When he was in Munich writing *Idomeneo* during Fall 1780, he asked his sister Nannerl for a report on the plays performed in Salzburg since his departure. She responded with an annotated list of all the performances he had missed.[1] "My only entertainment is the theater," he wrote Nannerl from Vienna on 4 July 1781. "I wish you were here so you could see a tragedy! On the whole, I know of no theater where all kinds of plays are performed really well. But they are here. Every part, even the smallest and poorest part, is well cast and understudied."[2] (As his fame as a composer grew during the 1780s, he could have had the added pleasure of hearing his own name spoken on the stage of the Burgtheater. In one of the greatest hit plays of the age, August von Kotzebue's *Menschenhaß und Reue* [Misanthropy and Remorse, 1789], the heroine Eulalia speaks of the pleasures of solitude: "I play for myself a sonata by Mozart or sing for myself an aria of Paisiello."[3])

Opera represented for Mozart a kind of alternate reality: a place he could return to in his imagination even when he was physically somewhere else. In November 1771, when he was in Milan to compose, rehearse, and perform *Ascanio in Alba*, his father's illness kept him from attending a performance of

Johann Adolf Hasse's *Ruggiero* (performed in alternation with *Ascanio*). But that did not keep him from enjoying Hasse's music: "Fortunately I know nearly all the arias by heart so I can see and hear it at home in my imagination."[4] Twenty years later his own final illness kept him from attending a performance of *Die Zauberflöte*, according to Ignaz von Seyfried: "On the evening of 4 December [1791] M. lay delirious, imagining he was attending *Die Zauberflöte* in the Theater auf der Wieden; almost his last words, which he whispered to his wife, were, Quiet, quiet! Hofer is just taking her top F; – now my sister-in-law is singing her second aria, 'Der Hölle Rache': how strongly she strikes & holds the B flat: 'Hört! hört! hört! der Mutter Schwur!'"[5]

It was not only on his deathbed that opera pervaded Mozart's thoughts and actions. As an eight-year-old in London, in the midst of the great tour of European capitals that the Mozarts made in 1763–66, he turned his homesickness into thoughts of opera. Leopold reported: "Not a day passes without Wolfgang talking at least thirty times of Salzburg and of his and our friends and patrons. Now he always has an opera in his head that he wants to produce there with several young people."[6] Wenzel Swoboda, a double bass player at the premiere of *Don Giovanni* in Prague in 1787, remembered as an old man "Mozart's habit of laying aside mere speech in favour of musical recitative, which even in public he would use as a means of making remarks and conveying requests to his circle of friends."[7] When Mozart's father, left wifeless in Salzburg when Wolfgang and his mother were in Mannheim in 1777, gave a poor girl a room in his apartment, Wolfgang responded as if anticipating a scene from *Figaro*: "Mamma is burning with indignation, rage, and jealousy at the thought that all Papa has to do is move the chest and open the door to get to that pretty young chambermaid."[8]

Salzburg and Vienna

Mozart's birthplace and the character and interests of the most influential person in his life, his father Leopold, cannot by themselves explain his passion for the theater. Neither the seat of the prince-archbishop of Salzburg nor Leopold was particularly interested in opera. During the 1750s and 1760s, when Mozart was growing up, Salzburg saw the performance of a few Italian operas; but it was no operatic center. Leopold composed prolifically during his early years in Salzburg, but as far as we know he wrote not a single opera. In letters written before his son began to write operas, he showed little interest in or fondness for the genre.

Yet one theatrical genre did flourish in Salzburg. Plays in Latin performed at the Benedictine university gave Mozart what seems to have been his first practical contact with the theater. In 1761 he had a role in *Sigismundus Hungariae Rex*; his name appeared in print for the first time in the libretto published for this production.[9] His appearance in the play had apparently nothing to do with his musical precociousness or training. Yet already as a five-year-old he experienced the thrill of being on stage, the pleasures of costumes, disguises, make-believe, and applause.

In considering the childhoods of other important operatic composers of the second half of the eighteenth century I can think of no similar theatrical debut. I suspect his appearance in a play at so young an age helped establish in his mind a desire that stayed with him throughout his life – a desire, simply put, to be on stage.

That desire surfaced clearly in 1783, when Mozart and a group of family and friends performed a *commedia dell'arte* sketch during a Carnival ball. The twenty-seven-year-old composer wrote to his father from Vienna:

> On Carnival Monday we performed our group's masquerade at the Redoute. It consisted of a pantomime that exactly filled the half hour set aside for it. My sister-in-law was Columbine, I was Harlequin, my brother-in-law Pierrot, an old dancing master (Merk) Pantalone, and a painter (Grassi) the doctor. The plot of the pantomine and the music for it were both by me; the dancing master Merk had the goodness to direct us, and I must say we played charmingly.[10]

Even in the last months of his life Mozart could not resist the urge to appear on stage – in sound if not in person. He wrote to his wife of a performance of *Die Zauberflöte* at which he circulated among the audience:

> But during Papageno's aria with the glockenspiel I went behind the scenes, for I felt an urge today to play it myself. Just for fun, at the point where Schikaneder has a pause, I played an arpeggio. He was startled, looked behind the wings, and saw me. When he had his next pause, I

didn't play it. Now he stopped and refused to go on. I guessed what he was thinking and again played a chord. He then struck the glockenspiel and said "Shut up." Everyone laughed. I think many people learned through this joke that he does not play the instrument himself.[11]

Mozart had relatively few opportunities to act; he sublimated his desire to be on stage into a passion to write operas. That passion differentiated him from some contemporary composers. Haydn, for example, while certainly a willing, skillful, and sometimes inspired composer of operas, never expressed in his letters what Mozart expressed repeatedly – his desire to write operas and the excitement and pleasure he received from their success.

The theater offered Mozart an opportunity not only to be on stage in front of an admiring audience, but also to mingle with a part of society that throughout his life constituted the ideal audience for his talents and accomplishments – the court and the aristocracy. He probably learned to associate the theater with contact with the upper reaches of society before he left Salzburg. But his early travels reinforced this association.

It is not clear whether he actually attended the theater on the first trips, to Munich during Carnival 1762 and to Vienna from September 1762 to February 1763. But we know that Leopold took in an opera in Vienna. He wrote home on 16 October 1762: "We are already being talked of everywhere; and when on the 10th I was alone at the opera, I heard Archduke Leopold say a number of things from his box to another, namely that there was a boy in Vienna who played the Clavier most excellently and so on."[12] From Leopold's letter we could not know that the opera performed that night was Christoph Gluck's epochal *Orfeo ed Euridice*.[13]

Typical of Leopold is his lack of interest in what was happening on stage; typical too was his recognition of the theater as a place of potentially advantageous social interaction. A few weeks later he wrote: "The lady-in-waiting Countess Theresa von Lodron recently conferred a great honor on us. She gave us a box at the play (which is very difficult to get) and gave my Wolferl shoe-buckles, which have little gold plates and look just like solid gold . . . Yesterday we lunched with Herr von Wahlau and in the evening Dr. Bernhard took us to a box at the opera."[14] If this "us" included Wolfgang, then he too witnessed a performance of Gluck's masterpiece.

Mozart, imitating his father, looked to the theater for contact with the court and nobility, contact that raised hopes of presents or even employment. Of the reception of *Ascanio in Alba* in 1771, Leopold wrote home to his wife from Milan:

> His Royal Highness the archduke and the archduchess not only caused two arias to be repeated by applauding them, but both during the serenata and afterwards leaned over from their box to Wolfgang down below and showed their gracious approval by calling out "Bravissimo, maestro" and clapping their hands. Their applause was taken up each time by the nobility and the whole audience."[15]

How similar is Mozart's report, written from Vienna twelve years later, of a concert he gave in the Burgtheater in March 1783 (which included arias from *Lucio Silla* and *Idomeneo*): "the theater could not have been more crowded and every box was full. But what pleased me most of all was that His Majesty the emperor was present and how delighted he was and how he applauded me."[16]

London and Paris

Mozart's travels constituted yet another aspect of his childhood in which he differed from most musicians of his era – they provided him with a vast array of theatrical experiences before the age of twelve, probably before most of his compositional contemporaries saw their first opera. These travels brought him to London, where he lived from April 1764 to July 1765, and where he celebrated his ninth birthday. His experiences in London, more than any other city, including Vienna, represented the single most important turning point in his relations with the theater.

In a letter of 8 February 1765 Leopold discussed Italian opera in London:

> This winter nobody is making as much money as Manzoli and a few others in the opera. Manzoli is getting 1500 pounds sterling for this winter . . . In addition he has a benefit, that is, a night's receipts for himself, so that this winter he will be making more than 20,000 German Gulden. He is the only person whom they have had to pay decently in order to set the opera on its feet again. On the other hand, five or six operas are being performed. The first was *Ezio*, the second *Berenice*, both so-called

pasticci by different masters; the third, *Adriano in Siria*, was newly
composed by Signor Bach. And I know that a newly composed *Demofoonte*
by Vento is coming, and then a couple of more pasticci.[17]

Leopold's principal interest in the London opera was financial – the money
that the musico (or castrato) Giovanni Manzoli made. As for the list of operas
being performed in London, two things stand out: the Italian repertory in
London during the Mozarts' visit consisted entirely of opera seria, and it
was dominated by settings of librettos by Metastasio. Of the four operas
mentioned by Leopold, three were based on librettos by the *poeta cesareo*. So
was the opera organized for Manzoli's benefit performance, a setting by Felice
Giardini of *Il re pastore*.

Compare Leopold's letter with Mozart's experience in London, which also
involved Manzoli, opera seria, and Metastasio (and more specifically two of
the dramas performed in London – *Ezio* and *Demofoonte*). Mozart heard Manzoli
not only on the operatic stage but also in private concerts, such as one given by
Margaret Clive, who wrote on 12 March 1765: "Tomorrow I shall have a great
deal of Company . . . to hear Manzoli sing here, accompanied by Mr Burton
on the harpsichord, on which the little Mozarts, the boy aged 8 and the girl
12 will also play most completely well."[18]

The famous account by Daines Barrington of Mozart's operatic improvisations has been frequently quoted; I do so again to emphasize the difference
between Leopold's reaction to opera in London and that of his son:

> Happening to know that little Mozart was much taken notice of by
> Manzoli, the famous singer, who came over to England in 1764, I said to
> the boy, that I should be glad to hear an extemporary *Love Song*, such as
> his friend Manzoli might choose in an opera.
>
> The boy on this (who continued to sit at his harpsichord) looked back
> with much archness, and immediately began five or six lines of a jargon
> recitative proper to introduce a love song.
>
> He then played a symphony which might correspond with an air
> composed to the single word, *Affetto*.
>
> It had a first and second part, which, together with the symphonies,
> was of the length that opera songs generally last: if this extemporary
> composition was not amazingly capital, yet it was really above mediocrity,
> and shewed most extraordinary readiness of invention.

Finding that he was in humour, and as it were inspired, I then desired him to compose a *Song of Rage*, such as might be proper for the opera stage.

The boy again looked back with much archness, and began five or six lines of a jargon recitative proper to precede a *Song of Anger*.

This lasted also about the same time with the *Song of Love*; and in the middle of it, he had worked himself up to such a pitch, that he beat his harpsichord like a person possessed, rising sometimes in his chair.

The word he pitched upon for this second extempory composition was, *Perfido*.[19]

On the same occasion Mozart and his father sang – at sight – a duet on a text from *Demofoonte*, the boy singing the higher part "in the truest taste, and with the greatest precision," Barrington reported: "His voice in the tone of it was thin and infantine, but nothing could exceed the masterly manner in which he sung." Mozart's singing is also attested to by Charles Burney, who wrote of the young boy's "fondness for Manzoli." Mozart imitated "the several Styles of Singing of each of the then Opera Singers, as well as of their Songs in an Extempory opera to nonsense words – to which were [added] an overture of 3 Movem[ts] Recitative – Graziosa, Bravura & Pathetic Airs together with Several accomp[d] Recitatives, all full of Taste imagination, with good Harmony, Melody & Modulation, after wh[ch] he played at Marbles, in the true Childish Way of one who knows Nothing."[20]

A catalogue of Mozart's works that Leopold compiled in 1768 refers to fifteen Italian arias written in London and shortly thereafter in Holland, but does not name them. They must have included "Va, dal furor portata," Mozart's earliest surviving vocal work, a setting of an aria text from Metastasio's *Ezio* dated 1765. Some of these arias were presumably written-out versions of those he improvised in London; "Va, dal furor portata" (though notated for tenor, and without the word "perfido") could have been the aria of rage that Barrington asked him to improvise (ex. 1.1). (It is also possible, of course, that some of what Barrington took for improvisation was simply Mozart's performance of arias he had composed and memorized earlier.)

In London opera became for the first time a way for Mozart to perform, as he did for Barrington and Burney: a way to earn admiration and praise. And by earning money for Leopold – since Londoners paid to see Mozart

Ex. 1.1   Mozart, "Va, dal furor portata," K. 21, mm. 17–28.

improvise – opera became a way for Mozart to earn his father's approval as well. Earlier in his travels he had amazed and delighted audiences with his sight-reading and improvisation at the keyboard and with his fluent violin playing. But in London he found a new outlet for his talents that allowed him to experience something of the thrill of being on the operatic stage. He wrote no real opera in London, but the "Extemporary opera to nonsense words" that Burney admired was the seed from which his career as an operatic composer grew.

London offered Mozart his first sustained contact with opera seria, a genre that dominated the first half of his career as an operatic composer. From

London also dates his attachment to Metastasio's poetry, and his recognition of it as a potential vehicle for the demonstration of his own talent. Many of his early arias are settings of Metastasio's texts, including several from *Demofoonte* and *Ezio*. Leopold, eager to demonstrate his son's ability as an operatic composer in Vienna in 1768, had Wolfgang compose arias on texts chosen at random from the librettos of Metastasio.[21] Another link in the chain that, in Mozart's mind, connected operatic success with Italian serious opera in general and Metastasio's poetry in particular was a lavish gift that he received in Milan in 1770 from his patron Count Carl Joseph Firmian – an edition of Metastasio's complete works. When Mozart, through Firmian's intercession, received his first commission for an opera in Italy, he recommended that the libretto be one of Metastasio's. Those responsible for choosing the libretto did not follow his advice (the opera was *Mitridate*); but five years later he composed *Il re pastore*, returning to a libretto that he almost certainly saw performed, with Manzoli in the title role, in London. At the end of his life he returned to opera seria and Metastasio for his last Italian opera, *La clemenza di Tito*.

What did Mozart learn from Manzoli in England, and of what did their relations consist? Parallels between his experiences and those of another musician suggest some possible answers. The Irish singer and composer Michael Kelly, born six years after Mozart, enjoyed a series of relations with musici that he recorded in his memoirs and that may help us understand what Mozart gained from Manzoli.

As a boy in Dublin in the early 1770s Kelly, when he was not practicing keyboard, studied singing with Nicolò Peretti, "a *vero musico*" who had sung in Italy, Germany, and London.[22] Later he met another musico:

> I was so fortunate as to be taken great notice of by Rauzzini, during his stay in Dublin. He gave me lessons, and taught me several songs, particularly that beautiful air of his own, which he sang divinely, "Fuggiam da questo loco, in piena libertà" . . .
> Rauzzini was so kind to me, and so pleased with the ardent feeling I evinced for music, that, previously to his leaving Ireland, he called upon my father, and said, "My dear Sir, depend upon it: your son will never follow any profession but that of a musician; and as there is no person in this country who can give him the instruction he requires, you ought to

send him to Italy. He is now at the time of life to imbibe true taste, and in Italy only is it to be found."[23]

Kelly's phrase "taken great notice of " duplicates almost exactly the phrase Barrington used to describe Manzoli's attitude to Mozart. Venanzio Rauzzini (like Peretti and Manzoli) was a specialist in opera seria, a musical genre that Kelly's contemporaries evidently believed to embody the techniques and ideals that serious young musicians were most in need of learning. Rauzzini, like many musici and some tenors too, was a composer as well as a singer – a reminder that the early stages in the musical training of singers and composers involved mastering many of the same skills.

That Manzoli gave Mozart any formal lessons is doubtful: if he had done so, Leopold would surely have mentioned it. But his singing constituted a valuable lesson in itself – in the shaping and spinning out of beautiful melody, in the ornamentation of vocal lines, in the dramatic potential of opera seria. Manzoli's lesson was probably heard and absorbed by Leopold as well as Wolfgang. Rauzzini's recommendation to Kelly's father that he send his son to Italy suggests the possibility that Manzoli made a similar recommendation to Leopold.[24]

Mozart's grand tour of 1763–66 brought him twice to Paris, where he lived for a total of seven months. His experiences with French opera, in so far as they can be extrapolated from Leopold's letters and notes, were very limited. There is no evidence of his presence at a single opera, either an opéra-comique or a tragédie lyrique.[25] Leopold shared with many eighteenth-century German and Italian musicians a distaste for French singing and for what he called *der französische Geschmack* (French musical style), and he passed it on to his son. In cultivating relations with musicians in Paris, Leopold took a particular interest in instrumentalists; he emphasized Wolfgang's talents as a keyboard player and (in the boy's first published works) a composer of keyboard music. Leopold and Wolfgang probably met Marie Fel and Pierre Jélyotte, two of the greatest French opera singers of the time; but in describing Jélyotte as a "singer renowned in France – that is to say, for their taste"[26] Leopold disqualified the tenor from becoming the kind of friend and mentor for Wolfgang that Manzoli was. London put Mozart on the path to success as a composer of Italian opera; Paris (as he experienced it through Leopold) offered him an operatic cul-de-sac. While several leading composers from outside of France, including Gluck, Antonio Salieri, Niccolò Piccinni, Antonio Sacchini, and Luigi Cherubini, wrote some of their finest operas in French and achieved some of their greatest triumphs in Paris, Mozart never wrote an opera in French, in Paris or anywhere else.

Verona and Mannheim

Mozart's experiences in London and Paris and their implications for the future are reflected in an account in Melchior Grimm's *Correspondence littéraire* dated 15 July 1766. Grimm, who lived in Paris, made no mention of any interest that Mozart might have shown in French opera. Instead he referred to Manzoli and to Mozart's singing as it benefitted from Manzoli's example; he raised the possibility (perhaps for the first time in writing) that Mozart would soon compose an opera in Italy: "He has even written several Italian arias, and I have little doubt that before he has reached the age of twelve, he will already have had an opera performed in some Italian theater. Having heard Manzuoli in London all one winter, he profited so well from this that although his voice is excessively weak, he sings with as much taste as soul."[27]

Grimm, a friend of Mozart's father, probably reported Leopold's opinions and ambitions here; he ended his report with exaggerated praise of Leopold's own talents. Despite Leopold's apparent lack of interest in opera, London was a turning point for him as it was for his son, whose experiences there – and in particular his relations with Manzoli – apparently gave Leopold the first idea of making an extended tour of Italy with the goal of making Wolfgang a composer of opera seria.

That idea approached fruition in December 1769, when Wolfgang and Leopold left Salzburg on their first trip to Italy. While Leopold hoped to win an operatic commission for his son, he probably intended the trip to serve above all as an educational experience – a resumption of the initiation into Italian serious opera that had begun in London. He timed the beginning of the trip to coincide with the Carnival opera season.

On 7 January 1770, in one of his first surviving letters, Mozart wrote to his sister of the opera that he had just attended in Verona. It is a fascinating and important letter because it reveals so much about his relations with the theater, bringing together almost every aspect of these relations that I have mentioned here.

The letter begins in German but soon switches to Italian, changes back into German and then Italian, and finally ends in French. This linguistic playfulness is a product of Mozart's travels and a manifestation of his theatricality – a kind of play-acting, an assumption of different roles:

> [German:] I have had an aching feeling, because I have been so long waiting in vain for an answer. I have had good reason too, because I have not yet received your letter. Here ends the German booby and the Italian one begins. [Italian:] You are more fluent in Italian than I had imagined. Please tell me the reason why you did not go to the play which the courtiers acted?
>
> At present we are always hearing operas, which is entitled *Ruggiero*.[28]

Mozart's ungrammatical switch from plural to singular reflects the Italian custom of attending several performances of a single opera, often on successive nights. *Ruggiero* was a serious opera by Pietro Guglielmi, first performed in Venice during the Ascension Fair, 1769, with a libretto by Caterino Mazzolà – the same poet who, twenty-one years later, reworked Metastasio's *La clemenza di Tito* for Mozart.

Playfully confusing the singers with the characters they were playing on stage, Mozart went on to discuss *Ruggiero*. He demonstrated his interest in the singers as people – an eagerness to establish relations with singers that he had shown in London with his friendship with Manzoli (whom he remembered here):

> [Italian:] Oronte, the father of Bradamenta [*recte*: Bradamante], is a prince (played by Signor Afferi), an excellent singer, a baritone, [German:] but forced when he sings falsetto, but not as much as Tibaldi in Vienna.[29] [Italian:] Bradamenta, daughter of Oronte, in love with Ruggiero but [German:] she is to marry Leone, but she does not want him; [Italian:] the part is played by a poor baroness who has had a great misfortune, but I don't know what it was. She is singing [German:] under an assumed name, but I don't know it; [Italian:] her voice is tolerably good and she doesn't look bad, but she sings devilishly out of tune.[30] Ruggiero, a rich prince, in love with Bradamenta, a musico, sings a little in the manner of Manzoli and has a very beautiful, strong voice, and is already old; he is

fifty-five years old and has a [German:] flexible throat.[31] Leone, who is to marry Bradamenta, is very rich, but whether he is rich off the stage, I do not know. [Italian:] He is portrayed by a woman, Afferi's wife.[32] She has a most beautiful voice, but there is so much noise in the theater that one cannot hear a thing. Irene is played by a sister of Lolli, the great violinist we heard in Vienna.[33] [German:] She has a nasal voice and always sings a sixteenth-note too late or too early. [Italian] Ganno [*recte:* Gano] is played by a gentleman whose name I do not know; he is singing for the first time.[34] [German:] After each act there is a ballet. There is a good dancer here called Monsieur Ruesler.[35] He is a German and dances very well.[36]

We get a wonderful sense here of Mozart being fully involved in every aspect of the opera – the plot, the performers (their personalities, their strengths and weaknesses, and their personal histories), and the behavior of the audience. The theater of Verona was not an important operatic center; most of the singers were second-rate and the opera itself of no great significance. Yet Mozart was clearly in his element.

Seven years later, in 1777, Mozart attended a performance of Ignaz Holzbauer's *Günther von Schwarzburg* in Mannheim. The twenty-one-year-old composer, now a mature artist and an experienced writer of operas, responded to Holzbauer's opera with a similar mixture of irreverence and enthusiasm, and with his attention mostly focussed on singers, especially the celebrated tenor Anton Raaff:

> Holzbauer's music is very beautiful. The poetry doesn't deserve such music. What surprises me most of all is that an old man like Holzbauer should still have so much spirit; for you can't imagine what fire there is in the music. The prima donna was Mme. Elisabetha Wendling, not the flutist's wife, but the violinist's. She is always indisposed and, what is more, the opera was not written for her, but for a certain Danzi, who is now in England; so it is not suited to her voice but is too high. On one occasion Raaff sang four arias, about 540 measures in all, in such a fashion as to call forth the remark that his voice was the strongest reason why he sang so badly. Anyone who hears him begin an aria without reminding himself at the same time that it is Raaff, the once famous tenor, who is singing, is bound to to burst out laughing. It's a fact. I thought to myself: "If I didn't know that this was Raaff, I should double up with laughing." As it is, I just pulled out my handkerchief and blew my

nose. Moreover, he has never been, so people here tell me, anything of an
actor; he must be heard but not seen; nor has he by any means a good
presence. In the opera he had to die, and do so while singing a very very
very long, slow aria; he died with a smile on his face, and toward the end
of the aria his voice gave out so badly that one really couldn't stand it any
longer. I was sitting in the orchestra next to the flutist Wendling. He had
objected beforehand that it was unnatural for a man to keep on singing
until he died, as it was too long to wait. Whereupon I remarked: "Have a
little patience. He'll soon be gone, for I hear it." "So do I," he said and
laughed. The second female singer is a certain Mlle. Strasser (but not one
of the Strasser sisters) who sings very well and is an excellent actress.[37]

Mozart's mockery (reflecting a part of his personality that did not win him
any friends) came in for poetic justice three years later, when Raaff, in the title
role of *Idomeneo*, held the success or failure of Mozart's opera in his hands.
His stilted acting and his aging voice were no longer laughing matters.

Returning to Italy and to Mozart's letter of 7 January 1770, we see that the
theater in Verona offered him and his father the same opportunities for social
climbing as theaters everwhere. Wolfgang casually dropped the name of a
nobleman, as proudly as his father had done when writing from Vienna in
1762: "One of the last times we were at the opera (but not the very last time) we
asked the dancer M. Ruesler to come up to our box (for we have free entrance
to the box of Marchese Carlotti, as we have the key) and there we had a talk
with him."[38]

The way to Milan

The next stops on the Mozarts' Italian tour brought Wolfgang back into
contact with Metastasio's librettos. In Mantua he admired *Demetrio* – either
a setting by an unknown composer or a pasticcio, with music by several
composers. In Cremona he saw Angelo Valentini's setting of *La clemenza di
Tito*, experiencing for the first time on stage the drama that he would himself
set to music. His comments on the operas and the ballets that accompanied
them sparkle with theatrical intelligence and earthy humor:

> The opera at Mantua was charming. They played *Demetrio*. The prima
> donna sings well, but very softly; and when you do not see her acting, but
> only singing, you would think she is not singing at all.[39] For she cannot

open her mouth, but whines out everything. However, we are quite accustomed to that now. The seconda donna looks like a grenadier and has a powerful voice too, and, I must say, does not sing badly, seeing that she is acting for the first time.[40] The primo uomo, il musico, sings beautifully, though his voice is uneven. His name is Caselli.[41] Il secondo uomo is already old and I do not like him. His name is —.[42] As for the tenors, one is called Otini.[43] He does not sing badly but rather heavily like all Italian tenors, and he is a great friend of ours. I do not know the name of the other one.[44] He is still young, but not particularly good.

Primo ballerino – good. Prima ballerina – good, and they say she is no dog, but I have not seen her close up. The rest are quite ordinary. A grotesco[45] was there who jumps well, but cannot write as I do, I mean, as sows pee. The orchestra was not bad.

In Cremona it was good. The first violin is called Spagnoletto. The prima donna is not bad; she is quite old, I think, looks like a dog, and does not sing as well as she acts. She is the wife of a violinist who plays in the orchestra; her name is Masi.[46] The opera is called *La clemenza di Tito*. Seconda donna, no dog on the stage, young, but nothing out of the ordinary.[47] Primo uomo, musico, Cicognani – a pretty voice and a beautiful cantibile.[48] The other two castrati, young and passable.[49] The tenor's name is: non lo so.[50] He has a pleasant way with him, and resembles, as though he were his natural son, Leroy in Vienna, who came to Geneva.

Ballerino primo good, Ballerina prima good and a real dog. There was a woman dancer there who did not dance badly and, what is very remarkable, is no dog either off the stage or on it. The others were quite ordinary. A grotesco was there too, who whenever he jumped let off a fart.[51]

Mozart's education in the music and stagecraft of opera and ballet did not keep him from demonstrating, in a series of concerts, his prowess in operatic improvisation and singing. During a concert in Verona "four verses [were] submitted to him, on which he composed on the spot an aria in the best taste in the very act of singing it."[52] And in Mantua "he sang a whole aria extempore, on new words never before seen by him, adding the proper accompaniments."[53]

He continued on to Milan, where he composed several arias in the hope of demonstrating his ability to compose an opera for the court theater. Having improvised an aria on four lines of text, as he had done in Verona, it was

Ex. 1.2 Mozart, "Per pietà, bell'idol mio," K. 78, mm. 1–32.

a small step to put that aria down on paper. One of his earliest surviving arias, "Per pietà, bell'idol mio," K. 78, is a setting of a four-line aria-text from Metastasio's *Artaserse*. Although possibly composed as early as 1766, this simple, tender cavatina in sonata form gives one a good idea of the

Ex. 1.2 (cont.)

kind of music that Mozart, singing "with as much taste as soul," might have improvised in Verona and Mantua (ex. 1.2).

To return to the adjective with which this chapter began, this music is hardly miraculous, but it does demonstrate the high level of craftsmanship that Mozart had achieved as a fourteen-year-old. More important, it is a kind of self-portrait in sound. In this music we can hear not only Mozart the composer, but Mozart the singer and the actor – the performer whose artistic and emotional life was already inextricably tied to the theater.

The Italian tour of 1770–71 brought Mozart into contact for the first time with Italian opera on its native soil and introduced him to the pleasures and headaches of operatic composition and production. This theatrical initiation, moreover, coincided with a physical coming of age. At the beginning of the tour he was a boy soprano, singing to audiences in Verona and Mantua arias that a musico might have sung on the operatic stage. Within a few months the effects of puberty had set in, as described by Leopold on 25 August 1770: "He has no longer any singing voice. It has gone completely. He has neither a deep nor a high voice, and not five pure notes. This annoys him greatly, since he cannot sing his own things, which he sometimes likes to do."[54] I suspect the father was more annoyed than the son at this turn of events, since the ruin of Mozart's soprano voice meant the loss of a source of income for Leopold. More important, it meant that Mozart was growing up, his status as a prodigy would eventually fade, and he would seek a life independent of his father. He would lead much of that life in the theater, depending on its singers to realize the theatrical impulses that, as a boy, he was able to express through his own soprano voice.

CHAPTER 2

Mozart's operas: function, genres, archetypes

Souvenons-nous d'abord qu'un opéra n'est point une tragédie, qu'il n'est point une comédie, qu'il participe de chacune et peut embrasser tous les genres.

Beaumarchais, Preface to *Tarare*, 1787

What purpose did Mozart's operas serve? What role did they play in the culture that produced them? The categories into which music historians of the nineteenth and twentieth centuries divided them will not help to answer these questions. In the sixth edition of the Köchel catalogue, *La finta semplice*, *La finta giardiniera*, the unfinished *Lo sposo deluso*, *Le nozze di Figaro*, and *Così fan tutte* are placed in the category of "opera buffa." *Mitridate*, *Idomeneo*, and *La clemenza di Tito* are called "opera seria"; *Lucio Silla* and *Il re pastore* "dramma per musica"; *Ascanio in Alba* "serenata teatrale"; the unfinished *L'oca del Cairo* and *Don Giovanni* "dramma giocoso." To *Bastien und Bastienne* and the unfinished opera we call *Zaide* is assigned the generic term "Singspiel"; *Die Entführung* is a "komische Singspiel"; *Die Zauberflöte* a "Deutsche Oper."

In the languages used for the generic designations the catalogue makes an implicit distinction between opera in Italian and opera in German – a distinction that suggests some essential difference between them. Within this overall dichotomy, another can be discerned (especially in the category of Italian opera): namely, the distinction between serious opera and comic opera.

Italian vs. German, serious vs. comic: these dichotomies have helped to shape much thought about Mozart's operas, including, for example, Alfred Einstein's chapters "Opera Seria," "Opera Buffa," and "German Opera" in his influential Mozart biography.[1] Mozart certainly used these terms. In the manuscript catalogue of his own works that he compiled from 1784, he used "opera buffa" for *Figaro*, *Don Giovanni*, and *Così fan tutte*, "opera seria" for *Tito*, and "teutsche Oper" for *Die Zauberflöte*. But he and his contemporaries also

19

used other terms, some of which may help us look with fresh eyes at and listen
with fresh ears to his operas. And they may also help us answer the questions
asked at the beginning of this chapter.

Let us begin with Leopold Mozart's account of opera in London during
the Mozarts' visit of 1764–65, quoted in chapter 1. Although from force of
habit we might refer to the works he mentions – *Ezio*, *Berenice*, *Adriano in Siria*,
Demofoonte – as serious operas, it is interesting to note that Leopold referred
to them simply as operas; the only distinction he made was between operas
newly composed by a single musician and others – pasticci – made up of
existing music by several different composers.

On their first trip to Italy, Mozart and his father arrived during Carnival and
began going to the opera as often as they could, in Verona, Mantua, Cremona,
and Milan. Again these operas were of the kind that we generally refer to
as serious operas – Guglielmi's *Ruggiero*, an anonymous *Demetrio*, Valentini's
La clemenza di Tito, and (probably) Piccinni's *Cesare in Egitto*. Yet the Mozarts
referred to them as "operas." Only once during a tour that lasted more than
a year did they acknowledge a distinction between serious and comic opera.
By mentioning explicitly that they had attended the opera buffa in Brescia,[2]
Leopold confirmed the impression that for him and Wolfgang "opera" by
itself meant what we would call serious opera.

Most Italian serious operas of Mozart's day were settings of librettos that
their authors generally called "drammi per musica" – dramas for music. Note
the neutrality of this literary term, corresponding to the Mozarts' tendency
to refer to the setting of such a libretto as an opera pure and simple. Only
toward the end of the eighteenth century did librettists emphasize with any
frequency the seriousness of their librettos with such terms as *dramma serio
per musica* or *dramma tragico per musica*. The dramma per musica tended to avoid
the extremes of tragedy (such as murders and suicides on stage) and comedy
(such as slapstick). Its royal and noble characters came from tragedy; its pairs
of lovers and happy endings from comedy.[3]

Leopold Mozart used the term "opera seria" only when he felt it necessary
to acknowledge the existence of comic opera as something distinct from the
dominant genre. Writing of the projected *La finta semplice* in 1768 he referred to
it first simply as "an opera for the theater." Only later he felt obliged to admit:
"It is not an opera seria, however, for there is no longer any opera seria here and

moreover people do not like it; but rather an opera buffa, but not a short opera buffa but about two and a half or three hours long." In emphasizing the length of *La finta semplice* Leopold was obviously trying to establish the importance of Wolfgang's project, despite the genre that local conditions forced on him. Likewise *La finta giardiniera*, composed for Munich in 1774, was simply an opera until Leopold started to discuss it in conjunction with the serious opera by Antonio Tozzi that he hoped Wolfgang's opera would surpass.

Wolfgang himself was under no such constraints when, in December 1772, he first mentioned comic opera: "I suppose Fischietti will soon be setting to work at an opera buffa, which, when translated, means 'crazy opera.'"[4] For him comic opera represented a kind of deviation from the norm – from the kind of opera he had composed for the Carnival in Milan.

The terms "opera seria" and "serious opera," however convenient, are misleading because they imply a uniform level of seriousness and lack of comedy that ill fits many such operas. Even when drawing a distinction between serious and comic opera Mozart acknowledged a continuum between them:

> I have not the slightest doubt about the success of the opera, as long as the libretto is good. For do you really suppose that I should write an opéra-comique the same way as an opera seria? In an opera seria there should be as little frivolity and as much seriousness and solidity, as in an opera buffa there should be little seriousness and all the more frivolity and gaiety. That people like to have comic music in an opera seria I cannot help. But in Vienna they make the proper distinction on this point.[5]

Mozart made that statement (in a letter to his father dated 16 June 1781) in reference to his projected opera *Die Entführung aus dem Serail*, and it is interesting to note the generic terms he used in connection with this German opera: opéra-comique and opera buffa. At the same time as he granted to serious opera a little frivolity and to comic opera a little seriousness, he alluded to his own project with terms that undercut the validity of historians' distinctions between Italian, French, and German opera.

On another occasion Mozart drew a distinction between French and Italian musical styles, but – again crossing generic borders that we take for granted – he found some contemporary tragédies lyriques, despite the language in which they were sung, more Italian than French. Joseph Frank, in memoirs published in 1852, recalled a conversation with Mozart that presumably took place in Vienna in the 1780s. His report constitutes a rare bit of evidence of the kind of music that Mozart examined in his spare time: "As I always found him busy studying the scores of French operas, I was bold enough to ask if he would not do better to devote his attention to Italian scores. 'In respect to melody yes, but in respect to dramatic effectiveness, no. Moreover, the scores you see here – apart from those of Grétry – are by Gluck, Piccini, and Salieri; they have nothing French about them but the words.'"[6] Assuming Mozart's views are represented here with reasonable accuracy, it is interesting to note that in referring to Italian opera he made no distinction between comic and serious.

Leopold Mozart's emphasis on the length of La finta semplice is not the only instance of his and Wolfgang's differentiating operas by length. Indeed length seems to have served in the eighteenth century as an important marker of genre, cutting across the generic borders that historians have grown used to. Thus Mozart referred to both Holzbauer's Günther von Schwarzburg (the German opera that he saw in Mannheim in 1777) and his own Idomeneo with the term "grosse Opera"; later a similar term ("grosse Oper") was used on the poster advertizing the first performance of Die Zauberflöte (see figure 7.3). When Leopold wrote of "Die operett Bastien und Bastienne, im Teutschen" – "the little opera Bastien und Bastienne, in German" – he first established the length of the opera with the diminutive "operett," and only later, as an afterthought, mentioned the language of its text.[7]

"Viva la libertà": opera as Carnival entertainment

The greatest librettist of dramma per musica – a dramatist and poet whose name became practically synonymous with the genre – was Pietro Metastasio. Between 1723 and 1771 he wrote twenty-seven three-act librettos, whose excellence was recognized by composers, singers, and audiences alike, and over the course of the century composers made hundreds of settings of them. Metastasio brought together elements of early eighteenth-century Italian opera, Italian epic poetry of the sixteenth and seventeenth centuries, and French classical tragedy (Corneille and Racine) to create librettos of great beauty and strength. He based most of them very loosely on historical or quasi-historical

events in Greek or Roman antiquity, and peopled them almost exclusively
with royal and noble characters. In their fine craftsmanship, liveliness, opti-
mism, accessibility, and cosmopolitan appeal to opera-lovers in many parts of
Europe, Metastasio's librettos embody many of the Enlightenment's ideals.
No wonder they appealed so strongly to Mozart, whose exposure to them in
London, Italy, Salzburg, and Vienna we noticed in chapter 1.

The derivation of plots from ancient history, the nobility of characters, the
inevitable triumph of virtue, the highly conventional alternation of recitative
and aria: all these aspects of Metastasian dramma per musica – together with
the term "opera seria" itself – might lead us to think of the operas based
on Metastasio's librettos as unremittingly serious, sober, and predictable: as
a product of the Enlightenment at its stiffest and dullest. Some historians
have dismissed them as just that. Those historians may have forgotten that
dramma per musica was very much a product of the Carnival season for which
it was largely conceived.[8]

"È aperto a tutti quanti/Viva la libertà," says Don Giovanni to the three
masked strangers who silently enter his ballroom in the finale of act 1. His
last three words, taken up by his guests and Leporello, constitute a perfect
motto for a season in which eighteenth-century Europe took a vacation not
only from organized religion but from the Enlightenment as well. The winter
weeks between Christmas and Lent saw a relaxation of codes of conduct, and
the pleasures of food, wine, and sex beckoned temptingly. Masks encouraged
social interaction unthinkable under other circumstances, as Mozart noticed,
to his great pleasure, during the first few days of his first trip to Italy, during
Carnival 1770: "Everyone is masked now and it is really very convenient when
you wear your mask, as you have the advantage of not having to take off your
hat when you are greeted and of not having to address the person by name.
You just say, 'servitore umilissimo, Signora Maschera.' Cospetto di Bacco,
what fun!"[9]

Carnival balls and similar festivities at other times of year often took place
in theaters, with dancing on stage as well as in the auditorium. In some
theaters machinery below the auditorium's floor allowed it to be lifted to
the same level as the stage. If the floor could not be raised, an elaborate
staircase was built in the area where the orchestra usually sat, as in the Teatro
San Benedetto in Venice during Carnival 1782 (figure 2.1), where a dinner and

Fig. 2.1. The stage and part of the auditorium of the Teatro San Benedetto in Venice, for which Mozart won a commission to compose an opera for Carnival 1773 – a contract eventually nullified because it conflicted with his obligations in connection with the composition and rehearsals of *Lucio Silla*. This engraving by Antonio Baratta after a drawing by Giovanni Battista Canal depicts a supper and Carnival ball in honor of Grand Duke Paul Petrovich (heir apparent to the Russian throne) and his wife Sophia Dorothea on 22 January 1782, with decorations by the scenographer Antonio Mauro. It was for the same grand-ducal couple's visit to Vienna a few weeks earlier that Mozart initially planned *Die Entführung aus dem Serail*. Deutsches Theatermuseum, Munich.

ball were given in honor of Grand Duke Paul Petrovich (heir apparent to the Russian throne) and his wife Sophia Dorothea. When Empress Maria Theresa gave birth to Archduke Leopold in 1747, her Milanese subjects expressed their joy with a ball in the Regio Ducal Teatro; there too the difference in height between the auditorium and the stage was bridged with a grand stairway (figure 2.2).[10] Forty-four years after Milan celebrated Leopold's birth, Prague celebrated his coronation as king of Bohemia with an opera, Mozart's *La clemenza di Tito*; a ball in the same theater marked the coronation of his wife (figure 2.3).

Fig. 2.2. Ball in the Regio Ducal Teatro, Milan (1747), in celebration of the birth of Archduke Peter Leopold. Both the Regio Ducal Teatro and Leopold were to play crucial roles in Mozart's operatic career. Engraving by Marc'Antonio dal Re, who (like the artists who made figures 2.3 and 2.4) enhanced the theater's grandeur by greatly reducing the size of the figures in relation to the rest of the image. Raccolta Bertarelli, Milan.

Another Habsburg festivity brought Mozart into a similarly carnivalesque mixture of theater and dance. The celebrations in Milan of the marriage of Archduke Ferdinand (another son of Maria Theresa) and Maria Beatrice d'Este in October 1771 included the following events, as listed in a printed calendar:

Wednesday 16	Opera [Hasse's *Ruggiero*] with illumination of the whole theater
Thursday 17	Serenata [Mozart's *Ascanio in Alba*] in the theater
Saturday 19	Serenata in the theater
Monday 21	Grand ball of His Serene Highness the Duke of Modena
Tuesday 22	Opera in the theater
Wednesday 23	Opera and masked ball in the theater
Thursday 24	Serenata with illuminations in the theater

Fig. 2.3. Ball in the Nostitz Theater, Prague on 12 September 1791 (six days after the premiere of *La clemenza di Tito*) celebrating the coronation of Empress Maria Luisa (wife of Emperor Leopold II) as queen of Bohemia. Detail of an engraving by Philipp and Franz Heger.

Saturday 26	Opera and gala ball at court
Sunday 27	Serenata and masked ball in the theater
Monday 28	Serenata with illuminations in the theater
Tuesday 29	Opera and masked ball in the theater
Wednesday 30	Opera and masked ball at court and in the theater[11]

The Cuvilliés Theater in Munich was the site not only of Carnival operas like Mozart's *Idomeneo* but of balls like one during Carnival 1765 for which the stage was embellished with magnificent decorations (figure 2.4). For those

Prospectus Decorationum festivæ Saltationis, quæ decimo quarto Ianuarij anno millesimo Septingesimo Sexagesimo quinto in Honorem Serenissimæ Dominæ Iosephæ Antoniæ Caroli Septimi Imperatoris gloriosissimæ memoriæ Dominæ Filiæ, jinioris Cæsareæ altitudinis, electæ, ác desponsatæ Regis Romanorum Coniugis apparatu Splendidissimo fuerunt productæ — *Valerian Funck Sculps.*
Ignatius Günter Bresgaviensis del. — *Franc: de Cuvilliés Militaris Architectura Contarius ac Imus Elisabeth Architedus invenit*

Fig. 2.4. Carnival ball (14 January 1765) on the stage of the Cuvilliés Theater in Munich, where sixteen years later Mozart presented his Carnival opera *Idomeneo*. Engraving by Valerian Funck after a drawing by Ignaz Günter, based on designs by François Cuvilliés.

who watched from the boxes, such occasions were spectacles as exciting as the operas with which they shared the stage. And just as Carnival balls became theatrical events, so operatic audiences became crowds of Carnival merrymakers (figure 2.5). The boundary between the stage and the auditorium, like other boundaries characteristic of everyday life, fell victim to the freedoms of the season and of the carnivalesque celebrations with which eighteenth-century subjects acknowledged their rulers' power.

Opera seria put Carnival on the operatic stage: elaborate costumes, disguises, cross-dressing, plots with only the flimsiest resemblance to the historical events on which they are supposedly based, and happy endings. Most

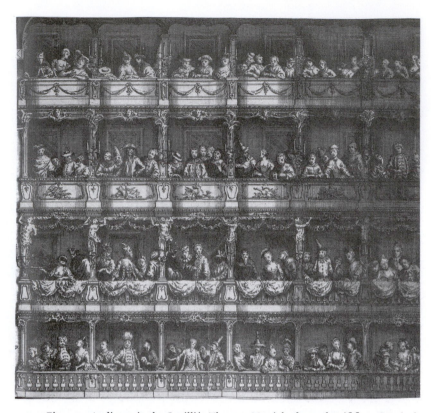

Fig. 2.5. Audience in the Cuvilliés Theater, Munich, dressed as if for a Carnival ball. Detail of figure 8.8.

carnivalesque of all – and most contrary to the spirit of the Enlightenment – was the appearance in opera seria of musici. The passionate declaration of love by men without testicles – at once sad, bizarre, and funny – was an essential element of opera seria throughout the century. Castrated singers, like Mozart's friend and mentor Manzoli, helped make opera seria Carnival entertainment at its most extravagant and exotic.

An engraving by Marc'Antonio dal Re depicts the performance of an opera seria, probably Giuseppe Carcani's *Tigrane* at the Regio Ducal Teatro in Milan during Carnival 1750 (figure 2.6).[12] It suggests something of the festive atmosphere that prevailed in an eighteenth-century theater. Apamia, attended by two pages, stands between cages containing wild animals and expresses

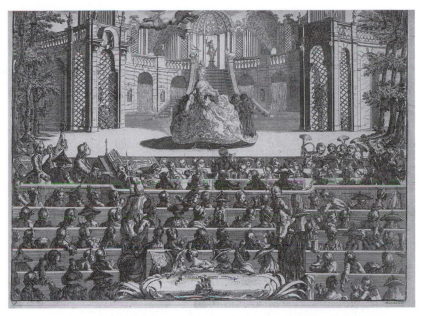

Fig. 2.6. Mid-eighteenth-century Italian operatic performance, probably Giuseppe Carcani's *Tigrane* in the Regio Ducal Teatro of Milan during Carnival 1750. Detail of an engraving by Marc'Antonio dal Re. Raccolta Bertarelli, Milan.

the conflicting emotions that so often torment the characters in dramma per musica. Her elaborate costume corresponds to no historical period – certainly not ancient Asia Minor, where *Tigrane* takes place – but suggests a fantastic world of the imagination, or a Carnival ball. The scenery, painted on a series of flats jutting out from the side of the stage and on a backdrop at the far end of the stage, likewise makes no attempt to represent anything from the real world.

The stage held up to the audience a kind of mirror: a make-believe Carnival reflecting the actual celebration taking place in the auditorium. In the light of candles that continued to flicker throughout the performance, the audience, the orchestra, and the singers enjoyed together an all-enveloping brilliance. The light allowed the audience to divide its attention between the stage and auditorium. Some people wore masks; some showed their backs to the stage and looked around at their neighbors; some engaged in conversation, pointing in various directions; some studied their librettos; some followed the action on stage.

Dal Re's engraving suggests that the seriousness of Carnival opera was one of its less important characteristics. Whether serious or comic, German, Italian, or French, eighteenth-century opera was above all a celebration embodying and expressing the spirit of Carnival.

It is by no means accidental that almost half of Mozart's operas – early and late, and regardless of genre – were first performed during Carnival: *Mitridate* (26 December 1770), *Lucio Silla* (26 December 1772), *La finta giardiniera* (13 January 1775), *Idomeneo* (29 January 1781), and *Così fan tutte* (26 January 1790). (*Der Schauspieldirektor*, a play with music rather than an opera, was also written for Carnival; it was first performed on 7 February 1786.) *Le nozze di Figaro* may have been conceived as a Carnival opera, though its premiere had to be delayed until after the festive season.[13] Most of Mozart's other operas can be understood as products of the transfer of carnivalesque traditions to other times of year in order to celebrate special political events – an archducal wedding (*Ascanio in Alba*), visits of members of royal families (*Il re pastore*, *Die Entführung*, *Don Giovanni*), and a coronation (*La clemenza di Tito*).

Both *Die Entführung*, conceived for a visit to Vienna of the same Russian crown prince whose reception in Venice is illustrated in figure 2.1, and *Don Giovanni*, whose premiere was intended to coincide with a visit to Prague of Archduke Franz (Leopold's son and successor) and his sister Maria Theresa and to celebrate Maria Theresa's wedding to Prince Anton of Saxony, came to the stage late, and well after the visits for which they were originally intended. In Prague, the festive function that *Don Giovanni* was meant to serve was served instead by a performance of *Figaro*. An account of that performance in a Prague newspaper conveys the carnivalesque qualities of the occasion:

> At half-past six o'clock [Their Highnesses] betook themselves to Count Nostitz's National Theater, embellished and illuminated for this occasion in a very distinguished manner. The auditorium was so much glorified by the finery of the numerous guests that one had to admit never having beheld such a magnificent scene. At the entry of Their Highnesses they were greeted with the most evident marks of joy by the whole public, which they acknowledged with gracious gratitude. At their request the well-known opera *Die Hochzeit des Figaro*, generally admitted to be so well

performed here, was given. The zeal of the musicians and the presence of Mozart, the composer, awakened a general approbation and satisfaction in Their Highnesses. After the first act a sonnet, ordered by several Bohemian patriots for this festivity, was publicly distributed.[14]

Dramma per musica and dramma giocoso per musica: *Semiramide* and *La finta giardiniera*

Metastasio's *Semiramide*, written for the Roman Carnival of 1729, is one of his most entertaining librettos, and contains some good examples of his comic talents. Mozart never set it to music, but he did write an opera, *La finta giardiniera*, that shares with *Semiramide* some important elements of plot. Thinking about Metastasio's libretto and Mozart's opera together may help us see the generic boundary between dramma per musica and dramma giocoso per musica as unnecessarily rigid.

The plot of *Semiramide* – while worked out with the clockwork precision and ingenuity characteristic of Metastasio – is itself so wonderfully and patently preposterous as to be funny. At some time before the action begins the Indian prince Scitalce, having been told that his beloved Semiramide was unfaithful to him and intended to kill him, stabbed her and left her for dead. (The wicked, deceitful Sibari, who also loved Semiramide, had given Scitalce this information, which was entirely false.) Semiramide survived the attack, and married the king of Babylonia. After his death, she ruled Babylonia disguised as her son Nino, since he, although heir to the throne, was too weak to rule. (As originally sung in Rome, where female sopranos were not allowed on stage, Semiramide was created by a musico, adding an extra layer of sexual ambiguity to the role.)

As the drama begins, Semiramide, acting as King Nino, supervises the choosing of a husband for Princess Tamiri. Three princely suitors arrive to compete for Tamiri's hand: the Egyptian Mirteo, the Scythian Ircano and, to Semiramide's shock, Scitalce, who is unaware that Semiramide is alive. The rivalry for Tamiri's hand and the amatory conflict between Semiramide and Scitalce (who, until near the end of the drama, believes he was justified in trying to kill Semiramide) are the two primary strands out of which Metastasio wove his drama, which ends with the revelation of Semiramide's identity and of Sibari's deceit, the reconciliation of Semiramide and Scitalce, and the engagement of Tamiri and Mirteo. (The names of the characters – three of which share the syllable "mir" and two of which are partially anagrammatic – add to the libretto's playfulness and quality of carnivalesque make-believe; one thinks of Tamino/Pamina and Papageno/Papagena, Bastien/Bastienne, Vitellia/Servilia, Sandrina/Arminda and Arminda/Ramiro in *La finta giardiniera*, Fracasso/Cassandro in *La finta semplice*, and Cecilio/Celia in *Lucio Silla*.[15])

The violent, uncouth barbarian prince Ircano, whose role one might almost call a *parte buffa*, makes a comic impression on his first appearance. Tamiri's three suitors arrive together; Mirteo tries to address Semiramide, but Ircano keeps interrupting him:

MIRTEO	Al tuo cenno, gran re, deposte l'armi,	Having laid down his arms at your command, great king,
	Si presenta Mirteo. L'Egitto . . .	Mirteo introduces himself. Egypt . . .
IRCANO	(*a Mirteo, interrompendolo*) Odi. La bella Che fra noi si contende, È quella?	(*to Mirteo, interrupting him*) Listen, the beautiful woman for whom we compete, is it she?
MIRTEO	(*ad Ircano*) È quella. (*a Semiramide*) L'Egitto è il regno mio . . .	(*to Ircano*) It is she. (*to Semiramide*) Egypt is my kingdom . . .
IRCANO	(*a Semiramide, interrompendo Mirteo*) Del Caucaso natio Vien dal giogo selvoso	(*to Semiramide, interrupting Mirteo*) From the forested mountains of his native Caucasus, comes
	L'arbitro degli Sciti amante e sposo.	the master of the Scythians, lover and bridegroom.
MIRTEO	Ircano, a quel ch'io veggo, Tu d'Assiria i costumi ancor non sai.	Ircano, from what I see, you do not yet know customs of Assyria.
IRCANO	Perché?	Why?
SEMIRAMIDE	Tacer tu dei: Parli il prence d'Egitto.	You must be quiet: let the prince of Egypt continue.

IRCANO	In Assiria il parlar dunque è delitto? (*si ritira indietro*)	In Assyria then speaking is a crime? (*he retires to the rear*)

(Metastasio, Semiramide, Act 1, Sc. 3)

Later in the opera Ircano learns of Sibari's plan to murder Scitalce by poisoning the drink that Tamiri is to give Scitalce as a sign that she offers him her hand in marriage. Scitalce is about to drink the poison (that is, he is about promise to marry Tamiri) when his love for Semiramide keeps him from doing so. Having been refused by Scitalce, Tamiri now offers her hand to Ircano by passing the drink to him. Ircano's surprise and confusion at this turn of events is amusing.

Mozart's *La finta giardiniera* is a setting of a libretto of unknown authorship, first set to music by Pasquale Anfossi in Rome in 1774. This dramma giocoso per musica grows out of a dramatic situation all but identical to the one that launches *Semiramide*: Contino Belfiore, groundlessly jealous of his lover Violante, has stabbed her and left her for dead. But Violante has survived and, pretending to be the gardener Sandrina, has entered the service of Don Anchise, mayor of Lagonero, who falls in love with her. Belfiore arrives in Lagonero intending to marry Anchise's niece Arminda. In the finale of act 1 Belfiore recognizes Violante, who accuses him of betrayal:

Barbaro senza fede,	Cruel man without faith,
È questa la mercede	is this the reward
Del mio costante amor?	for my constant love?

Violante's question echoes Semiramide's, addressed to Scitalce, in act 3 of Metastasio's drama:

È questa la mercede	Is this the reward
Che rendi a tanto amore,	that you give me for so much love,
Anima senza legge e senza fede?	soul without law and without faith?

After much confusion and excess of sentiment that lead Belfiore and Violante to temporary spells of madness, she reveals her identity and forgives him, he breaks off his engagement to Arminda, and the opera ends with a celebration of the marriage of Belfiore and Violante (as well as the marriages of two subsidiary couples).[16]

There is more comedy in *La finta giardiniera* than in *Semiramide*, of course; and that is enough to justify our calling the one a comic opera and the other a serious opera. But those terms, by themselves, obscure the fundamental similarities between Mozart's opera and Metastasio's libretto – two dramas located on different parts of a continuum between tragedy and comedy. Mozart made a musical allusion to the connections between dramma per musica and dramma giocoso per musica in the *introduzione* – the opening ensemble – of *La finta giardiniera*, the principal melody of which he took from the concluding *finale col coro* of his previous opera, *Lucio Silla*. Daniel Heartz, in pointing this out, remarked: "the composer literally picks up where he left off in the operatic domain."[17]

An archetypal plot: two lovers and a second man

The broadly similar function that most of Mozart's operas served helps to explain why most them, regardless of operatic subgenre, language, or place of performance, can be understood as elaborations of a single basic dramatic archetype. A young man and a young woman love one another, but their path to married happiness is blocked by a second man, older and/or more powerful (the "obstructing character" in Northrop Frye's classification of dramatic archetypes[18]), who often gives the opera his name. The young lovers eventually overcome the obstacles in their way, while the second man remains alone. Jessica Waldoff has pointed out that this resolution typically arrives by way of what she calls a recognition scene: "The conclusions of these operas, whether buffa or seria, whether Italian or German, culminate in a truth that recognition brings, not for the individual alone, but for the whole stage and the world it represents."[19] Table 2.1 is a list of all of Mozart's operas save one (*La finta semplice*, which does not use the archetype in question); in column 2 are the pairs of young lovers at the center of each opera; in column 3 the second men.

Mary Hunter, focussing on Italian comic operas performed in Vienna during the 1770s and 1780s, sees this repertory as representing several plot archetypes, one of which, exemplified by *Le nozze di Figaro*, she describes as the "theme of a virtuous lower-class woman importuned by a nobleman and

Table 2.1. *Operas by Mozart based on the archetype of two lovers and a second man*

Opera	Pair(s) of Lovers	Second Man
Ascanio in Alba	Ascanio, Silvia	Aceste
Bastien und Bastienne	Bastien, Bastienne	Colas
La clemenza di Tito	Sesto, Vitellia	Tito
Così fan tutte	Ferrando, Dorabella Guilelmo, Fiordiligi	Alfonso
Don Giovanni	Ottavio, Anna Masetto, Zerlina	Giovanni
Die Entführung aus dem Serail	Belmonte, Constanze	Selim
La finta giardiniera	Belfiore, Violante	Anchise
Idomeneo	Idamante, Ilia	Idomeneo
Lucio Silla	Cecilio, Giunia	Silla
Mitridate re di Ponto	Sifare, Aspasia	Mitridate
Le nozze di Figaro	Figaro, Susanna	Almaviva
Il re pastore	Aminta, Elisa	Alessandro
Zaide	Gomatz, Zaide	Soliman
Die Zauberflöte	Tamino, Pamina	Sarastro

eventually allowed to return to her proper lover."[20] A second archetype, involving the "triumph of young love over rigidity, lust, or greed in the form of a father, uncle, or guardian who tries to prevent his daughter, niece, or ward from marrying the young man of her choice," is exemplified by Giovanni Paisiello's *Il barbiere di Siviglia*.[21] A third archetype

> involves elopement or abduction. Here an already married or betrothed couple find themselves in a foreign environment, with the heroine about to be wed to the local ruler or patriarch; sometimes (as in Mozart's *Die Entführung* and Haydn's *L'incontro improvviso*) the heroine spends some time alone in the exotic location before the hero finds her. The happy outcome in this case always depends on the generosity of the ruler or head of household.[22]

I would argue that all three of these plot archetypes constitute subcategories of the more basic archetype presented here, which covers serious as well as comic opera, German as well as Italian.

In several of Mozart's operas the second man is sexually or amorously attracted to the young woman. The Roman dictator Lucio Silla wants to marry Giunia; only when he gives her up to Cecilio can the young lovers find happiness. Mitridate, similarly, is engaged to Aspasia, who loves Mitridate's son Sifare. In *Zaide* and *Die Entführung* Soliman and Pasha Selim are attracted to Zaide and Constanze; Constanze's refusal inflames Selim's passion, just as Lucio Silla admits that he finds Giunia attractive despite her resistance.[23] Don Anchise, the mayor of Lagonero in *La finta giardiniera*, wants to marry his gardener Sandrina (he is unaware that she is really the Marchesa Violante in disguise). And in *Figaro* Count Almaviva, already married, wants to seduce Susanna.

In the other operas the second man has other reasons to frustrate the desires of the young lovers, or does so unintentionally. Colas, in *Bastien und Bastienne*, keeps the young lovers apart – by advising Bastienne to pretend that she no longer loves Bastien – only to strengthen their love for one another. Idomeneo, in sending his son Idamante into exile (and separating him from Ilia), hopes to avoid having to fulfill the vow he made, during a storm at sea, to sacrifice to Neptune the first person he saw on reaching land. In *Il re pastore*, Alessandro, unaware that young Aminta loves Elisa, arranges for him to marry someone else. Sarastro keeps Tamino and Pamina apart until Tamino proves himself wise and virtuous. Aceste, in *Ascanio in Alba*, resembles Sarastro in being a high priest who acts as a guardian for a young woman, Silvia. She loves a man whose face she has seen in a dream. Aceste, in telling Silvia that she is to marry Ascanio, causes her distress because she believes that she will not be able to marry her true love. But – symptomatic of this opera's lack of dramatic tension – Silvia's distress is shortlived; Aceste tells her almost immediately that the man of her dreams is in fact Ascanio.

Two of Mozart's late operas, *Don Giovanni* and *Così fan tutte*, represent a variation on the archetype in which the second man interferes with the marriage of not one but two young couples. (There are subsidiary couples in several of Mozart's operas – for example, Annio and Servilia in *La clemenza di Tito*, Agenore and Tamiri in *Il re pastore*, Pedrillo and Blonde in *Die Entführung* – but only in *Don Giovanni* and *Così fan tutte* are the two couples of equal importance.) Don Giovanni tries to seduce both Donna Anna and Zerlina; and in killing Anna's father he sets in motion events that will delay her marriage to Don Ottavio by at least a year. Don Alfonso first separates two pairs of lovers by proving to Guilelmo[24] and Ferrando that their fiancées are capable of infedelity, and then reunites them. In doing so, he plays a role analogous to, and probably inspired by, that of the magician Trofonio in Salieri's *La grotta di Trofonio*, another opera in which the archetypal pair of young lovers has been doubled.[25]

La clemenza di Tito offers another variation on the archetype. Vitellia and Sesto make an odd pair of operatic lovers in that Vitellia's feelings for Sesto are, until near the end of the opera, entirely overwhelmed by her desire to avenge the death of her father at the emperor's hand and by her ambition to be empress herself. Tito fulfills the conventional role of second man by asking for Vitellia's hand in marriage, unaware that Sesto loves her. But Tito decides to marry Vitellia only after she has seduced Sesto into taking part in a plot to assassinate the emperor. The opera's ending leaves in doubt the future relations of Sesto and Vitellia.

Although the archetypal second man is left alone at the end of most of Mozart's operas, in three exceptional cases he has a different fate. Count Almaviva, having failed to seduce Susanna, returns to married life with Countess Rosina. And in two operas the second man dies. The last words of Mitridate, mortally wounded, are "Moro felice appieno" (I die supremely happy), while Don Giovanni can only cry out "Ah!" as he descends into the flames. Neither Mitridate nor Giovanni takes part in the last ensemble of the opera named after him.

Mozart normally differentiated the young male lover from the second man by writing the role of the younger man for a singer with a higher voice. In his settings of drammi per musica, the highest male voices are those of musici, who created the roles of Sifare, Ascanio, Cecilio, Aminta, Idamante, and Sesto. The second man in these operas – Mitridate, Aceste, Lucio Silla, Alessandro, Idomeneo, and Tito – is a tenor. In the German operas and the comic operas in Italian, the second man is a bass or baritone, except in three cases (in the harem operas Sultan Soliman is a tenor and Pasha Selim does not sing at all; in *La finta giardiniera* Anchise is a tenor), while the young male lovers are tenors, with three exceptions: Figaro, Masetto, and Guilelmo. In writing these parts for basses, Mozart called attention to the important ways in which these characters differed from the archetypal young lover. Figaro is not necessarily younger than the count, nor is Masetto necessarily younger than Don Giovanni. Figaro and Masetto are both of humble birth (young lovers are often noblemen). Masetto and Guilelmo are both "extra" young lovers, their bass voices differentiating them musically from Don Ottavio and Ferrando. In Paisiello's *Il barbiere di Siviglia*, Count Almaviva, a young lover, is a tenor; in Mozart's *Figaro* the count, now second man, is a baritone.

These characters interact in settings far from the real world of the audience and performers – but in some ways close to the make-believe world of Carnival. Operas take place in a fairy-tale realm with ancient Egyptian elements (*Die Zauberflöte*), Homeric Crete (*Idomeneo*), the Middle East recently conquered by Alexander the Great (*Il re pastore*), Asia Minor (*Mitridate*), ancient Rome (*Tito*, *Lucio Silla*), Muslim North Africa (*Die Entführung* and probably *Zaide*), or bizarre versions of modern Italy and Spain in which Christianity does not exist. (The wall that protected Carnival from religious interference also kept opera from incorporating explicitly Christian elements. References to Christ, the Trinity, and the saints were strictly banned.)

The remarkable letter that Mozart wrote from Verona during Carnival 1770 (quoted and discussed in chapter 1) expresses the excitement he felt on seeing his first opera in Italy. A few words of his description of the opera – "Oronte, the father of Bradamante, is a prince played by . . . a baritone . . . Ruggiero, a rich prince, in love with Bradamante, a musico" – are enough to let us know that Guglielmi's *Ruggiero* was yet another elaboration of the archetype that would serve Mozart well throughout his career. By 1770 he had seen so many operas and read so many librettos that the archetype from which many of them were derived was probably second nature to him: something to be noticed only when it was absent. From the relations between Bradamante, Ruggiero, and Oronte – a pair of lovers and a second man – Mozart drew his wonderfully diverse operatic oeuvre.

CHAPTER 3

Commissions, fees, and the origins of Mozart's operas

Eighteenth-century writers occasionally sent librettos to composers in the hope of having their words set to music and performed on stage. No dramatist aimed higher in her musical aspirations than the novelist and playwright Isabelle de Charrière, so proud of her libretto *Les Phéniciennes* (The Phoenician Women) that she thought of Mozart, Paisiello, Salieri, Domenico Cimarosa, and Giuseppe Sarti as possible collaborators. In 1788 she sent the libretto to Mozart in Salzburg, unaware that he had not lived there since 1780. Receiving no response, she consoled herself with the thought that he did not, after all, suit her needs: "In Vienna M. Stahl knows Salieri and believes that the Phoenician women would not fare badly in his hands . . . He has certainly written some nice numbers in *Tarare* and he knows French perfectly. As for Mozart, whom he also knows, he does not find his genius sufficiently controlled by taste and experience."[1] In the end *Les Phéniciennes* received no musical setting.

That Mozart ever saw Charrière's libretto is doubtful; but he did receive, three years earlier, a libretto in the mail from another dramatist, Anton Klein, with a request that he set it to music. Firmly established in Vienna as a freelance musician and a veteran composer of operas, Mozart responded diplomatically, asking for more time and more information: "If I should feel inclined to set it to music, I would like to know beforehand whether its production has actually been arranged for a particular place; since a work of this kind, from the point of view both of the poetry and the music, deserves a better fate than to be composed to no purpose."[2] In that sentence he expressed plainly an attitude that he shared with most composers of his age. No matter how attractive an operatic project might be from a purely artistic point of view, a composer rarely put music on paper without a reasonable expectation that it would be paid for and without knowing where, when, and by whom it would be performed.

Teachers of composition sometimes assigned the writing of an opera to an advanced student as a pedagogical tool. Paisiello gave his student Giacomo Ferrari a libretto by Carlo Goldoni, *Le pescatrici*, to set to music.[3] Under the tutelage of Florian Gassmann the young Salieri wrote several "small compositions that were to serve as preparations for larger works," including an Italian opera, *La vestale*.[4] Salieri later taught composition to Joseph Weigl, whom he directed to compose *La sposa collerica*.[5] None of these operas was apparently performed in public. Indicative of Mozart's childhood talent is that he apparently skipped this purely pedagogical stage of operatic composition. The first act of the sacred drama *Die Schuldigkeit des ersten Gebots*, which the eleven-year-old composed in Salzburg in early 1767 and which constitutes his first known large-scale theatrical work, was no schoolboy exercise: it was performed in public in March 1767.

The arrangements by which composers came to understandings with impresarios and other theatrical managers fall into several categories. In Italy they usually took the form of *scritture*: commissions for individual operas, formalized by contract. Many theaters outside Italy engaged music directors whose responsibilities included the composition of operas. In exchange for a salary, and sometimes a future pension, the Kapellmeister or maestro di cappella promised to compose a certain number of operas per year.[6] That was sometimes the case in Vienna; during the 1790s Weigl and Salieri both agreed to supply the impresario Peter von Braun with new operas every year.[7] But during Mozart's residence in Vienna, when Emperor Joseph II managed the court theaters through his chamberlain Count Franz Xaver Rosenberg, a more informal policy for operatic commissions (commissions that did not necessarily involve written contracts) allowed a wide range of composers to write operas for the court theaters. And these composers earned an equally wide range of fees.

The origins of Mozart's operas reflect, in their variety, the variety of arrangements under which eighteenth-century operas came to be written. He wrote his early Italian operas under the terms of scritture. The operas that he composed for Munich and Prague, *La finta giardiniera*, *Idomeneo*, *Don Giovanni*, and *La clemenza di Tito*, probably fulfilled the terms of contracts (although no copies of the contracts have apparently survived). In Vienna he quite successfully adapted to a theatrical administration in which personal relations and the emperor's whim often played a role in operatic decision-making, bringing four operas to the stage of the Burgtheater – *Die Entführung aus dem Serail*, *Le nozze di Figaro*, a revised version of *Don Giovanni*, and *Così fan tutte*. With the death of Joseph II in 1790 and the accession of Leopold II, whose theatrical tastes and policies led to a repertory in the court theaters in which the operas that Mozart, Salieri, and Vicente Martín y Soler wrote during the 1780s had little place, Mozart declared his independence of the court theaters by agreeing, for the first time since his arrival in Vienna in 1781, to write an opera for one of the suburban theaters, Emanuel Schikaneder's Theater auf der Wieden.

An impresario's contract

In the case of one of Mozart's operas a document survives that gives us an overview of the entire process of creating and performing an opera, and an insight into the role that the composer played in that process. The document vividly illustrates the centrality of the roles of the impresario and of singers in the opera business. On 8 July 1791 representatives of the Estates of Bohemia – for all practical purposes, the Bohemian nobility and the Catholic Church – concluded with Domenico Guardasoni, impresario of the Italian opera in Prague, an agreement in which Guardasoni promised to present, two months later, a "grand opera seria" to celebrate the coronation of Leopold II as king of Bohemia. Here is part of the contract:

> Specification of the items that I, the undersigned, promise the exalted Estates of Bohemia to honor, and that I require of Their Excellencies, above mentioned, in connection with a grand opera seria to be performed in this National Theater on the occasion of the coronation of His Imperial Majesty within the space of the beginning of the month of September next, when I will be presented and granted six thousand Gulden, or six thousand five hundred, if the musico should be Marchesi.
>
> First, I promise to give them a primo musico of the first rank, for example either Marchesini or Rubinelli, or Crescentini, or Violani, or another, as long as he is of the first rank. Likewise I promise to give them a prima donna also of the first rank, and certainly the best of that rank who is free, and to fill the rest of the cast with members of my own company.
>
> Second, I promise to have the poetry of the book composed on one of the two subjects given to me by His Excellency the governor and to have it

set to music by a famous composer; but in case it may not be possible to do that because of the shortness of time, I promise to procure an opera newly composed on the subject of Metastasio's Titus.

Third, I promise to have two new changes of scenery made expressly for this spectacle. Likewise I promise to have new costumes made, and especially for the leading roles in the opera.

Fourth, I promise to illuminate and to decorate the theater with garlands, to present the said opera complete, and to perform it gratis for one evening, to be specified by the High Estates, within the above mentioned time.[8]

In the order in which he listed his promises, Guardasoni made clear his priorities and those of his patrons. His most important and expensive task was to engage the singers, of whom the musico was of paramount interest. The representatives of the Estates were so eager to have the great Luigi Marchesi sing at the coronation that they were willing to pay Guardasoni an extra 500 Gulden if he could manage to engage him. That the prima donna mattered less to the Estates is suggested by the absence of the names by which they could have, if they had wished, more clearly defined what was meant by "a prima donna also of the first rank."

The next priority was the libretto, about which the representatives of the Estates felt strongly enough that they supplied Guardasoni with the choice of two subjects for a new libretto. The impresario, for his part, was so concerned that time might be too short for a new libretto to be written that he gave himself a loophole: if necessary the opera could be a new setting of an old libretto by Metastasio.

Evidently the representatives of the Estates had no particular interest in who would compose the music for the coronation opera, as long as he was "un celebre Maestro." And Guardasoni, in agreeing to this stipulation, was reasonably confident that he would be able to persuade such a composer to write the score and to bring it to performance in less than two months.

Guardasoni mentioned in the contract his intention of going to Vienna as part of a trip that would eventually take him to Italy. In Vienna he repeatedly asked Salieri to write the coronation opera.[9] It was presumably after Salieri refused that he turned to Mozart, who interrupted his work on *Die Zauberflöte* to write *La clemenza di Tito*.

We tend to think of Tito, like all of Mozart's operas, as a more or less immutable work of art embodied in the musical score. But for those who commissioned it, Tito was an event – one of several events organized to celebrate a coronation – in which the score was by no means the most important element. Mozart probably felt the same way. When he attended his first operas in Italy, in Verona, Mantua, and Cremona during Carnival 1770, he wrote excitedly (in letters quoted in chapter 1) of the singers, the plots, the masks worn by members of the audience, the noise in the auditorium, the dancers; but he rarely mentioned the music and never the name of a composer.

The Italian operatic season and the scrittura

Librettos published for the performance of operas in most Italian cities during the eighteenth century mention a season (Spring, Summer, Fall, or Carnival) or an occasion (a royal birthday or nameday in Naples, the Ascension Fair in Venice). The operatic calendar was organized around such occasions and seasons.

Carnival, the most important season (and the only operatic season in Rome), usually ran from the day after Christmas to the beginning of Lent; in Rome it did not usually begin until Epiphany – 6 January. (Throughout this book I will follow the eighteenth-century practice of referring to a particular Carnival by the year in which it ended; thus the Carnival that began in Milan on 26 December 1770 with the premiere of Mozart's *Mitridate* was Carnival 1771.) Most theaters presented two operas during Carnival, the second replacing the first around the end of January or the beginning of February (depending on the popularity of the first opera and the length of the season, which itself depended on where the beginning of Lent fell in the calendar). Impresarios who ran the theaters generally assembled singers for a single season, at the conclusion of which these singers dispersed to other cities in preparation for the next season.

Only the theaters in a few major cities, including Venice, Milan, Turin, Rome, and Naples, specialized in the performance of new works. For the impresarios of such theaters each new season required, in addition to the engagement of a company of singers, the commissioning of operas from one or two composers, preferably other than those who had presented operas in the previous season. The contracts enabled the impresario responsible for organizing a particular season to know several months in advance what singers would perform during a particular season and what composer – if the impresario intended to present a new opera – would write the music. They enabled itinerant singers and composers to plan their travels around Italy.

Engaging singers

The first step in organizing an operatic season was often to engage the leading singers, especially the musico.[10] The most important theaters often had to put singers of the first rank – singers in demand all over Europe – under contract more than a year in advance. The Teatro Regio in Turin, for example, engaged the great soprano Caterina Gabrielli for Carnival 1762 with a contract dated 18 February 1760 (almost two years earlier).[11] In less important theaters impresarios generally waited longer to engage singers who had not been snapped up earlier by the major houses. Guardasoni, in promising less than two months before the premiere of Mozart's *Tito* to bring to Prague a musico and a prima donna of the first rank, must have been counting on the month of September, when the opera was to be performed, to be a period of relatively little operatic activity in Italy.

In the case of Mozart's first Italian opera, *Mitridate*, two of the three principal singers, the prima donna and the tenor, had been engaged before the composer received his contract in March 1770 (about nine months before the premiere). In the same letter in which Leopold announced that Wolfgang would write the opera, he mentioned that three of the singers had already been engaged: "The prima donna and seconda donna are Signora Gabrielli and her sister. The tenor is Signor Ettore . . . The primo uomo and the others have not yet been chosen. Possibly Manzoli will sing."[12]

The very early engagement of the principal singers came with the risk that such singers might, on one pretext or another, break their contracts, leaving an impresario scrambling for replacements. That seems to have happened with *Mitridate*. Within a month of Mozart's joining the project Gabrielli's participation came into doubt, while Manzoli's had become definite, if we are to believe what the composer wrote from Rome on 21 April:

> Manzoli is under contract with the Milanese to sing in my opera. With that
> in view he sang four or five arias for me in Florence, including some which
> I had to compose in Milan . . . Manzoli is demanding 1000 ducats. It is not
> known whether Gabrielli will come. Since she stood up the Bolognese,
> some think she will stand up the Milanese as well, in which case she will
> remain in Palermo. Some say De Amicis will sing. We are to see her in
> Naples. I wish that she would sing, together with Manzoli. Then there
> would be two good aquaintances and friends of ours.[13]

Mozart's account is a little confused. If Manzoli were really under contract,
then surely his fee would have been already settled; yet Mozart implied that
negotiations were still under way. If Manzoli had indeed been engaged at
1000 ducats, that fee would have covered his singing in two Carnival operas in
Milan; the 500 ducats he would have received for his appearance in *Mitridate*
would have been five times what Mozart was paid to compose the music.

All these statements, suppositions, and wishes corresponded very little to
the cast eventually assembled for the Milanese Carnival of 1771, which in
itself suggests how difficult it was to assemble a first-rate company, even for
Carnival in one of Italy's most important theaters. Manzoli's contract (if it
ever existed) fell through. Of all the singers mentioned by Leopold and his
son, only one, the tenor Guglielmo d'Ettore, created a role in *Mitridate*. By
30 June they knew only that Pietro Benedetti (known as Santorini) would be
primo uomo. Finally, on 27 July they received the libretto and a list of the
singers who were to create the five most important roles.

Singers mattered a great deal to Mozart. He knew he would have to tailor
his music to the strengths and weaknesses of a particular cast. He followed
with great interest the selection of singers for *Mitridate*, but he could do very
little to influence it. His powerlessness had less to do with his youth than
with the fact that, as composer, he had very little influence over the choice of
singers. Ten years later, when he was writing *Idomeneo*, he complained bitterly
about the musico who was to create the role of Idamante but understood that
replacing him was out of the question.

The most experienced and successful composers could, on occasion, contribute to the selection of singers. One such composer, the Bohemian Joseph
Mysliveček, told Mozart in 1777 that he had been invited to compose several
operas for Naples: "The troupe for next year is good: all singers whom I

have recommended. You see, my credit in Naples is so high that when I say 'Engage this man,' they engage him."[14] Mysliveček was probably exaggerating his influence; Mozart, in any case, could never have honestly made such a claim.

Engaging the composer

First-rate composers were rare enough to give rise to strong competition among the relatively few impresarios who commissioned new works; they were sometimes willing to issue scritture more than a year in advance in order to secure the services of the best composers. Leopold Mozart reported in August 1770 that Mysliveček had agreed to write an opera for the Milanese Carnival of 1772 – almost a year and a half later.[15] Less fashionable composers might have to wait much longer to find work. When Antonio Vivaldi, late in his career and not much in demand, wrote *Ginevra principessa di Scozia* for the Teatro della Pergola in Florence for Carnival 1736, contracts were not signed until June 1735.[16]

In a few exceptional cases composers were engaged even later. Guardasoni probably did not bring Mozart into the project that resulted in *La clemenza di Tito* until the middle of July 1791 – a month and a half before the premiere. It was probably less than a month before the opening of a new theater in Vicenza in July 1784 that Cimarosa agreed to compose the inaugural opera, after the composer originally engaged, Giovanni Battista Borghi, withdrew because of illness.[17]

Leopold and Wolfgang made their first trip to Italy in late 1769 in the hope of winning a scrittura. During their short visits to Verona, Mantua, and Cremona they attended the opera, but since these cities rarely presented new operas, they made no effort, as far as we know, to obtain a contract. For this purpose their goal was Milan. The Regio Ducal Teatro of Milan usually presented two new operas every Carnival. Its impresario was under the influence of Count Carl Joseph Firmian, Empress Maria Theresa's plenipotentiary minister in Lombardy and *de facto* governor of this Austrian province. Firmian was the brother of one of Leopold Mozart's close associates at the court of Salzburg – Franz Lactantius Firmian, chief steward and inspector of the court music.

Leopold Mozart was not alone in using such connections in an attempt to secure an operatic contract. Emperor Joseph II, Salieri's steadfast patron, pulled dynastic strings in Italy and France, though not always successfully. In 1772 he wrote to his brother Leopold, grand duke of Tuscany:

> À *propos*, I have been asked to make you a proposition. Gasman's student Salieri, this young man whom you know and whose scores are very successful, would like to find a theater in Italy where he could write an opera, buffa or seria, to make himself better known. Would there be an occasion in Florence this spring to commission one from him? I believe that it would please. If you find the means, have him contacted directly, because I do not want to get involved in this intrigue.[18]

Leopold responded cautiously:

> As for what you mentioned concerning Salieri, Gasman's student, I will find out more, but our theatrical impresarios in Florence, who do not like to spend money, much prefer to give to the public opere buffe that are already known, changing a few arias that the musicians bring with them, rather than to make new ones. As for opere serie, these are given only during Carnival, and it is always a pasticcio; and this year the impresario wanted a new score for the second opera, and offered a young Florentine composer 12 sequins for the entire score. That is only to give you an idea of the generosity of our impresarios.[19]

Sequins were *zecchini* – small gold coins similar in size and value to Austrian ducats. Some zecchini carried the image of a lily, and were known as *zecchini gigliati*, or simply *gigliati*.

Joseph's family tree finally bore operatic fruit six years later. With the arrival of Archduke Ferdinand (one of Joseph's younger brothers) as governor of Lombardy in 1771 Milan became less hospitable to Mozart (who received the commission for his last Milanese opera, *Lucio Silla*, before Ferdinand became governor) and correspondingly more welcoming to the emperor's protégé. In 1778 Salieri received a commission for *Europa riconosciuta*, the opera that celebrated the opening of the Teatro alla Scala.

All of Leopold Mozart's skillful exploitation of Firmian's family connections would not have won a commission if Wolfgang had been unable to demonstrate his skills as a composer of Italian arias. For a concert given on

12 March 1770 by Firmian, and attended by the cream of Milanese society, he wrote three arias and an accompanied recitative. Mozart knew that the concert was a kind of test; he told his sister he wrote the arias "because no one had heard any theatrical music by me, in order thereby to see that I am capable of writing an opera."[20] He passed the test. On 13 March, the very next day, Leopold wrote of negotiations: "Between this evening and tomorrow another matter will be decided. For Wolfgang has been asked to write the first opera for next Christmas."[21] A few days later: "The scrittura or written contract has already been made and exchanged between the parties; so now it comes down to the permission of His Grace [the archbishop of Salzburg]. The contract was made in Count Firmian's house. We are to receive 100 gigliati and free lodging."[22]

The success of *Mitridate* encouraged Leopold to try to parlay Firmian's support into another contract for Wolfgang elsewhere in Italy. In January 1771, after the first few performances of *Mitridate*, Leopold and Wolfgang made a short trip to the nearby city of Turin. A letter recently discovered in the Archivio di Stato in Milan suggests that the principal aim of their visit to Piedmont was to obtain a contract to write an opera for Turin's Teatro Regio. The letter, from Carlo Flaminio Raiberti in Turin to Antonio Greppi in Milan, shows how effectively Leopold Mozart used Firmian's letters of recommendation; but it also shows how difficult it could be, in spite of the good will of powerful patrons, to win a scrittura:

> Besides the various letters that Sig. Amedeo Wolfango [sic] Mozart brought from Milan, and particularly the one from His Excellency Count Firmian, who recommended him to His Excellency Count Lascaris, which would have been enough to interest one in favor of that worthy virtuoso, but having seen how much it pleased Your Illustrious Lordship to praise him in the much esteemed letter with which you wished to accompany him, I did not neglect, according to the idea presented to me by the same Sig. Mozart, to speak personally, independently of what Count Lascaris already did, to the directors of the theater in order to do him a service. Committed as they are for the two operas of next year [i.e. Carnival 1772], having already granted the scrittura, I succeeded in finding out that they are extremely well disposed toward the person recommended by you for the following year; and although in the negotiation of a business that

depends on the goodwill and approval of many people things can always
be subject to many circumstances, as Your Illustrious Lordship likewise
understands from your extensive experience in similar affairs,
nevertheless you can be sure that I will make a special effort, in
discussions with the directors [of the opera], to promote, in so far as I am
able, the true suitability and qualifications of Sig. Mozart, for nothing
weighs more heavily on my heart than to convince you at every opportunity
of the true delight it gives me to obey you.[23]

Leopold's machinations in Turin came to nothing; his son was never to write
operas for any Italian city except Count Firmian's Milan.

It was probably indicative of Mozart's low status – his youth and inexperience as a composer of opera seria – that he received the scrittura for *Mitridate*
only about eight months before the premiere. Its success, in turn, was reflected
in the much longer time that separated Mozart's next commission for a Carnival opera from the date of its performance. The scrittura for *Lucio Silla* is
dated 4 March 1771; the opera did not reach the stage until December 1772,
almost two years later. For *Lucio Silla* Mozart was to be paid 130 *gigliati* – a
significant increase over his fee for *Mitridate*. But other than this, the terms of
the contract closely resemble those to which Mozart and his father agreed in
connection with the earlier opera:

> It is agreed that Sig. Amadeo Mozart will set to music the first drama to be
> performed in the Teatro Regio Ducal of Milan in the Carnival of the year
> 1773 and as honorarium for his artistic services are to be assigned to him
> one hundred and thirty *Gigliati* viz. 130 g. and furnished lodgings.
>
> It is further agreed that the said Maestro is to deliver all the recitatives
> set to music within the month of October of the year 1772 and to be in
> Milan again at the beginning of the subsequent month of November to
> compose the arias and be present at all the rehearsals required by the said
> opera. With the usual reservations in case of theatrical misfortunes and
> Princely intervention (which God forbid).

Milan, 4 March 1771
>   The Associates of the Lessee of the Theater
>   Federico Castiglione[24]

Having entered into this contract for the first Carnival opera in Milan,
Leopold accepted another scrittura for the second opera of the same Carnival

season at the Teatro San Benedetto in Venice (see figure 2.1). In that contract Mozart promised "to present himself in Venice by 30 November 1772 in order to be present at all the rehearsals and performances to be held at that time" – a promise that he could not possibly keep if he honored the contract with Milan. Whether Leopold two-timed the impresarios of Milan and Venice out of greed and recklessness or out of fear that one of the contracts might fall through, he must have eventually decided that he had embarked on a risky course. He withdrew from the agreement with Venice, but not before a good deal of time had elapsed; he was still boasting of the Venetian scrittura in a letter of 7 February 1772.[25] Leopold's attempt to manipulate the system for his own benefit may have had something to do with the fact that Mozart never received another scrittura from Italy after composing *Lucio Silla*.[26]

Mozart's contract for *Lucio Silla* is remarkable – though by no means atypical – for what it does not contain. It does not say anything about the subject of the opera he was to write. It does not mention the opera's title, nor does it name a librettist, nor does it say if the libretto will be one that had been set to music before or a new one. And the contract says nothing about the singers.

Over all these matters, which were crucial to the success or failure of the opera, and indeed the opera's very character, Mozart and most other composers had little or no influence.

Choosing a libretto

Impresarios and those they served (rulers, courts, academies) generally had the final say in what libretto would be used for a particular opera. That decision – in effect, a decision about how the plot archetype discussed in chapter 2 was to be elaborated – was often made quite late, after the engagement of singers and composer. Composers' contracts rarely include the title of the opera they are promising to write.[27] A composer could give his advice, but that advice was not necessarily followed. Vivaldi, having agreed to write an opera for Florence in 1735, and having been told by the Florentine impresario Luca Casimiro degli Albizzi that the libretto was to be Antonio Salvi's *Ginevra*, repeatedly asked that he be allowed to set to music Apostolo Zeno's *Merope* instead. Albizzi repeatedly refused, and eventually Vivaldi relented.[28]

The management of the Teatro Alibert in Rome, in contrast, reacted quite solicitously to the preferences expressed by Tommaso Traetta, the celebrated composer it had engaged to write an opera for Carnival 1767.[29] Apparently the management had originally proposed a libretto entitled *Talestri*; Traetta responded that he did not have a copy of that libretto, and suggested instead *Ricimero*. The management answered by saying that it had requested a copy of *Ricimero* and would study it; but in the meantime it asked Traetta to consider Metastasio's *L'olimpiade*. Traetta refused *L'olimpiade* and suggested three other possible librettos. (The negotiations came to nought, since Pope Clement XIII cancelled the Roman opera season of Carnival 1767.)

Mozart, like Traetta, expressed his preference for a libretto to those organizing the Carnival opera in Milan three years later. He wrote of the first opera he was to write for Milan: "We do not yet know the libretto. I recommended one by Metastasio to Don Ferdinando and Herr von Troger."[30] But he obviously lacked Traetta's clout. His recommendation went unheeded by those responsible for the opera in Milan; they sent him Vittorio Amadeo Cigna-Santi's *Mitridate* instead, and Mozart accepted it as a matter of course.

Mozart's next two operas, *Ascanio in Alba* and *Lucio Silla*, were his first settings of new librettos. The poets Giuseppe Parini and Giovanni De Gamerra, both closely associated with the Regio Ducal Teatro, probably chose the subjects for these operas as part of the task of creating librettos from scratch. Just as the success of *Mitridate* led to the scrittura for *Lucio Silla*, so the plot of *Mitridate* led De Gamerra to the choice of Lucius Cornelius Sulla (also spelled Sylla, Italianized as Silla in De Gamerra's libretto) as the subject of Mozart's next dramma per musica. Both operas deal with the same period of Roman history, that of the Mithridatic Wars (88–64 BC). Sulla, before becoming dictator of Rome, defeated King Mithridates in a battle to which Aufidio alludes in Act I of *Lucio Silla*:

Ma Silla, il fiero terror dell'Asia,	But Silla, fierce terror of Asia,
Il vincitor di Ponto,	the conqueror of Pontus,
L'arbitro del Senato,	master of the Senate,
E che si vede un Mitridate	at whose great feet Mitridate
Al suo gran pié sommesso,	kneeled in submission,
S'avvilirà d'una donzella appresso?	will allow himself to be humiliated by a young woman?

Although in the chronology of the Mithridatic Wars the action of *Mitridate* (which ends with the king's death) takes place well after that of *Lucio Silla*, De Gamerra probably intended *Lucio Silla* as the second in a pair of operas by Mozart based loosely on the lives of the ancient adversaries who gave the operas their names.

Singers generally exercised more influence in the selection of librettos than composers did. An impresario or a librettist might choose a particular subject to suit one or more leading singers who had already been chosen. In Naples in 1770 the engagement of Anna de Amicis and Giuseppe Aprile as prima donna and primo uomo led the librettist Francesco Saverio de Rogati to choose Armida and Rinaldo (from Tasso's *Gerusalemme liberata*) as his principal characters. An admirer of Niccolò Jommelli, the composer who set *Armida* to music, wrote of De Rogati: "He adapted so well the part of Rinaldo to the ability of the man [i.e. Aprile] and the part of Armida to the ability of the woman [i.e. De Amicis], that neither he nor she could be anything but delighted."[31] The impresario who engaged Luigi Marchesi to sing in the opera being organized to celebrate the opening of the theater in Vicenza in 1784 repeatedly invited the musico to choose the libretto for the inaugural opera.[32]

There are good reasons to think that singers played an important behind-the-scenes (and thus largely undocumented) role in the choice of librettos for at least four of Mozart's operas: *La finta semplice* (the origins of which will be discussed later in this chapter), *Mitridate*, *Il re pastore*, and *Don Giovanni*.

The tenor Ettore was one of the singers engaged to perform in Milan during Carnival 1771 before Mozart won a scrittura to write one of the operas for that season. Ettore knew Cigna-Santi's libretto *Mitridate*, having created the title role in an earlier setting of it, by Quirino Gasparini, in Turin in 1768.[33] His insistence that Mozart incorporate into Mitridate's part music from one of Gasparini's arias suggests strongly that he helped to persuade the Regio Ducal Teatro in Milan to stage Cigna-Santi's libretto.

The Salzburg court engaged the musico Tommaso Consoli to take part in musical events celebrating the visit to Salzburg of Archduke Maxmilian in April 1775. Those celebrations included a performance of Mozart's setting of an abridged version of Metastasio's *Il re pastore*. A few months earlier, in Munich, Consoli had sung in a setting by Guglielmi of the same version of the libretto. Since Mozart's cast almost certainly included Consoli, it seems quite likely that this musico, as part of the negotiations that brought him to Salzburg, recommended that the Munich version of *Il re pastore* be set to music for Maximilian's visit.[34]

The tenor Antonio Baglioni was probably involved in the decision-making that resulted in *Don Giovanni*. In Venice during Carnival 1787 he sang in *Il capriccio drammatico*, on a libretto by Giovanni Bertati that depicts an Italian opera troupe in Germany arguing with their impresario about what opera to perform. The second act of the opera consisted of a performance – a play within a play – of a Don Juan opera entitled *Don Giovanni o sia Il convitato di pietra*, with music by Giuseppe Gazzaniga. Shortly after appearing in that production, Baglioni became a member of the Italian opera company in Prague – precisely the kind of troupe depicted in *Il capriccio drammatico*. Later the same year he created the role of Don Ottavio in Mozart's *Don Giovanni*, on a libretto by Da Ponte that made obvious and repeated use of Bertati's *Don Giovanni*. Da Ponte's claim that Guardasoni, the impresario of the Italian opera in Prague, asked Mozart to set Bertati's libretto to music (before Mozart insisted on having Da Ponte write a new treatment of the Don Juan story),[35] strengthens the possibility that Baglioni, as the only direct link between the two Don Juan operas of 1787, brought Bertati's libretto with him to Prague and urged his new employer to have it performed.

The Munich operas

The operatic center closest to Salzburg, both in actual distance and in the personal relations that could be of help in arranging for Mozart to write operas, was the court of the elector of Bavaria in Munich. No contracts survive for either of Mozart's Munich operas, *La finta giardiniera* and *Idomeneo*, and much is still unknown about the arrangements that led to their being composed. The New Court Theater in Munich (also known as the Cuvilliés Theater) traditionally presented a single new serious opera during Carnival, which in Munich began at Epiphany (6 January). In addition to the Carnival opera, during much of the 1770s Count Joseph Anton von Seeau, director of the court opera, also put on Italian comic operas in the Old Court Theater (also known as the Theater am Salvatorplatz or Salvatortheater).[36]

In early December 1774 Mozart, accompanied by his father, went to Munich to complete and perform La finta giardiniera.[37] Their timing was odd, for three reasons. First, a comic opera with a very similar title, Sarti's La giardiniera brillante, received its Munich premiere on 12 December, a few days after the Mozart's arrival.[38] Second, Carnival was approaching, and with it the performance of the Carnival opera, Antonio Tozzi's Orfeo ed Euridice (which was probably already in rehearsals in December). And third, during Carnival the opera buffa troupe traditionally performed not only in the Salvatortheater but on a stage at one end of the Redoutensaal, the court ballroom, where it presented comic operas during breaks in the dancing. Leopold wrote later: "after that [5 January 1775] no more comic operas will be performed in the theater, but only the Redoutensaal – and then only intermezzi – while hundreds of masks stroll around, chatter, jest, and gamble at the different tables. Thus nothing intelligent can be performed after that."[39] Leopold was mistaken that performances in the Salvatortheater stopped entirely during Carnival.[40] But the opera buffa troupe's activities in the Redoutensaal must have severely limited the number of performances it gave in the Salvatortheater.

Early December 1774 was thus an inauspicious time for Mozart to arrive in Munich with the intention of presenting a big, complex, and difficult work like La finta giardiniera. But Leopold had his own reasons for bringing his son to Munich at precisely this time, as we will see.

Leopold's first letter from the Bavarian capital, written on 9 December, suggests that he and his son arrived with little knowledge of what the future had in store. More likely he feigned ignorance, omitting any reference to the impending production of Sarti's La giardiniera brillante: "So far I have nothing to tell you about the opera. We only made the acquaintance today of the people connected with it, all of whom, and in particular Count Seeau, were very kind to us."[41] Seeau had presumably commissioned Mozart to compose a comic opera for the Salvatortheater. But it is unlikely that he intended the production of Mozart's opera to coincide with (and thus to compete with) Sarti's comedy, Tozzi's Orfeo, or Carnival balls.

In Leopold's next letter, dated 14 December, he gave his wife a farfetched explanation of why Wolfgang's opera was to be performed later than he originally expected:

An opera for which the public has to pay cannot be performed here more than twice in succession, for otherwise the attendance would be poor. So for two or three weeks other operas have to be performed and then the first one may be trotted out again, just as is done in the case of plays and ballets. Thus the singers know the parts for at least twenty operas which are performed in turn, and at the same time they rehearse a new one. So Wolfgang's will be produced for the first time before Christmas and, I believe, [again] on the 29th.[42]

A number of points in this passage call for comment. What Leopold called "an opera for which the public has to pay" was specifically a comic opera performed in the Salvatortheater (entrance to the Cuvilliés Theater for the Carnival opera was free). He surely exaggerated the number of comic operas in the repertory at any one time. From 1769 to 1776 forty-three comic operas are known to have been performed in Munich.[43] That almost half of these operas were being performed in succession in December 1774 is hard to believe.[44] By stating that Wolfgang's opera would be performed before Christmas, with a second performance on 29 December, Leopold made clear that he did not think of *La finta giardiniera* as a Carnival opera. Rather he had come to Munich with the intention of having it performed before Carnival, probably to give it an advantage in a competition that he secretly hoped would emerge between *La finta giardiniera* and Tozzi's *Orfeo ed Euridice*.

Leopold's ambitions came to the surface in a letter of 30 December, after the premiere of *La finta giardiniera* had been postponed, again, to early January:

You must know that this time last year Maestro Tozzi, who this year is writing the opera seria, wrote an opera buffa, and contrived to write it so well that it killed the opera seria written by Maestro Sales [Pietro Pompeo Sales' *Achille in Sciro*]. Now it so happens that Wolfgang's opera is being performed before Tozzi's, and when people heard the first rehearsal, they all said that Tozzi was being paid back in his own coin, for Wolfgang's opera would certainly kill his. I do not like these bickerings, I try as far as possible to suppress such remarks and I keep protesting.[45]

In staging this operatic duel, Leopold hoped to win for his son a commission for the Carnival opera the following year. He was still optimistic on this account on 11 January 1775: "Up to the present it seems that there is every likelihood that Wolfgang will compose the grand opera here this time next year."[46]

But in the end Leopold's machinations and self-righteous protestations failed. The production on 12 December of Sarti's comic opera about a female gardener probably caused the initial delay in the production of *La finta giardiniera*. Leopold's belief that Wolfgang's opera would have to be performed before Carnival turned out to be incorrect. *La finta giardiniera* reached the stage only on 13 January, after Tozzi's opera. *Orfeo* received seven performances (more than most Carnival operas in Munich during the 1770s),[47] while *La finta giardiniera* was given only three performances, at least one of which had to be shortened because of a singer's illness. As for a future Carnival opera, Mozart had to wait for five years to pass, and for a new elector to be installed, before he won the commission for *Idomeneo*.

Commissioning operas in Vienna: Mozart's *La finta semplice* and Salieri's *Le donne letterate*

Mystery surrounds the commissioning of operas in Vienna during Mozart's lifetime. Even the word "commissioning" may be misleading in this context, since there is no evidence that most of the operas written for Vienna – and not only by Mozart – were commissioned at all, at least by way of formal contracts. Many Viennese operas seem to have been conceived in discussions between librettists and composers, who together initiated projects that they presented only later, when some of the music was done, to the management of the court theaters for possible performance.

During the decade from 1765 to 1776 a series of impresarios ran the court theaters, the Burgtheater and the Kärntnertortheater. They presented operas, ballets, concerts, and spoken dramas under the court's supervision. Florian Gassmann served the impresarios as operatic music director for most of the decade. Since he wrote nine operas during between 1766 and 1774, at a rate of one per year, his conditions of employment probably included the requirement that he provide the court theaters with one new opera every year.

When Mozart and his father spent several months in Vienna in 1768 the court theaters were under the control of the impresario Giuseppe Affligio. There is no reason to think that Leopold came to Vienna with the intention of winning a scrittura for his twelve-year-old son. Yet Wolfgang's operatic improvisations in London three years earlier and Grimm's prediction that he would soon compose an Italian opera must have made Leopold susceptible to the idea of using operatic composition as yet another way of demonstrating his son's astonishing musical abilities and of increasing his income. Some casual remarks by the young Emperor Joseph II – who asked Wolfgang if he would like to compose an opera – put the idea in Leopold's head and, once there, it gave him no peace. Leopold's dissatisfaction with the admiration and the money his son was winning in Vienna suddenly transformed itself into a plan by which Wolfgang, by writing an opera for Germany's largest city, would establish his reputation and his fortune once and for all.[48]

The first steps that Leopold took in putting this plan into action were successful. He recorded them in a petition that he later submitted to Joseph II after failing to bring Wolfgang's opera to performance.[49] Leopold won the informal support of Affligio and two of the singers in his company, Francesco Carattoli and Gioacchino Caribaldi. One of these singers, Leopold wrote to his friend Hagenauer in Salzburg, "has given me all the suggestions for the work,"[50] probably meaning that Carattoli or Caribaldi supplied Wolfgang with a libretto, Goldoni's La finta semplice. With their encouragement Wolfgang composed the first act, and he and Leopold played the music for the two singers. On the basis of their approval, Leopold concluded a scrittura with Affligio, who promised to pay 100 ducats for the opera (the same as Wolfgang would receive for his first opera for Italy, Mitridate, two years later). This was a remarkable feat for Leopold, given that the impresario already had, in Gassmann, a dependable supplier of new operas, and no financial incentive to commission operas from anyone else. Moreover, throughout the entire period of Mozart's activity in Vienna, I know of no other opera composed in fulfillment of a formal scrittura.

Mozart finished the opera, but as he did so problems began to surface. From Leopold's petition to the emperor, it appears that the tide of opinion turned against Wolfgang, Leopold, and La finta semplice at a poorly prepared rehearsal. It was probably at that point that Affligio began to delay preparations for the performance.

Leopold, frustrated by the delay, began to see conspirators everywhere. In a remarkable letter to Hagenauer he gave his rage and self-righteousness full vent, rising unstoppably to a climax of religious zeal. There is no more vivid expression, in the whole correspondence of the Mozart family, of the passion that eighteenth-century operatic production could arouse:

> But at this point the mask fell from the face. For in the meantime all the composers, among whom Gluck is a leading figure, undermined everything in order to prevent the success of this opera. The singers were talked over, the orchestra worked up and every means was used to stop its performance. The singers, who, moreover, hardly know their parts and one or two of whom have to learn everything entirely by ear, were now put up to say that they could not sing their arias, which they had approved of, applauded, and described as quite suitable for them. The orchestra was now supposedly unwilling to be conducted by a boy, and a hundred similar things. Meanwhile some people spread the report that the music was not worth a fig; others said that it did not fit the words, or was against the meter, thus proving that the boy had not sufficient command of the Italian language. As soon as I heard this, I made it quite clear in the most eminent quarters that Hasse, the father of music, and the great Metastasio had stated that the slanderers who spread this report should go to them and hear out of their own mouths that thirty operas have been performed in Vienna, which in no respect can touch this boy's opera which they both admire in the very highest degree. Then it was said that not the boy, but his father had written it. But here too the credit of the slanderers began to fall. For they dropped *ab uno extremo ad aliud* until they were in the soup. I asked someone to take any portion of the works of Metastasio, open the book and put before little Wolfgang the first aria which he should hit upon. Wolfgang took up his pen and with the most amazing rapidity wrote, without hesitation and in the presence of several eminent persons, the music for this aria for several instruments. He did this at the house of Kapellmeister Bonno, Abbate Metastasio, Hasse, and the Duke of Braganza and Prince Kaunitz. Meanwhile arrangements have been made for another opera and, as no more objections can be raised, little Wolfgang's is to be performed immediately afterwards. Hundreds of times I have wanted to pack up and go off. If this opera had been an opera seria, I should have left immediately and at the very first moment, and should have laid it at the feet of His Grace [the archbishop of Salzburg]. But, as it is an opera buffa, and, what is more, an opera that demands certain types of *persone buffe*, I must save our reputation in Vienna, cost what it may. The honor of our most gracious prince is also involved. His

Grace has no liars, charlatans, and deceivers in his service, who with his foreknowledge and permission go to other towns in order, like conjurors, to throw dust in people's eyes. No, he sends honest men, who to the honor of their prince and of their country announce to the world a miracle, which God has allowed to see the light in Salzburg. I owe this act to almighty God, otherwise I should be the most thankless creature. And if it is ever to be my duty to convince the world of this miracle, it is so now, when people are ridiculing whatever is called a miracle and denying all miracles. Therefore they must be convinced. And was it not a great joy and a tremendous victory for me to hear a Voltairian say to me in amazement: "Now for once in my life I have seen a miracle; and this is the first!" But because this miracle is too evident and consequently not to be denied, they want to suppress it. They refuse to let God have the honor. They think that it is only a question of a few years and that thereafter it will become natural and cease to be a divine miracle. So they want to withdraw it from the eyes of the world. For how could it be more visibly manifested than at a public show and in a large and populous town? But why should we be surprised at persecutions away from home, when almost the same thing has taken place in this child's native town? What a disgrace! What inhumanity![51]

We can only imagine how Vienna's nobility and professional musicians reacted to Leopold's behavior; they may well have considered him something of a clown. It was almost certainly partly in reaction to Leopold's extraordinary belligerence that Affligio eventually decided to cancel the production of La finta semplice altogether.

But how could an impresario legally refuse to produce an opera that he had commissioned by scrittura? In light of the survival of Leopold's petition, which refers repeatedly to the contract, it is strange that the text of the contract itself seems not to survive. But we know it contained (at Leopold's insistence) a provision that the opera be performed before the scheduled departure of Joseph II for Hungary. That deadline could not be met, thanks to a delay caused at least in part by Mozart's having to rewrite some of the music at the singers' request. Affligio may have cited that delay as grounds for his refusal to bring the opera to performance. Or the contract might have contained a clause that, in view of Wolfgang's youth and inexperience, made performance of the opera contingent on the approval of the complete score by the management and singers.

Compare Leopold's clumsy and ultimately self-defeating attempts to have *La finta semplice* performed in Vienna to the way in which Salieri, two years later, brought his first opera, *Le donne letterate*, to the stage. Salieri had an important advantage over Mozart in being Gassmann's handpicked apprentice; and Salieri's librettist was a protégé of another influential man of the theater, Gluck's librettist Ranieri de' Calzabigi. Salieri, moreover, had the patience to let these connections have their desired effect. The longest autobiographical fragment published in Ignaz von Mosel's early biography of Salieri begins with an account of how he began composing the opera:

> Gaston Boccherini, a dancer in the Viennese opera theater who passionately loved poetry, had written, with Calzabigi's help . . . an Italian opera entitled *Le donne letterate*, which he intended for Gassmann. Calzabigi advised him to entrust it to me instead, since I, a beginner in composition as he was a beginner in poetry, would more easily come to an understanding with him.
>
> So Boccherini came to me one morning and, after greeting me, asked me without further preliminaries: "Would you like to set to music a comic opera libretto that I have prepared?" I calmly answered: "Why not?" And then he told me with complete honesty the plan he had, and how Calzabigi had advised him. "Ah ha," I said to myself, "so they think you are already able to write an opera! Courage! We cannot let this opportunity slip away!"[52]

During the month that followed Salieri composed two-thirds of the opera, without knowing if it would be performed. The turning point in the opera's fate, as in the case of *La finta semplice*, was a rehearsal, but a rehearsal that differed greatly from the one that doomed Mozart's opera:

> The impresario had just brought to the stage an opera that did not please the public and felt it necessary to replace it quickly with another work. Boccherini, without telling me anything, had whispered to Calzabigi that I had already made good progress with my opera. The latter, a friend of the impresario, wished to hear in his apartment a small rehearsal of what I had composed. He invited me and, without guessing the reason, I went there with my poet and with the completed numbers. I was a little surprised to find the impresario and the Kapellmeisters Gluck and [Giuseppe] Scarlatti, but I thought they were there only out of curiosity

and was delighted by their presence. I sang and played what I had finished; Gluck and Scarlatti sang with me in the ensembles. Gluck, who had always liked me and encouraged me, showed himself pleased with my work from the very beginning; Scarlatti, who from time to time pointed out small mistakes in the composition, praised every number as a whole, and at the end both masters said to the impresario that if I could soon fill in what was missing the opera could be rehearsed and performed without delay, for (in Gluck's words) the work had "what it takes to please the public."

Who can imagine the joyful surprise that this statement gave me, through which I immediately saw the object of the rehearsal? Full of confidence – "superbo di me stesso" [proud of myself; the beginning of an aria in Metastasio's *L'olimpiade*] – I promised my judges to show the greatest diligence until the opera reached the stage.[53]

Viennese opera under Joseph II and Count Rosenberg

Emperor Joseph II ruled the Austrian monarchy as co-regent with his mother Maria Theresa from 1765 to 1780 and as sole ruler from 1780 to his death in 1790. Joseph loved opera, but he brought to his patronage of it all the inconsistency and impulsiveness that characterize other aspects of his reign. Mozart, initially drawn into the fiasco surrounding *La finta semplice* by an innocent question posed by the emperor, felt the effects of Joseph's personality several times later in his career as an opera composer.

In 1776 Joseph dismissed the last of the impresarios who had run the court theaters since 1765 and took control of the theaters himself, transforming the Burgtheater into a "Nationaltheater" devoted to the performance of spoken plays in German. To his troupe of German actors he added, in 1778, a Singspiel company. In 1783 the emperor changed his mind yet again. He ended the performance of opera in German, bringing several fine Italian singers to Vienna to form an opera buffa troupe.

Joseph made Count Rosenberg, his chief chamberlain, manager of the court theaters. But true to his personality, the emperor himself made frequent but unpredictable interventions. Sometimes he worked through Rosenberg; sometimes he subverted the chain of command by dealing directly with singers and composers.

Under Joseph and Rosenberg the court theaters maintained a permanent opera company (as opposed to the temporary companies that impresarios in Italy assembled for a single season) that presented a repertory that gradually evolved as new operas replaced older ones. The opera buffa troupe founded by Joseph in 1783 depended for much of its repertory (especially during its early years) on operas imported from Italy and Saint Petersburg. Joseph seems to have treated the commissioning of operas very casually, as exemplified by the fact that when the Italian troupe made its debut, it did so not with a new opera by its musical director Salieri, but with an opera that he had written four years earlier for Venice, *La scuola de' gelosi*. Salieri subsequently wrote several operas for the opera buffa troupe; and the rate at which he wrote them, about one opera per year, suggests that as music director he was subject to an obligation to write one opera every year for the court theaters.[54]

The arrival of distinguished composers from abroad sometimes gave rise to commissions. Paisiello's *Il re Teodoro in Venezia* (1784), Gazzaniga's *Il finto cieco* (1786), and Martín y Soler's first Viennese opera, *Il burbero di buon core* (1786) all seem to have fulfilled commissions from the emperor or the theater management.[55] But during the 1780s Mozart was the only long-term resident of Vienna other than Salieri to whom the court theaters repeatedly turned for new operas.

Even before Joseph's Singspiel company made its debut in 1778, Leopold Mozart investigated the possibility of Wolfgang applying for a job as its music director – in effect, its resident composer. But Franz Heufeld, a Viennese friend, firmly refused to recommend Wolfgang to the emperor, instead suggesting another strategy for gaining access to imperial patronage:

> For the present no musical composer will be specially taken on,
> particularly as Gluck and Salieri are in the emperor's service. To
> recommend anyone to the sovereign would be a sure means of not
> finding a place for the person recommended. Nor is there any middleman
> through whom he could be approached, since, being himself a
> connoisseur, he arranges and chooses everything according to his own
> idea and fancy. Everybody knows this, and no one dares to come forward
> with suggestions and recommendations. In this way His Majesty has made
> his own choice of Gluck, Salieri, and, for some time now, of most of the
> people in his service. I might give you some examples, too, of people who

appealed straight to the sovereign and failed to succeed. I cannot approve
of the way in which you intend to go about it, and that is the reason why I
refrained from taking any steps by means of a petition, because I am
convinced in advance that it would be useless, and indeed
disadvantageous.

At the same time, however, another, more laudable and surer way
remains open whereby good talents may find their fortune with the
sovereign, namely by their works, for in this respect all men are
considered eligible. If your son will take the trouble of setting some good
German comic opera or other to music, to submit it, to leave his work to
the imperial judgment and then to await a decision, he may succeed in
being admitted, if the work pleases. In that case, however, it would
probably be necessary to be here in person.[56]

Given Mozart's reluctance to compose operas for which performances were
not assured, his response to this sensible advice, which Leopold forwarded to
him, was predictable: "You should not have sent me Heufeld's letter, which
gave me more annoyance than pleasure. The fool thinks I will write a comic
opera – and will do it without knowing anything definite and at my own risk."[57]
But in fact Mozart did eventually write a comic opera for Joseph's Singspiel
troupe, *Die Entführung aus dem Serail*, and the way in which that project got
underway, as we will see, conformed quite closely to Heufeld's suggestions.
He may have also written the opera we now know as *Zaide* in the hope of
having it performed in Vienna, leaving it unfinished (and untitled) when he
(or someone in Vienna whose judgment he trusted) decided that it would not
appeal to Viennese taste.

The emperor could, on occasion, commission an opera himself, as he did
in the case of Salieri's *Der Rauchfangkehrer*. According to Mosel, in April 1780
Joseph asked the composer, who had just returned from a long tour of Italy, to
attend a performance of the Singspiel troupe that the emperor had assembled
in Vienna. The next day he asked Salieri his opinion of the troupe:

Salieri, who was in fact delighted with what he had heard and seen,
answered that he found this musical theater wonderfully perfect in every
respect.

"Now you must compose a German opera," said the emperor.

Salieri suggested that one of the five operas he had written in Italy be translated into German.

"No translation," replied the emperor, smiling. "An original Singspiel!"

"Your Majesty," answered Salieri, "I would not know how to begin composing an opera in German; I speak it so badly . . . "

"Well," the emperor interrupted, still smiling, "then this work will serve as an exercise in the language. Tomorrow morning I will direct Count Rosenberg to have a German libretto prepared for you."[58]

No talk of a contract here; but this was clearly an offer that Salieri could not refuse.

Although the emperor did not think of asking Salieri about what plot he might like to use as the basis for his opera, or about what librettist he might like to work with, Salieri may have had a say in both. Evidently Joseph did not follow through on his promise to instruct Rosenberg to supply Salieri with a libretto; or Rosenberg, if he did receive such an order from the emperor, did not carry it out. According to Mosel, in response to Joseph's commission Salieri set to music a libretto "which a friend gave him, and which he set to music as an exercise while waiting for the management to provide him with another libretto."[59]

Mozart's *Entführung* had a very different – but equally informal – origin, which in many respects resembled the origin of Salieri's *Le donne letterate*. Mozart's first reference to the collaboration that would eventually produce the opera is in a letter to his father dated 28 April 1781, a few weeks after arriving in Vienna (and two days before the premiere of Salieri's Singspiel). He made no mention of the emperor or of Rosenberg: "Stefani is going to give me a German opera to write."[60]

Johann Gottlieb Stephanie, an actor and playwright, belonged to a committee of actors who helped Rosenberg run the Burgtheater. He was therefore in a perfect position to give Mozart an opportunity to compose an opera for the Singspiel company. But whether he wanted to do so is open to question. It was not until 9 June that Mozart mentioned Rosenberg in connection with the project, but without Stephanie as the go-between: the count had "commissioned Schröder (the distinguished actor) to look around for a good libretto and to give it to me to compose."[61] A week later Mozart described a complicated web of intrigue and influence-peddling that thrived under Rosenberg's theatrical management, and he concluded: "Even if I already had a libretto, I would not put pen to paper, since Count Rosenberg is not here. If at the last moment he did not approve of the book, I would have had the honor of composing for nothing. I won't touch it."[62]

Yet six weeks later he contradicted himself, saying that he had gone ahead and started to compose without Rosenberg's explicit approval. Stephanie had reentered the picture, not as the author of an original libretto but as the supplier (and potential arranger) of a libretto by Christoph Friedrich Bretzner:

> The day before yesterday Stephani junior gave me a libretto to compose. The libretto is very good. The subject is Turkish and the title is *Belmonte und Konstanze*, or *Die Verführung aus dem Serail* . . . The grand duke of Russia is coming here, and that is why Stephani begged me, if possible, to compose the opera in this short time. For the emperor and Count Rosenberg will return soon and their first question will be whether anything new is being prepared. He will then have the satisfaction of being able to say Umlauf's opera (which he has had for a long time) will be ready and that I am composing another one for the occasion. And he will certainly count it a merit on my part to have agreed to compose it for this purpose in so short a time.[63]

Mozart and Stephanie had already made crucial decisions about the cast: "Mlle. Cavalieri, Mlle. Teyber, M. Fischer, M. Adamberger, M. Dauer, and M. Walter will sing in it." And he had started to plan the music and to compose: "I will make the overture, the chorus in the first act, and the final chorus with Turkish music . . . I am so delighted at composing this libretto that Cavalieri's first aria, Adamberger's aria, and the trio that closes the first act are already finished."[64]

So Mozart did begin the opera, despite his declarations to the contrary, as a kind of speculative venture (as Salieri began *Le donne letterate*), in collaboration with a librettist who (like Boccherini) had powerful contacts within the theatrical administration, and who took responsibility to present it to the emperor and Count Rosenberg. But notice, again, that the opera's subject was a *fait accompli* as far as Mozart was concerned – he apparently had no input in the opera's basic concept, but simply accepted what Stephanie presented him. Once he began working on the opera Mozart formulated very strong ideas about changes that needed to be made in the libretto, as we will see in chapter 4. But the idea to make a new opera on Bretzner's libretto was Stephanie's, not Mozart's.

Librettists in Vienna had more opportunity than composers to choose an opera's subject matter. Of Martín y Soler's first Viennese opera, Da Ponte claimed in his memoirs: "I chose *Il burbero di buon core* for the subject of our drama, and I went to work."[65] Of Gazzaniga's *Il finto cieco* he wrote amusingly:

> I received an order from the directors of the theater to write a libretto for
> Gazzaniga, a composer of some merit but in a style no longer in fashion.
> To get rid of it quickly I chose a French comedy entitled *L'Aveugle*
> *clairvoyant* and dashed off a libretto from it in a few days. It had no success
> at all, either the words or the music. A passing infatuation for a lady of
> fifty, which unsettled the mind of that good man at the time, prevented
> him from finishing the opera by the specified date. I was therefore obliged
> to introduce into the second act pieces written twenty years earlier, to take
> various scenes from other operas, both his and by other masters, in short,
> to make a pasticcio, a pot-pourri with neither rhyme nor reason, which
> was performed three times and then put to sleep.[66]

When Da Ponte had more time he gave a composer a choice of several subjects. He wrote of the collaboration with Salieri that would result in *Il ricco d'un giorno*: "I proposed to him various plans, various subjects, leaving the choice to him. Unfortunately he liked the one that was perhaps least susceptible to beauty and theatrical effectiveness."[67]

With Mozart's *Le nozze di Figaro* it was a different matter.[68] Da Ponte, in his memoirs, generally credited himself with good ideas when he felt that he could get away with it. But the idea of turning Beaumarchais' play *Le Mariage de Figaro* into an opera he explicitly attributed to Mozart. This is particularly remarkable, because we find this attribution in a passage designed mostly to reflect well on Da Ponte himself:

> I could easily see that the sweep of his genius demanded a subject of great
> scope, something multiform, sublime. In conversation with me one day
> in this connection, he asked me if I could easily make an opera from the
> comedy by Beaumarchais entitled *Le Mariage de Figaro*. I liked the
> suggestion very much, and promised him to write one. But there was a
> very great difficulty to overcome. A few days earlier the emperor had
> forbidden the company of the German theater to perform that comedy,

which he said was too licentiously written for a decent audience; how then to propose it to him for a libretto? Baron Vetzlar offered, with noble generosity, to pay me a handsome price for the words, and then to have the opera performed in London or France, if it was not possible in Vienna. But I refused his offers and proposed to write the words and the music secretly and then to await a favorable opportunity to show them to the directors of the theater or to the emperor himself, for which I bravely volunteered to assume the responsibility.[69]

Da Ponte's account of the origins of *Figaro* has often been dismissed as untrustworthy. He almost certainly exaggerated the importance of his own role in persuading the emperor to allow the opera to come to performance. But in light of the way in which Mozart began composing *Die Entführung*, with the assurance that Stephanie would present it to the emperor and Rosenberg, it seems quite likely that he began composing the music for *Figaro* before Joseph approved the project. More important, Da Ponte's memoirs can, I think, be trusted on the question of who thought of turning Beaumarchais' play into *Le nozze di Figaro*. This was a rare occasion when Mozart himself came up with the idea for an opera.

What we know of Mozart's relations with Stephanie and Da Ponte suggests that librettists played a crucial role in the origins of his Viennese operas, regardless of whether they revised existing librettos or wrote new ones. Mozart occasionally looked for an existing libretto to set to music (as if to make a librettist unnecessary), but no such search resulted in a completed opera. Stephanie and Da Ponte gave him two things that he needed to get an opera off to a successful start: the idea for an opera's subject, and influence over the theatrical management. The main reason why Mozart had to wait until 1782 to present an opera in the Burgtheater is that before settling in Vienna in 1781 he had developed no working relations with any of the librettists employed in the Viennese court theaters.

Composers' fees in Vienna

The money that composers earned from their operas in Vienna was, like other aspects of theatrical life during the 1780s, very much subject to the emperor's personal tastes and whims. In so far as there was a standard fee for a full-length opera in Vienna, it was 100 ducats (the same as Mozart would have received if *La finta semplice* had reached performance in Vienna in 1768, and equivalent to what he got in Milan in 1770 for *Mitridate*). But between 1778 and 1792 fees actually ranged from 36 ducats (the most frequent payment for a new Singspiel) to 300 ducats (the enormous fees that Paisiello received for *Il re Teodoro in Venezia* of 1784 and Cimarosa received for *Il matrimonio segreto* in 1792). Mozart's *Die Entführung* was one of only five Singspiele to earn 100 ducats (the others were Salieri's *Der Rauchfangkehrer* and three operas by Dittersdorf). On the other hand, neither *Figaro* nor *Così fan tutte* earned more than 100 ducats, while two of Salieri's operas, *La grotta di Trofonio* and *Axur re d'Ormus*, earned 200 ducats each. For the Viennese version of *Don Giovanni* Mozart received 50 ducats.[70]

We can discern some patterns in this apparently wild variety of fees. The low payment earned by most Singspiele corresponds to the amount of music they contained and the amount of musical rehearsal they required, both of which were generally smaller than was the case with opera buffa: Singspiele lacked simple recitative and often included strophic songs. The extraordinarily large fees that Salieri earned for some of his operas probably reflects Joseph's special fondness for the composer and his music, while the large fee that Mozart earned for *Die Entführung* probably reflects both its great popularity and its exceptional musical richness. Both Paisiello and Cimarosa, international stars of a magnitude far outshining Mozart and Salieri, were special guests in Vienna, stopping there on their way to Italy from Russia (where they had enhanced their prestige by serving at the court of Empress Catherine the Great), when they received commissions to write *Il re Teodoro* and *Il matrimonio segreto*.

The system's apparent inequities annoyed Mozart. The success of *Die Entführung*, measured by large audiences, frequent performances, and hefty box-office receipts, caused him to resent the fact that his own share of the winnings was a flat fee of 100 ducats (despite this fee being much larger than what most Singspiel composers earned).[71] His sense of having been taken advantage of boiled over as he wrote to his father, fantasizing about becoming an impresario for his next opera: "I will write an opera, but not to look on with a hundred ducats in my pocket as the theater makes four times as much in two weeks. Instead, I will produce my opera at my own expense, and will make at least 1200 Gulden in three performances, and then the management may have it for fifty ducats [roughly 225 Gulden]. If they refuse to take it, I shall have made some money and can produce the opera anywhere."[72]

Mozart was not entirely raving here. A few months later he wrote: "I am now writing a German opera for myself. I have chosen Goldoni's comedy *Il servitore di due padroni*, and the first act is already completely translated. The translator is Baron Binder. But it is all still a secret until everything is ready."[73] This project, completely at odds with the operatic practices of Mozart's time and those of Mozart himself, came to nothing.

Paris and London: missed opportunities

Among the major operatic centers for which Mozart never wrote operas were Paris and London. He knew both cities well, and had chances to write operas in both. But he failed to capitalize on those opportunities.

Traveling rather reluctantly to Paris in 1778, Mozart found the same distinctively French style of singing and vocal composition for which, thanks partly to his father, he had developed a distaste during his childhood visits in the 1760s. He wrote to Leopold:

> What annoys me most of all in this business [of composing for French audiences] is that our French gentlemen have only improved their *goût* to the extent that they can now listen to good music as well. But to expect them to realize that their own music is bad or at least to notice the difference – heaven preserve us! And their singing – ouch! As long as a Frenchwoman never sings Italian arias, I can forgive her for her French screeching. But to ruin good music! It's unbearable.[74]

In addition to his emotional and aesthetic antipathy to French vocal music, another barrier stood in the way of Mozart writing an opera for Paris. The Opéra, France's most prestigious operatic institution and its sole producer of tragédie lyrique, operated under its own special rules and traditions that made it difficult for foreign composers to gain a foothold. It was only after an energetic publicity campaign by his partisans that Gluck had been able to present his *Iphigénie en Aulide* in 1774; and Salieri needed the support of

Queen Marie Antoinette, enlisted by her brother Emperor Joseph II, to have
Les Danaïdes performed in 1784.

Mozart had influential friends in Paris, such as the choreographer Jean
Georges Noverre, but even with Noverre's support and encouragement he
did not feel sufficiently confident that, if he wrote an opera, it would be
performed. In writing to his father from Paris in September 1778, near the
end of his stay, Mozart expressed an attitude toward operatic fees entirely
different from the one he was to express after the success of Die Entführung:

> Because I said that I'm leaving, I now hear that I should really write an
> opera. But I told Noverre, "If you guarantee for me that it will be
> performed as soon as it is ready, if I am told exactly what I will get for it, I
> will stay for another three months and write it." . . . Nothing came of it,
> and I knew beforehand that that would be the case, because this is not the
> way things are done here. What happens here, as perhaps you already
> know, is that when the opera is finished, it is rehearsed and if the stupid
> Frenchmen do not like it, it is not performed – and the composer has
> written it for nothing. If they find it good, it is put on stage; after that it
> wins applause, and after that is the payment. There is no certainty at
> all.[75]

Unmentioned in these letters – and hidden behind Mozart's uncharacteristic
displays of xenophobia – lies another, probably more important reason for
his reluctance to write a French opera. He was in love with Aloysia Weber, the
young soprano he had met a few months earlier in Mannheim. Aloysia, whom
he dreamed of transforming into a great singer of Italian opera, personified
all of Mozart's operatic interests during the months he spent in Paris. His
passion for her blinded him to the dramatic and musical potential of tragédie
lyrique.

After settling in Vienna in 1781 Mozart made plans to return to Paris (he
now found the prospect of operatic commissions in Paris more congenial)
and London. "I have been practicing my French daily and have already taken
three lessons in English," he wrote to his father during the summer of 1782.[76]
He studied scores of French operas by André Grétry, Gluck, Salieri, and Piccinni. The idea that emerged during early discussions of Figaro of presenting
the opera in Paris or London if a Viennese production failed to materialize

probably reflected Mozart's interest in returning to the capitals of France and Britain.

London, the city where in 1764–65 Mozart first discovered the magic of Italian opera and improvised his first Italian arias under the inspiration of a great male soprano, continued to beckon. His travel plans were still in the air in 1790, when an invitation to compose two operas for London arrived in a letter from the impresario Robert Bray O'Reilly:

> To Monsieur Mozart
> Celebrated Composer of Music in
> Vienna
> London, 26 October 1790
>
> Sir,
> Through a person attached to H. R. H. the Prince of Wales I learn of your design to undertake a journey to England, and as I desire to know people of talent personally and am at present in a position to contribute to their advantage, I offer you, Sir, such a position as composers have had in England. If you are thus able to be in London towards the end of the month of December next, 1790, and to stay until the end of June 1791, and within that space of time to compose at least two operas, serious or comic, according to the choice of the Directorate, I offer you three hundred pounds Sterling, with the advantage to write for the Professional Concerts or any other concert-hall with the exception only of other theaters. If this proposal seems agreeable to you and you are in a position to accept it, do me the favor of letting me have a reply by return, and this letter shall serve you as a contract.
> I have the honor to be,
>
> > Sir,
> > Your very humble servant
> > Rob. Bray O'Reilly[77]

The fee of 300 pounds that O'Reilly offered contrasts dramatically with the 1500 pounds that Manzoli earned in London during 1764–65; the ratio of those fees (1:5) is exactly the same as that of the fees that Mozart received for and that Manzoli demanded to sing in *Mitridate* in 1770. But by 1790 Mozart must have been used to the idea that for writing operas he would earn substantially less than the principal singers who brought his operas to life.

How, or even if, Mozart responded to O'Reilly's letter we do not know. In any case, the invitation arrived at the wrong time. Emperor Joseph II had died only a few months earlier, and the new emperor, Leopold II, was about to embark on a major reorganization of the court theaters. Mozart must have felt that it would be unwise for a member of the imperial *Kammermusik* to be absent from Vienna for six months – including the whole Carnival season – during the first phase of Leopold's reign.

CHAPTER 4

Mozart and his librettists

Many eighteenth-century theaters had a house poet, a librettist whose responsibilities went beyond the writing of librettos and the revision of existing texts. The house poet often staged operas, directing the movements and gestures of the singers and coordinating various aspects of each production – costumes, scenery, and so forth. His duties included those of the person we call today the stage director.[1]

A contract for a librettist who worked for the court theaters of Vienna in the early 1770s survives. Dated 15 January 1772, it indicates what a house poet was expected to do in Mozart's time. Giovanni Gastone Boccherini (brother of the famous cellist and composer) had made his debut as a librettist two years earlier with Salieri's *Le donne letterate*; now he agreed

> First. To shorten or otherwise adjust all the librettos of the Italian operas that the management wishes to present in these theaters.
>
> Second. To supervise the preparation of scenery, costumes, and everything necessary for the performance of said operas.
>
> Third. To be present at all the rehearsals held before the opera is staged, and to be present in the theater where the operas are being presented at all the premieres that may occur, in order to observe and to make sure that everything happens in an orderly fashion and with the greatest possible precision.
>
> Fourth. To compose three new librettos every year. These, if the theatrical management so desires, must be written by him on the subjects that it pleases the same management to assign him; otherwise he is free to write them on any subject he pleases.[2]

Notice that the contract made no provision for a composer to choose the subject of an opera; that decision was the management's to make or to delegate to the house poet.

Mozart never worked with Boccherini, but he did work with Da Ponte, house poet for the Italian opera troupe in Vienna from 1783 to 1791, and author, probably in 1786, of a comic poem about the work of a house poet that refers to many of these tasks; he exaggerated for comic effect, but the gist of the poem reflects reality:

> You know – everyone knows – that for three years I have served, for better or worse, as theatrical poet; that it is one of the hardest, toughest jobs that could have caused long suffering Job to lose his patience. One must first satisfy the maestro di cappella, into whose head always comes one trifle or another. Here he wants to change the meter or the rhyme, and to put an A where there is a U. There he needs a verse, or would like the first verse to be the second. Even worse for you if, to awaken the inspiration of the constipated maestro, you have to add, in the normal way (especially in the finale), the singing of birds, the rushing of brooks, the beating of hammers, the ringing of bells, the wheel, the tambourine, the grindstone, the mill, the frog, the cicada, the *piano*, the *crescendo*, and the *diminuendo*. Then, when he is satisfied, a thousand troubles remain, as you fight against a hundred heads full of caprice. Even if the principal singers are reasonable in their dealings with the composer and poet, there is the third man, the fourth buffa, who cause a commotion – one wants his part improved, because he is the second actor; another wants an aria di bravura, because it makes her look more important; one does not want these words, another does not want the music . . . Finally the first performance arrives. Oh heavens, what heartbreak! One sings badly, another acts badly, one has a cough or a cold. And in the audience, which judges from what it sees and hears, only the poet comes to harm, he alone is considered an idiot.[3]

Later in the poem Da Ponte referred to the contract under which he was employed in Vienna. It required him to write only one libretto each year; presumably the management expected him to devote most of his time to the revision and production of existing operas.[4] Joseph II had priorities quite different from those that shaped Boccherini's contract a decade earlier, at least in so far as he understood the house librettist's duties.

We should add to the functions of the house poet in Vienna one discussed in chapter 3: that of liaison between operatic composers and the theatrical administration. The librettist maintained contacts with composers and recommended to the management operatic projects that seemed likely to succeed. And, on the instructions of the management, the poet initiated collaborations with particular composers, choosing librettos for them to set to music.

Under Leopold's control

One might suppose that a composer so often involved in operatic production as Mozart should have come into frequent and intensive contact with librettists, and that this contact involved far more than just operatic texts. Yet Mozart's early experiences with opera are remarkable for the lack of contact with librettists. Before *Idomeneo*, Mozart seems to have considered his work on an opera to have been more or less completely separate from the multiple tasks for which the house poet was responsible. Working closely with the singers, he set the words to music without involving himself in any intensive, active way in shaping the opera's text. Although his compositional activities in connection with *Mitridate*, *Ascanio in Alba*, and *Lucio Silla* are well documented in the family correspondence, the letters say almost nothing about Mozart's relations with librettists, and there is very little evidence in these or Mozart's other early operas (up to and including *La finta giardiniera*) of changes made in the librettos by him or at his wishes.[5]

Mozart was only fourteen years old when he wrote *Mitridate*, eighteen when he wrote *La finta giardiniera*. His youth probably made him reluctant to consider the librettist a colleague with whom he might discuss, on a more or less equal basis, the dramaturgy of an opera and from whom he might request changes in the libretto. Furthermore, his being German might have discouraged him from actively collaborating with Italian librettists in the shaping of Italian operas.

If we compare the young Mozart's relations with librettists (or lack thereof) to the young Salieri's relations with the novice librettist Boccherini as they began working together on *Le donne letterate*, it is clear that Salieri and Boccherini, as a pair, had considerable advantages. Both Italian, both beginners, they fell immediately into a fruitful collaboration, as Salieri wrote:

> So I asked the poet with great impatience to share with me the plot of his opera and to read the poem out loud to me. He did both; and after we had distributed the roles according to the skills of the opera troupe then

in residence, Boccherini said: "Now I will leave you, and in the meantime make your annotations, and if you desire changes here and there in consideration of the musical effect, we will make them together when I return."[6]

After Salieri passed a sleepless night in composition, Boccherini reappeared: "He could not believe I had sketched the whole *introduzione* and half of the first finale. I played him at the keyboard what I had written; he was extraordinarily pleased with it; he embraced me, and he seemed no less delighted than I was myself."[7]

When these conversations took place Salieri and Boccherini were alone, unsupervised by a strongly opinionated older man. That suggests another reason why Mozart interacted little with librettists during the composition of his early operas: his father actively supervised the composition of these operas. Leopold not only looked over his son's shoulder as he composed but also controlled his relations with everyone involved in the production of the operas. Leopold's view of the proper relation between an opera's music and text shaped his son's early relations with librettists.

In Leopold's letters describing the performance of his son's operas, or any other operas for that matter, one very rarely gets a sense that operatic drama or operatic spectacle stirred much excitement in him. Leopold deeply loved literature – he especially admired the poet and playwright Christian Fürchtegott Gellert[8] – and it seems to have been the literary side of opera that most interested him. He loved music too, of course, but for him operatic music meant little more than a succession of beautiful arias. Anticipating the success of *La finta giardiniera* in Munich, he reported that "the whole orchestra and all who heard the rehearsal say that they have never heard more beautiful music, in which all the arias are beautiful."[9]

Six years later, as *Idomeneo* neared performance in the same city, Mozart realized that the opera was too long. He wrote to his father, who was serving as an intermediary between the composer and the librettist, Giovanni Battista Varesco, asking him to have Varesco shorten the recitative. One of the scenes that Mozart suggested for shortening was that in which Idomeneo, having survived a shipwreck, meets his son Idamante. Leopold responded at great length, expressing Varesco's reluctance to cut anything, and defending the recitatives mostly on literary grounds. In the absence of any letters written to Mozart by any of his librettists, Leopold's letter has special value as a clear statement of a librettist's interests and values, which coincided with Leopold's:

> we [that is, Leopold and Varesco] have read it [the recognition scene] backwards and forwards, and both of us find no opportunity to shorten it. It is translated from the French, as the plan required. Indeed, the plan demanded that this recitative be lengthened a little, so that they would not recognize one another too quickly. And now they want to make it ridiculous by having them recognize one another after only a few words. Let me explain. Idamante must surely say why he is there; he sees the stranger and offers his services. Idomeneo now goes so far as to speak of his sufferings, and yet must return his greetings. Then Idamante will tell him that he can sympathize with misfortune, as he himself has experienced misfortune. Idomeneo's reply is a necessary question. Idamante now recounts the king's misfortune and Idomeneo, by his mysterious words "non più di questo," gives Idamante a ray of hope. Idamante asks eagerly "Dimmi, amico, dimmi dov'è?" This eagerness makes Idomeneo ask "Ma d'onde," etc. Is it not necessary for Idamante to explain things at this point in such a way as to depict himself as a son worthy of his father and to awaken in Idomeneo admiration, respect, and longing to hear who this youth is – a young person who, when Idomeneo recognizes him as his son, makes the whole story more interesting? Keep in mind that this is one of *the finest scenes in the whole opera*, indeed *the principal scene*, on which the entire remaining story depends. This scene moreover cannot weary the audience, *as it is in the first act*.[10]

Leopold's remarks nicely express the primacy of his literary concerns, which almost certainly played a role in keeping his son, in his earlier operas, from encroaching on what Leopold must have considered the librettist's responsibility for the opera's text.

Mozart as dramatist: *Idomeneo*

Although possibly already in *Il re pastore* Mozart played a role in the adaptation of the libretto,[11] *Idomeneo* represents a much more important turning point in Mozart's operatic career. This was the first opera that Mozart wrote without his father's personal supervision. Mozart was alone in Munich when he wrote most of the opera – a mature artist of twenty-four, with a vast amount of operatic experience behind him. No wonder the letters between him and his father regarding *Idomeneo* constitute one of the most fascinating and important parts of the Mozart correspondence.

The situation was a rather odd one. Varesco, probably suggested as librettist by Leopold, was a priest and bureaucrat in Salzburg. He had some skill as a poet but very little experience as a librettist for the theater, with all the varied responsibilities that such a position involved. Leopold and Varesco stayed in Salzburg, while Wolfgang went to Munich to finish, rehearse, and perform the opera. The arrangement, which kept Mozart from interacting directly with Varesco and kept Varesco from directly contributing to the opera's staging, reflected both the librettist's lack of experience in the theater and Leopold's view of the libretto as a work of literature that could exist independently of the staged opera.

Mozart obviously took into account his father's opinions, and those of Varesco as reflected in his father's letters. But he was much more under the influence of the theatrical personnel in Munich – the singers and instrumentalists, the choreographer Jean-Pierre Legrand (who took responsibility for the stage-direction that Varesco, if he had been in Munich, might have overseen), the scenic designer Lorenzo Quaglio, and the opera director Count Seeau. He also fell under the influence of the opera itself as it took shape during rehearsals, offering perspectives and insights unavailable to Varesco and Leopold. In his letters we can see Mozart discovering, as if for the first time, the secrets of operatic dramaturgy, and trying to establish a new working relationship with his librettist in which he took an increasingly large responsibility for bringing the opera to dramatic life.

Mozart was not alone in establishing this kind of relationship with a librettist. The idea that the composer had a legitimate role in the shaping of a libretto was explicitly stated two years before *Idomeneo*, when a libretto written for Mozart was set to music by another composer. *Lucio Silla*, with music by Michele Mortellari, was performed in Turin during Carnival 1779. The libretto printed for that production describes itself as "adapted to the convenience of the composer of the music."[12]

In Mozart's first letter concerning *Idomeneo* he wrote:

> I have a request to make of the Abbate [Varesco]. I would like to have
> Ilia's aria in the second act, second scene changed a little for what I need.

> "Se il padre perdei, in te lo ritrovo": this strophe could not be better. But now comes what has always seemed unnatural to me (I mean, in an aria), namely *a spoken aside*. In a dialogue these things are completely natural – a few words can be spoken aside quickly – but in an aria, where the words have to be repeated, it makes a bad effect.[13]

The request was completely reasonable, and Varesco complied with it without complaint. But more important changes were to come.

One was suggested by the scenographer, as Mozart wrote to his father on 13 November 1780. In referring to Varesco as "Herr Abbé" he subtly alluded to his lack of theatrical experience:

> In the first act, scene 8 Quaglio has made the same objection that we made originally, namely that it is not fitting that the king should be all alone in the ship. If the Herr Abbé thinks he can be reasonably represented in the terrible storm, forsaken by everyone, without a ship, swimming all alone and in the greatest peril, then let it stand; but please cut out the ship, for he cannot be alone in the ship; but if the other situation is adopted, a few generals who are in his confidence (extras) must land with him. But then he must address a few words to his people, namely that they must leave him alone, which in his present melancholy situation is quite natural.[14]

"Natural" and "unnatural," eighteenth-century aesthetic buzzwords, come up frequently in Mozart's wrestling with the problems of musical dramaturgy. That his sense of what was natural in the theater did not preclude the supernatural is clear from his discussion of the oracle scene: "Tell me, don't you think that the speech of the subterranean voice is too long? Consider it carefully. Picture to yourself the stage. The voice must be terrifying – it must penetrate – one must believe that it really exists. How can this work if the speech is too long, and from this length the listeners will become more and more convinced that it means nothing?"[15]

Mozart suggested another change to the libretto, again based on the actual staging of the opera as it evolved in Munich:

> In the last scene of act 2 Idomeneo has an aria or rather a sort of cavatina between the choruses. Here it will be better to have a mere recitative, well supported by instruments. For in this scene, which will be the finest in the whole opera (on account of the action and grouping which were settled recently with Legrand), there will be so much noise and confusion on the

stage that an aria at this particular point would not work well; and
moreover there is the thunderstorm, which is not likely to subside during
Herr Raaff's aria, is it? And the effect of a recitative between the choruses
will be infinitely better.[16]

Mozart, referring to a scene as "the finest in the whole opera," used the same
phrase his father used when trying to dissuade Mozart from drastically shortening the recognition scene in act 1. The difference between what father and
son perceived as the opera's finest scene speaks volumes about the difference
in their understanding of operatic dramaturgy.

From the beginning of his career as an opera composer, Mozart had willingly – indeed enthusiastically – collaborated with singers, studying their
voices and stage personalities and writing arias that made the most of their
strengths. One aspect of his new working relationship with the librettist
involved advocacy for the singers. He relayed to Varesco a request from the
tenor Raaff for a new aria near the end of the opera, but was dissatisfied with
the result:

> The aria text for Raaff that you have sent me pleases neither him nor
> me . . . The aria is not at all what we wished it to be; I mean, it ought to
> express peace and contentment . . . for we have seen, heard, and felt
> sufficiently throughout the whole opera all the misfortune which
> Idomeneo has had to endure; but he can certainly talk about his present
> condition [that is, the happiness he feels as his troubles dissipate].[17]

Varesco supplied another aria text, but this one too drew criticism from
the tenor and Mozart, on the basis of the poet's use of odd, harsh-sounding
words, and especially his overuse of the vowel "i": "The other day he was
very much annoyed about some words in his last aria – 'rinvigorir' – and
'ringiovenir' – and especially 'vienmi a rinvigorir' – five i's! – It is true that
at the end of an aria this is very unpleasant."[18] Here Mozart was opening up
a whole new area of possible collaboration between singer, composer, and
librettist, involving the libretto's vocabulary and vowel sounds.

"Signor Raaff is far too picky," wrote Leopold in response to this complaint.
But Varesco did write yet another aria text, which Mozart set to music as the
lovely "Torna la pace al core." It is ironic – and it must have enraged or at least
annoyed Varesco – that when *Idomeneo* finally came to performance, this aria,

whose text Mozart had requested from the poet, and whose text the poet had rewritten twice, was omitted because, even with all the other cuts, the opera was still too long.

The new relation between composer and librettist that Mozart established during the composition of *Idomeneo* probably prevailed in all his later collaborations with librettists. Although there is little or no documentary evidence about some of these collaborations, we can safely accept Schikaneder's reference to *Die Zauberflöte* as "an opera that I thought through diligently with the late Mozart"[19] as applying equally well to all the operas that Mozart wrote in the last decade of his life.

Turning librettos into "vera opera": *Die Entführung aus dem Serail* and *La clemenza di Tito*

Idomeneo was a product of the independence from his father, and from his father's conception of opera, that Mozart established in Munich. That declaration of artistic independence was followed just a few months later by another, when the twenty-five-year-old composer broke his ties with the Salzburg court and settled in Vienna.

With his first Viennese opera, *Die Entführung aus dem Serail*, Mozart was even more assertive in his relations with the librettist than he had been with *Idomeneo*, insisting that Stephanie make major changes in Bretzner's *Belmont und Constanze, oder Die Entführung aus dem Serail*.[20] Exactly ten years later he set to music a libretto of Metastasio, *La clemenza di Tito*, but not before Mazzolà substantially revised it, along lines remarkably similar to those adopted by Stephanie, into what Mozart called a "vera opera."

"The libretto is very good," Mozart wrote of *Belmont und Constanze* on 1 August 1781,[21] at a time when he thought the composition of the work would have to be very rushed, with the possibility of a performance in the middle of September (just a month and a half away – about the same time he had to compose *La clemenza di Tito*). But soon the performance was postponed, giving him time to consider the libretto at leisure. He became increasingly dissatisfied. His famous letter of 26 September 1781 shows him more or less taking over from Stephanie principal responsibility for the opera's dramaturgy: "The original text began with a monologue, and I asked Herr Stephanie to make a little arietta of it – and then to put in a duet instead of making the two chatter together after Osmin's short song."²² Act 2 required even more alterations:

> The first act has been finished for more than three weeks. One aria in act 2 and the drunken duet (for the Viennese audience) is already done. But I cannot do any more with it, because the whole story is being altered – indeed, at my own request. At the beginning of act 3 there is a charming quintet or rather a finale, but I would prefer to have it at the end of act 2. In order to make this practicable, great changes must be made, in fact an entirely new plot must be introduced – and Stephanie is up to the eyes in other work. So we must have a little patience . . . But after all he is arranging the libretto for me – and, what is more, as I want it – exactly – and, by heaven, I do not ask anything more of him!²³

Mozart's idea of transferring Bretzner's "charming quintet" from act 3 to the end of act 2 eventually proved unworkable; but he did not abandon the idea of a finale in act 2, for which Stephanie produced a new text.

No letters document the revision of Metastasio's *Tito*, but it would not be surprising if Mozart made similar recommendations to Mazzolà, who was in Vienna, serving as the Italian troupe's house poet, during the summer of 1791. Shifting material from the beginning of an act to the end of the previous act in order to make a finale is precisely what Mazzolà did in *Tito*: he built the great quintet and chorus at the end of Mozart's act 1 out of dialogue in scenes 1–6 of Metastasio's act 2.²⁴ Mozart's idea of replacing spoken dialogue for Belmonte and Osmin in the first scene of *Die Entführung* with a Lied and duet ("Wer ein Liebchen hat gefunden") found realization also in the first scene of *Tito*, where Mazzolà and Mozart turned part of a conversation in blank verse between Vitellia and Sesto into a duet ("Come ti piace imponi").

Mazzolà's reduction of Metastasio's three acts to two has no precedent in *Die Entführung*; but Mozart had personal experience with two-act arrangements of Metastasio's three-act drammi per musica. He had already set one such arrangement to music: *Il re pastore*, in 1775. Later that same year a two-act version of Metastasio's *L'olimpiade*, with music by Luigi Gatti, was performed in Salzburg.²⁵ Mozart was almost certainly in the audience if not the orchestra.

Mozart's collaboration with Stephanie required him to resume the role of the singers' advocate that he had played in the preparation of *Idomeneo*, making sure the libretto allowed him to take advantage of a singer's strengths:

> As we have given the part of Osmin to Herr Fischer, who certainly has an excellent bass voice . . . we must use such a man, particularly as he has the whole Viennese public on his side. But in the original libretto Osmin has only this short song and nothing else to sing, except in the trio and the finale; so he has gotten an aria in act 1 and will have another in act 2. I have given Stephanie complete specifications for the aria – and the substance of the music for it was already finished before Stephanie knew a word about it."[26]

In composing Osmin's "Solche hergelauf'ne Laffen" without the text and requiring the librettist to adjust his poetry to existing music (even if that music was not yet written down), Mozart took another step in his gradual appropriation of duties normally assigned to the librettist. It was a step for which he was well prepared. Already as a child in London he had improvised a "Song of Rage" to nonsense words. And in composing *Idomeneo* he had written part of Ilia's aria "Se il padre perdei" without words, finding inspiration instead in the purely musical idea of a soprano interacting with four wind instruments in moderately slow tempo.[27]

Mozart continued in *Die Entführung* to exercise some control over literary aspects of the libretto, explaining his replacement of a word (hui) that he found out of keeping with the opera's tone and the character of the heroine Constanze: "I really don't know what our German poets are thinking of. Even if they do not understand the theater, or at any event opera, yet they should not make their characters talk as if they were addressing a herd of swine."[28] Leopold, in a letter to Wolfgang that does not survive, must have joined him in complaining about the literary quality of the libretto. The composer responded by defending the words that Stephanie had provided for Osmin's aria as good, functional operatic poetry:

> As far as Stephani's work is concerned, you are quite right. Still, the poetry is perfectly in keeping with the character of the stupid, surly, malicious Osmin. I am well aware that the verse is not of the best quality, but it fits my musical ideas, which were already going around in my head,

so well that it could not fail to please me; and I would like to bet that when it is performed no deficiencies will be found.[29]

Operatic poetry, in short, should be judged by how it expresses character and dramatic situation, how it fits the music, and how it is perceived by an audience in the theater, not by how it might please a literary critic reading it in print.

This led Mozart to one of his most celebrated and important declarations on the relation between the music and the libretto of an opera:

> In an opera the poetry must be absolutely the obedient daughter of the music. Why do Italian comic operas please everywhere – in spite of their miserable librettos? Because there the music reigns supreme and all else is forgotten. An opera is sure to please when the plot is well worked out; the words, in contrast, need only be written for the music alone, and not put here and there to suit a miserable rhyme . . . Best of all, if a good composer, who understands the stage and is talented enough to make a contribution himself, and an able poet, that true phoenix, come together; then one has no need to be anxious about the applause even of the ignorant.[30]

This statement is very much based on Mozart's own experience. He could certainly not have written it before *Idomeneo*. When he wrote of a "good composer" he had in mind himself, of course. He understood the stage as well as any composer of the time, and better than most. He was not only "talented enough to make a contribution" to the libretto, but confident enough to make demands of librettists, Italian as well as German – to regard himself as a librettist's equal or even his superior in operatic dramaturgy. The "able poet" whom he envisioned as his perfect partner was not only a skillful wordsmith who knew the theater well, but also – and just as important – he had to be willing to put his own literary interests second to the primary goals of musical theater. Indeed, in saying "the poetry must be absolutely the obedient daughter of the music" Mozart meant that the librettist must be subservient to the composer. And in calling the revision of *La clemenza di Tito* that he set to music a "vera opera," he expressed approval of the transformation of Metastasio's *dramma per musica* that Mazzolà produced, in all probability, at Mozart's request and under Mozart's supervision.

What Metastasio, who died in 1782, would have thought of the "vera opera" that Mozart composed in 1791 we can only guess; but we are lucky to have Bretzner's amusing and thoroughly sarcastic response to what Stephanie did with his *Belmont und Constanze*:

> An unnamed person in Vienna has been pleased to adapt my opera, *Belmont und Constanze*, for the I. & R. National Theater, and to have the piece printed in this altered shape. The changes in the dialogue being insignificant, I ignore this altogether; but the adapter has at the same time interpolated a large number of songs containing truly heartbreaking and edifying verselets. I should not like to deprive the improver of the fame due to his work, and I therefore find myself under the necessity of specifying here the songs interpolated by him according to the Viennese edition and Mozart's composition.

After a list of the aria and ensemble texts added by Stephanie, Bretzner quoted some particularly egregious examples of "the improver's" poetic clumsiness, from the quartet "Ach Belmonte! ach mein Leben" with which Stephanie replaced Bretzner's quartet "Mit Pauken und Trompetten." He commented: "That is what I call an improvement!"[31] One imagines that Leopold Mozart would have strongly sympathized with Bretzner.

Crisis and failure: *L'oca del Cairo*

"That true phoenix," the theatrical poet with whom Mozart in 1781 imagined working, appeared two years later in the person of Da Ponte. But it was not until 1786 that the first fruit of their theatrical collaboration reached the stage. For three years Mozart found his operatic ambitions repeatedly frustrated, as he relearned lessons that he should have remembered from his experiences with *Idomeneo* and *Die Entführung*.

Da Ponte came to Vienna as part of a new opera buffa troupe assembled by Joseph II. The debut of this company filled Mozart with excitement and eagerness to compose an Italian comic opera, as he wrote to his father in May 1783:

> The Italian opera buffa has started again here and is very popular. The buffo is particularly good; his name is Benucci. I have looked through at

least a hundred libretti and more, but I have hardly found a single one with
which I am satisfied; that is to say, so many alterations would have to be
made here and there, that even if a poet would undertake to make them, it
would be easier for him to write a completely new text – which indeed is
always best to do. Our poet here is now a certain Abbate Da Ponte. He has
an enormous amount to do in revising pieces for the theater and he has to
write *per obbligo* an entirely new libretto for Salieri, which will take him two
months. He has promised after that to write a new libretto for me. But
who knows whether he will be able to keep his word – or wants to? As you
know, these Italian gentlemen are very polite to your face. Enough! We
know them! If he is in league with Salieri, I shall never get anything. But
indeed I should dearly love to show what I can do in an Italian opera as
well [as a German one]![32]

Mozart's problematic collaboration with Varesco on *Idomeneo* taught him the
usefulness of working closely with a librettist willing and capable of turning
the composer's dramatic impulses into usable words. His work with Stephanie
on *Die Entführung* showed him the importance of having a librettist with whom
he could work in person, and who could present the work-in-progress to the
theatrical management. But facing an operatic genre with which he had not
dealt since 1775, Mozart forgot these lessons. He proposed to his father the
idea of another long-distance collaboration with Varesco:

> So I have been thinking that unless Varesco is still very much annoyed with
> us about the Munich opera, he might write me a new libretto for seven
> characters. Basta! You will know best if this can be arranged. In the
> meantime he could jot down a few ideas, and when I come to Salzburg we
> could then work them out together. The most essential thing is that on the
> whole the story should be really comic; and, if possible, he ought to
> introduce two equally good female parts, one of these to be *seria*, the other
> *mezzo carattere*, but both parts equal in importance and excellence. The
> third female character, however, may be entirely *buffa*, and so may all the
> male ones, if necessary. If you think that something can be got out of
> Varesco, please discuss it with him soon.[33]

Several things in this passage did not bode well. The supercilious tone betrays
the barely disguised contempt that Mozart evidently felt for Varesco, which
was not likely to inspire the poet to do his best work; nor does it suggest that

the composer expected a libretto of high quality from Salzburg. In the rigidity and specificity of his requirements we can sense that Mozart's conception of opera buffa was based less on personal experience in the theater than on conventions that had grown out of the popularity of Goldoni's librettos in the second third of the eighteenth century.

Varesco responded to Mozart's halfhearted invitation with a proposal for a libretto to be called *L'oca del Cairo*, about a lover who finds his way into a tower where his beloved is imprisoned by hiding inside a mechanical goose. Mozart liked the idea, but in accepting it he showed his contempt for the poet again, his self-confidence as a musical dramatist turning quickly into an ugly ruthlessness:

> But that Herr Varesco has doubts about the success of the opera I find very insulting to me. I can assure him of this: his libretto will not be successful if the music is no good. The music is the main thing in every opera. So if the opera is to be a success and Varesco hopes to be rewarded, he must alter and recast the libretto as much and as often as I wish and he must not follow his own inclinations, for he has not the slightest knowledge or experience of the theater. You can always have him keep in mind that it doesn't much matter whether he writes the opera or not. I know the story now; and therefore anyone can write it for me as well as he can.[34]

During the next several months Mozart made sporadic attempts to turn Varesco's fragmentary libretto into an opera buffa. The letters to his father concerning changes that he wanted the poet to make in *L'oca del Cairo* show him gradually coming to understand the limitations of his view that "in an opera the poetry must be altogether the obedient daughter of the music."[35] What Mozart needed from a librettist was not filial obedience but theatrical experience, verbal skill, and a willingness to work with him – not for him. Collaborating with a librettist without "the slightest knowledge or experience of the theater," who was far away and who had no institutional connections with or firsthand knowledge of the Viennese court theater, and working within an antiquated conception of opera buffa, Mozart continued to compose. But the project reached a crisis in February 1784, when he wrote to Leopold: "At present I don't have the slightest intention of producing" *L'oca del Cairo*.[36] He seems to have abandoned the opera shortly thereafter.

Mozart and Da Ponte

An intelligent and witty writer of prose and verse, Da Ponte had only a little theatrical experience when he began working as house poet of the Viennese court theater in 1783. But he was willing to let composers guide him. When he finished the first draft of *Il ricco d'un giorno* (the new libretto that Mozart mentioned) he gave it to Salieri. He recorded the composer's response in his memoirs: "It is well written, but we must see it on the stage. There are some very good arias, and scenes that I like very much. But I will need you to make some small changes, more for the musical effect than for anything else." We can imagine Mozart saying something very similar on reading the first draft of the libretto for *Le nozze di Figaro*. In particular, Salieri's phrase "we must see it on the stage" reminds us of Mozart's saying to his father, in letters about *Idomeneo*, "picture to yourself the scene" and "picture to yourself the stage."

Da Ponte's account of his collaboration with Salieri on *Il ricco d'un giorno* continues:

> I began to hope that my drama might not be as bad as I had judged at first. But what did these "small changes" [required by Salieri] consist of? Of mutilating or lengthening most of the scenes; of introducing new duets, terzets, quartets, etc.; of changing meters halfway through arias; of mixing in choruses . . . of deleting almost all the recitatives, and consequently all of the opera's plot and interest, if there was any. When the drama went on stage I doubt whether there remained a hundred verses of my original.[37]

The librettist is certainly exaggerating here, but the anecdote suggests that he was willing to go a long way to satisfy the composers with whom he worked. Such willingness must have endeared him to Mozart as well, when they finally began to work together. But their collaboration did not begin until well after Mozart reached and retreated from the artistic dead end represented by *L'oca del Cairo*.

We know little about Mozart's relations with Da Ponte. By the time they began working together on *Figaro* Mozart had stopped telling his father much about his work, and *Don Giovanni* and *Così fan tutte* were both written after Leopold's death. One of Leopold's last surviving comments about his son's operatic working methods is in a letter to Nannerl dated 11 November 1785, from which it appears that Mozart was as assertive with Da Ponte as he had been with Varesco and Stephanie:

> He begs forgiveness because he is up to his ears in work, having to finish the opera *Le nozze di Figaro* . . . I know the play; it is a very complicated work, and the translation from the French will surely have to be very freely altered in order to become an opera, if it is to be effective as an opera. God grant that the action comes off; about the music I have no doubt. That will cost him much running to and fro and arguing, until he gets the libretto arranged as he wishes for his purpose.[38]

Another hint of the closeness with which Mozart and Da Ponte worked is in the preface to the libretto of *Figaro*, in which the poet, writing of his efforts to recast Beaumarchais' play as a libretto of reasonable length, referred to Mozart as an equal partner: "But despite the labor and diligence that the maestro di cappella and I expended in the interest of brevity, the opera will not be among the shortest that have been presented on our stage."[39]

Da Ponte left us a tantalizing glimpse of him and Mozart working on *Don Giovanni*. As an old man in New York he reminisced with a friend, who recorded the remarks many years later:

> His accounts strengthened the reports of the ardent, nay, almost impetuous energy and industry of Mozart; his promptness in decision, and his adventurous intellect. The story of Don Juan had indeed become familiar in a thousand ways; Mozart determined to cast the opera exclusively as serious, and had well advanced in the work. Da Ponte assured me, that he had remonstrated and urged the expediency on the great composer of the introduction of the vis comica, in order to accomplish a greater success, and prepared the rôle with Batti batti, Là ci darem, Etc.[40]

The fact that Salieri began to compose the libretto that, with Mozart's music, came to be known as *Così fan tutte* allows us another kind of insight at what Mozart brought to the purely verbal dimension of opera buffa. The fragmentary evidence of Salieri's attempted setting includes some simple recitative that follows the opening trio. The recitative text differs entirely from the one that Mozart set, which is more lively, more amusing, and in every other respect more theatrically effective.[41]

Figaro, *Don Giovanni*, and *Così* are not only full of purely musical beauties, but they crackle with theatrical intelligence, energy, and wit in a way that differentiates their librettos even from those that Da Ponte wrote for Salieri, Martín y Soler, and his other Viennese collaborators. That is a clear indication that the assertiveness that Mozart showed in helping to shape the librettos of *Idomeneo* and *Die Entführung*, and the lessons learned from his failure to complete *L'oca del Cairo* in 1783–84, contributed decisively to the making of the three masterpieces on which he worked with Da Ponte.

CHAPTER 5

Composition

"I can adopt or imitate more or less any kind and style of composition," wrote Mozart in February 1778, assuring his father of his ability to write an opera for Paris.[1] His approach to writing opera varied greatly not only according to the kind of opera he was writing but also according to the system of production in which he was involved. An opera staged under the Italian system – that is, commissioned for a particular season or occasion, and written for a particular cast – required compositional strategies different from those suitable for an opera written for a gradually evolving troupe like the one that sang opera buffa in Vienna during the 1780s. Also affecting the way Mozart composed an opera was the degree of haste with which it was to be staged, and his knowledge of the singers, the orchestra, the theater, and the audience for which he was to compose it.

All eighteenth-century composers depended on such knowledge when writing operas. They knew that an opera written for a particular time and place might not succeed if performed elsewhere and later. Haydn in 1787 refused a request that he send one of his comic operas to Prague, "since all my operas are too closely bound up with our personnel (at Eszterháza in Hungary), and moreover would never produce the effect which I calculated according to local conditions."[2]

It was only in those rare cases when composers tried to write an opera at a distance from performers and audience that they put into words ideas that they usually took for granted. Jommelli, composing operas for the Portuguese court while living near Naples, expressed frustration: "It becomes increasingly difficult . . . to have to write so far removed from the people who must hear and execute my music."[3] He complained of the aesthetic vacuum in which he had to work: "I do not know, by having seen with my own eyes, either the taste of His Most Faithful Majesty or the thousands and thousands of other very necessary things that would give me more certainty, frankness, and facility. Ah! We are too far from each other!"[4] Such laments encourage us to imagine the various kinds of stimulation that Mozart felt in Vienna, Milan, Munich, and Prague as he wrote operas for the musicians and audiences in those particular cities.

Despite the variety of ways in which Mozart adapted to and found inspiration in local conditions, it is possible to make a few generalizations about how he composed operas, as Franz Xaver Niemetschek did in his early biography: "He never touched the piano while writing . . . When he received the text for a vocal composition, he went around with it for a long time; he concentrated on it, stimulating his imagination. Then he worked out his ideas at the piano; and only then did he sit down and write. That is why he found the writing itself such easy work, and often joked and dawdled."[5] If we understand Niemetschek's anachronistic use of "piano" to mean keyboard instruments in general (clavichord, harpsichord, or piano), and if we understand "writing" to mean putting a fully worked out composition down on paper, his statement probably reflects Mozart's practice quite accurately.

The crucial role that Niemetschek attributed to the keyboard in Mozart's vocal composition is consistent with other evidence. Shortly after Mozart and his mother arrived in Paris in 1778, Maria Anna Mozart wrote of their lodging: "The doorway and the stairs are so narrow that it would be impossible to bring up a Clavier. So Wolfgang has to compose away from home, at the residence of Monsieur Le Gros, for there is a Clavier there."[6] One of the projects he hoped to begin work on was an opera. On 1 August 1781 he wrote to his father from Vienna: "I am now going off to rent a Clavier, for until it is in my room I cannot live in it, because I have so much to compose, and not a minute to lose."[7] The principal work for which he needed the keyboard was Die Entführung. On a clavichord now displayed in the house in Salzburg where Mozart was born, a label written by his wife declares that he used this instrument to compose, among other works, Die Zauberflöte and Tito.

Niemetschek's brief account of Mozart's compositional process does not mention sketches. The surviving sketches (some 320 items) suggest that the autograph scores, including those of the operas, were often preceded by a great deal of preparatory written work.[8] Contrapuntal complexity sometimes required sketches. Mozart worked out on paper the simultaneous sounding of three dances (each in a different meter) in the first-act finale of Don Giovanni,

Fig. 5.1. Continuity sketches for two arias in Le nozze di Figaro, act 3: "Dove sono
i bei momenti" (staves 1–3) and "Vedrò mentr'io sospiro." At this stage in
working out his ideas, Mozart was interested in shaping the melodic line,
instrumental as well as vocal; he wrote down neither the words nor the bass line.
Such sketches, made for the composer's private use, often did without key
signatures, time signatures, and clefs. The sketch for the count's aria, beginning
on the fourth staff, is in D major. It starts with four measures of the first violin
part (implied treble clef), then continues (implied bass clef) with the beginning
of the vocal line. At the bottom of the page are attestations of the manuscript's
authenticity signed by Mozart's son (who shared his father's name) and by the
nineteenth-century collector Aloys Fuchs. Biblioteca Estense, Modena.

the canon in the finale of act 2 of Così fan tutte, and the fugal exposition in
the overture to Die Zauberflöte. But he also found sketches useful in the composition of arias, for which he sometimes made continuity sketches: single
lines combining the vocal part (often without text) and important instrumental passages. One sketchleaf (figure 5.1) contains continuity sketches that
Mozart used in the process of reaching final versions of two arias in act 3 of
Figaro: the Countess's "Dove sono i bei momenti" (staves 1–3) and the Count's

"Vedrò mentr'io sospiro" (staves 4–9). That some of the operatic autographs (such as that of *Così fan tutte*, discussed and illustrated later in this chapter) look almost like fair copies means not that the operas came to Mozart's imagination complete and ready to be written down in their final form, but rather that by the time he made these scores he had done most of the hard work of composition.

Composition in fulfillment of a scrittura

Theatrical managements in Italy differed in the schedules they imposed on composers. Those who ran the Teatro Regio in Turin generally required composers to finish the first two acts of a three-act opera before arriving in Turin, to send this music several months in advance, and to bring the completed third act with them.[9] In other words, composers were expected to write operas for Turin without necessarily having firsthand knowledge of the singers who were to perform the music. When Baldassare Galuppi agreed to compose the second opera for the Turin Carnival of 1764 he signed a contract that stated, in part:

> the said Signor Maestro must submit and send the first two acts of the same opera at the end of the month of October of the current year [1763], and must bring the third act with him on his arrival in this capital no later than the end of the month of December of the current year, in order to stage the opera and to play [the keyboard] during [the first] three or four performances of the same.[10]

Since the second Carnival opera typically came to performance in late January, this contract required Galuppi to arrive in Turin only about a month before the premiere.

Not far away, in Milan, the management assigned Mozart a different schedule. His contracts for *Mitridate* and *Lucio Silla* required him to arrive much earlier than was customary in Turin (about two months before the premiere) but in compensation for this allowed him to compose everything except the simple recitatives in Milan. Of the commission that would result in *Mitridate* Leopold Mozart wrote: "The opera begins in the Christmas holidays. The recitatives must be sent to Milan in October and on November 1st we must be in Milan so that Wolfgang can write the arias."[11]

About six months before the premiere of *Mitridate*, the Mozarts did not yet know what libretto Wolfgang was to set to music:

> You ask if Wolfgang has already begun the opera. He is not even thinking of it. You should ask us again when we have reached Milan on November 1st. So far we know neither the cast nor the libretto. We do know the primo uomo and the tenor. The primo uomo is Herr Santorini, who sang during the last Carnival in Turin, and the tenor is Signor Ettore. We found Santorini here in Rome; he visited us yesterday and said he thinks the first opera [that is, the opera that Mozart would compose] would be [Metastasio's] *Nitteti*. Basta! There is still plenty of time.[12]

Mozart waited another month before the libretto for *Mitridate*, together with a list of the singers who were to create the main roles, arrived on 27 July 1770.

Knowing the singers' names was not the same as knowing their particular strengths, weaknesses, and tastes. It would not be for another three or four months that Mozart would be able to hear the singers who were to perform in *Mitridate* and get to know their musical personalities. For this and the other operas he wrote in response to Italian scritture in the early 1770s he began the compositional process with parts of the opera that did not require an intimate knowledge of the singers.

In a letter of 14 November 1772, about a month and a half before the premiere of *Lucio Silla*, Leopold left a valuable picture of Mozart composing what he could while waiting in Milan for the singers to show up:

> None of the singers is here yet except Signora Suarti, who sings the part of the secondo uomo, and the ultimo tenore. The primo uomo, Signor Rauzzini, is expected any day. But Signora De Amicis will not arrive until the end of this month or the beginning of the next. Meanwhile Wolfgang has had sufficient amusement from writing the choruses, of which there are three, and from altering and partly rewriting the few recitatives he made in Salzburg, since the poet sent the libretto to Abbate Metastasio in Vienna for his approval and the latter corrected and changed a good deal and added a whole scene in the second act. Wolfgang then wrote all the recitatives and the overture.[13]

The highly conventional musical language of simple recitative made it particularly susceptible to early composition. All Mozart needed was the libretto and a general idea of what kind of singer (soprano, alto, tenor, or bass) was to take each role. In the case of *Mitridate*, Mozart began composing the recitatives on 29 September 1770, during a long stay in Bologna (a little less than three months before the premiere). But it was probably not until his arrival in Milan on 18 October that he made substantial progress on the recitatives. On 20 October he wrote: "I cannot write much, for my fingers hurt from writing so much recitative."[14]

The conventionality of simple recitative meant that composers sometimes assigned its composition to assistants. In many of Paisiello's autograph scores the simple recitative is in the hand of a copyist, suggesting that Paisiello did not compose it himself. Mozart allowed himself this shortcut only in composing *Tito*, for which he had very little time, and a performance date that, unlike those of many of his other operas, could not possibly be postponed. The autograph score of *Tito* resembles some of Paisiello's in containing almost no simple recitative. An account of the premiere published shortly afterwards reported: "only the arias and choruses were by his [Mozart's] hand; the recitatives were by another."[15] Franz Xaver Süssmayr, Mozart's student and assistant, came with him to Prague, probably to help with copying, proofreading, and rehearsals. He may also have composed the simple recitative.

But another kind of recitative – accompanied by orchestra, and in particular the *recitativo obbligato* in which the orchestra took responsibility for much of the melodic content – offered composers unparalleled opportunities for the display of their skills as musical dramatists, opportunities of which Mozart was eager to take advantage. We can see him doing so already in *Lucio Silla*, which, as Kathleen Hansell points out in the preface to her edition of that opera in the *Neue Mozart Ausgabe*, has much more orchestrally accompanied recitative than most other Milanese operas of the period. Sergio Durante finds in these richly crafted recitatives early evidence of Mozart's eagerness to expand his role (vis à vis the librettist and singers) in the creation of musical drama. In setting as orchestrally accompanied recitative texts that other composers might have set as simple recitative,

> the sixteen-year-old composer was actually exploiting to his own
> advantage the obligations of the local system, that is, the expectation that
> the recitatives be a "fait accompli" before meeting with the singers (in

order to write the set pieces). In this way he was somehow submitting his personal view of the place of music in the *dramma per musica* or, in a more pragmatic light, his desire and ability to manipulate the collective process of operatic production.[16]

Composing operas for Vienna

Vienna's repertory system, the presence there of resident opera troupes, and the informality with which operatic projects sometimes came into being together encouraged an approach to operatic composition quite different from the approach that prevailed in Italy.

We saw in chapters 3 and 4 how the nineteen-year-old Salieri came to write his first opera buffa in 1769 and how his collaboration with the librettist Boccherini began. Salieri's reminiscence continues with an account of the early stages of the composition of *Le donne letterate*. It is worth quoting at some length, because we have nothing quite like it for Mozart:

> When I was alone I locked myself in, and with burning cheeks – which was normal for me, whenever I undertook a project with pleasure and love – I read the poem through again, found it certainly well suited to music; and, after I had read the aria and ensemble texts a third time, I first of all determined, as I had seen my teacher do, the key appropriate to the character of each number. Since it was already noon, and I consequently could not hope to begin composing before lunch, I used the remaining hour to read through the libretto again.

Later the same day, Salieri got back to work, turning to the opera's first ensemble:

> As soon as I was alone, I felt an irresistable urge to set to music the opera's introduzione. I tried to imagine as vividly as possible the personalities of the characters and the situations in which they found themselves, and suddenly I found a motive in the orchestra that seemed to me to carry and to unify the piece's vocal line, which was fragmentary on account of the text. I now imagined myself in the parterre, hearing my ideas being performed; I tried them again, and when I was satisfied with them, I continued further. So, in half an hour, a sketch of the introduzione was down on paper. Who was happier than I!
> It was six in the evening and darkness had fallen; I called for a light. Tonight, I decided, you will not go to bed before twelve. Your imagination

is alight, this fire must be made use of. I read the first finale, which
began, as far as the words were concerned, much like the introduzione. I
read it again, and made a plan of meters and keys suitable to the whole,
devoting three hours to this work without writing a note.

I felt tired, and my cheeks burned. So I paced back and forth in my
room, and soon I was drawn back to my writing desk, where I began the
first draft [of the finale], and when midnight came, I had made such
progress that I went to bed in a state of great joy.

My head had been too full of music and poetry the whole day for me
not to dream of them as well. Indeed, I heard in my dream a strange
harmony, but so distant and so confused that it gave me more pain than
pleasure, and I finally awoke. It was four in the morning, and all my efforts
to go back to sleep were in vain. So I lit a candle and looked through
everything I had sketched with a pencil the day before, continued the
sketch further, and had come to the halfway point of the first finale when
the clock struck eight and, to my surprise, my poet entered the room.[17]

Salieri made no mention of a keyboard instrument until he came to the part
of the story (quoted in chapter 4) in which he played his music for Boccherini.
There he revealed that he had a *Clavier* in his room. Perhaps it was a clavichord,
whose delicate sound might have allowed him to use it while the rest of the
household slept.

There is no reason to think that Mozart's approach to the early planning and
sketching of an opera differed much from Salieri's, especially when he was
faced with an opera buffa libretto containing abundant ensembles.[18] Even
the intense pleasure and excitement that Salieri felt in beginning an opera
correspond to the feelings that Mozart expressed on 1 August 1781, two days
after receiving the libretto for *Die Entführung*: "I rush to my desk with the
greatest eagerness and remain seated there with the greatest delight."[19]

Work with singers: composing arias

In his eagerness to begin writing *Die Entführung*, Mozart made use of his
knowledge of the voices of Cavalieri and Adamberger to write (or at least to
sketch) some of their arias without consulting them. Under calmer circumstances he much preferred to postpone the composition of arias, even for
singers he knew well, until he could work with them closely and in person.

In Italy, the singers, coming together from various cities, often arrived at different times, and often later than expected. Their tardiness forced Mozart to delay his work, or even – in rare cases – to compose an aria for an absent singer. Of the late arrival of the primo uomo for *Mitridate* Leopold Mozart wrote, about a month before the premiere: "Wolfgang has his hands full now, as the time is pressing and he has made only one aria for the primo uomo, because he has not yet arrived and because Wolfgang does not want to do the work twice and prefers to wait for his arrival so as to fit the costume to the figure."[20] A week later Leopold began to betray some anxiety: "You think the opera is already finished. You are greatly mistaken. If it were up to our son, two operas would be done. But in Italy everything is mad . . . The primo uomo has not yet arrived. He will certainly arrive today."[21]

The late arrival of singers drew similar complaints from Leopold during the composition of *Lucio Silla*. He wrote on 12 December 1772: "During the coming week . . . Wolfgang will have his heaviest work. For these blessed theatrical people leave everything to the last minute."[22]

As the singers for *Lucia Silla* arrived, Mozart set to work on the arias. The primo uomo Rauzzini was the first leading singer to appear, shortly before 21 November 1772; "so now there will be more to do and things will become increasingly lively," wrote Leopold.[23] Indeed during the following week Mozart wrote Rauzzini's first aria, "Il tenero momento," of which Leopold reported on 28 November: "it is incomparable and he sings it like an angel."[24]

Anna de Amicis, the prima donna in *Lucio Silla*, did not reach Milan until 4 December, delayed on her journey from Venice by flooded roads. Mozart must have devoted the next few days to intensive composition of arias for her; on 12 December Leopold wrote: "She is exceptionally happy with the three arias she has so far. Wolfgang has introduced into her principal aria passages that are new, unusual, and amazingly difficult, which she sings astonishingly well."[25]

In the weeks before the first performance of *Ascanio in Alba* Mozart was likewise in frequent contact with the primo uomo and the leading tenor: "Signor Manzoli often comes to see us, but we have only been to see him once. Signor Tibaldi comes almost every day at about eleven o'clock and remains seated at the table till about one, while Wolfgang is composing."[26]

But easily the most vivid testimony of the amazing productivity of Mozart's collaboration with singers is his famous letter of 26 September 1781, in which he told his father about some of the music he had written for Ludwig Fischer and Valentin Adamberger, who were to create the roles of Osmin and Belmonte in *Die Entführung aus dem Serail*. More than any other letter by Mozart, this one gives us a picture of the musical dramatist at work, thinking simultaneously about the dramatic situation and the singer for whom he was writing:

> I am enclosing only the beginning and the end [of Osmin's aria "Solche hergelauf 'ne Laffen"], which is bound to have a good effect. Osmin's rage is rendered comical by the use of the Turkish music. In working out the aria I have . . . allowed Fischer's beautiful deep notes to glow. The passage "Drum beim Barte des Propheten" is indeed in the same tempo, but with quick notes; and as Osmin's rage gradually increases, there comes (just when the aria seems to be at an end) the Allegro assai, which is in a totally different meter and in a different key; this is bound to be very effective. For just as a man in such a towering rage oversteps all bounds of order, moderation, and propriety and completely forgets himself, so must the music too forget itself. But since passions, whether violent or not, must never be expressed to the point of exciting disgust, and as music, even in the most terrible situations, must never offend the ear, but must please the listener, or in other words must never cease to be *music*, so I have not chosen a key foreign to F (in which the aria is written) but one related to it – not the nearest, D minor, but the more remote A minor.[27]

Mozart went on to comment on Belmonte's aria "O wie ängstlich, o wie feurig," again with reference to the singer who was to create the role:

> Would you like to know how I have expressed it – and even indicated his throbbing heart? By the two violins playing octaves. This is the favorite aria of all those who have heard it, and it is mine also. I wrote it expressly for Adamberger's voice. You see the trembling – the faltering – you see how his throbbing breast begins to swell; this I have expressed by a crescendo. You hear the whispering and the sighing – which I have indicated by the first violins with mutes and a flute playing in unison.[28]

Although the dramatic situation and the singer were Mozart's main sources of inspiration, he sometimes welcomed other, stranger musical stimuli. In the building in Milan where he wrote *Ascanio in Alba* he was surrounded by musicians: "Upstairs is a violinist, downstairs another one, in the next room a singing master gives lessons, and in the last room opposite ours is an oboist. That is good fun for composing! It gives you plenty of ideas."[29]

Orchestration

After working out his ideas at the keyboard and in sketches, Mozart usually began the process of putting his music down on paper with the vocal lines and the bass, from which a copyist produced a *parte cantante* (a kind of vocal score, but on just two staves) for each singer. Using these *parti cantanti* the singers could learn their parts while Mozart continued to fill in the orchestral accompaniment. He wrote to his wife on 2 July 1791, referring to his student and assistant: "Please tell that idiotic fellow Süssmayr to send me my score of the first act, from the introduction to the finale, so that I may orchestrate it." That must be a reference to the autograph score of the first act of *Die Zauberflöte*, from which the *parti cantanti* were copied (possibly by Süssmayr himself) while Mozart worked on act 2. But if he began scoring that opera in July 1791, he interrupted the task in order to write *La clemenza di Tito*, which he had to complete in time for it to be performed at the coronation of Leopold II as king of Bohemia in early September. According to Seyfried's reminiscences, by the time Mozart went to Prague to complete and conduct *Tito* in August 1791,

> all the ensembles of *Die Zauberflöte*, up to the last finale, were ready; that is, the vocal parts, the bass line, and the main instrumental motifs; from this short score my friend Henneberg got busily to work on the rehearsals. After Mozart's return – 10 or 12 September – he quickly got down to the task of scoring & of catching up with the small numbers which had not yet been composed; not till the 28th, as the autograph thematic catalogue shows, did the Priests' March and the Overture flow from his pen; the parts for the latter, indeed, came wet to the dress rehearsal.[30]

With *Così fan tutte* as well rehearsals and orchestration took place more or less simultaneously. The Viennese composer Joseph Eybler served as Mozart's assistant during rehearsals. He later wrote that he worked with Adriana Ferrarese (see the frontispiece) and Luigia Villeneuve, who created the roles of Fiordiligi and Dorabella, as Mozart completed the opera's orchestration.[31]

Procrastination

When the methodical Leopold accompanied his son to a city where Wolfgang was to write an opera, he kept him on a strict compositional schedule. But once Mozart was by himself, he began to show a tendency to procrastinate, especially in the tedious work of putting the notes down on paper. He admitted as much in a letter to his father concerning the composition of *Idomeneo*, making a clear distinction between the mental act of composition (which, as we have seen, often involved sketches) and a final draft:

> It is true that in Munich, without wishing to do so, I put myself in a false light as far as you were concerned, for I amused myself too much. But I swear to you on my honor that until the first performance of my opera I had never been to a theater, or gone anywhere but to the Cannabichs. It is true that I left the greatest and most difficult things to the last minute; yet this was not from laziness or negligence – but because I had spent two weeks without writing a note, simply because I found it impossible to do so. Of course I wrote a lot, but not the fair copy. I admit I lost a great deal of time this way, but I do not regret it.[32]

In Vienna, Joseph's opera director Rosenberg took over from Leopold the job of keeping Mozart on schedule. Leopold wrote to his daughter, in reference to the composition of *Le nozze di Figaro*, that Wolfgang "will always put things off and lose valuable time, according to his charming habit; now he must go to work seriously because he is being prodded by Count Rosenberg."[33]

Overtures

Although in some of his early operas Mozart wrote the overture very early, since this was an item that did not require knowledge of or collaboration with singers who had not yet arrived for rehearsals, the adult Mozart tended to put off the composition of the overture until just before the premiere. By the time he wrote *Idomeneo* he had come to agree with Gluck that the most effective overtures were those that anticipated the character and musical content of the opera. Such overtures were most easily written after the rest of the opera, though in the case of *Die Entführung* Mozart had composed enough of the opera by September 1781 (ten months before the premiere) to write the overture. He sent the first fourteen bars to his father, describing the overture to him as "very short, with alternate fortes and pianos, the Turkish music always coming in at the fortes. The overture modulates through different keys; and I doubt whether anyone, even if his previous night was a sleepless one, could go to sleep over it."[34]

But Mozart wrote the overture to *La clemenza di Tito* almost literally at the last minute, according to an anecdote told by a nineteenth-century owner of Villa Bertramka, the house in the outskirts of Prague where Mozart stayed when finishing *Tito*, and recorded by a woman who, in 1825, spent a summer in the villa.

> Bertramka's owner showed Frau von Pichler the place in my room where Mozart's spinet had stood, and told her how, when *Titus* was about to be performed just at the time of the reception of the Emperor Leopold, messenger after messenger was sent out by the Vienna [*sic*] orchestra for the missing overture. Mozart paced up and down in the room; but when his friend Frau Dussek [*recte*: Duschek; she and her husband were Mozart's hosts] (who was constantly urging him on) spied the leader of the orchestra among those panting up the hill, and Mozart calmly answered the reiterated injunction with "Not a single idea will come," she shouted at him "Then for heaven's sake begin it with a cavalry march!" He flew to the spinet and after the first two bars of the cavalry march, with which the overture really does begin, the melodies tumbled into place, the overture was finished, was quickly orchestrated, and the messengers hurried off with the sheets, still wet.[35]

That anecdote (which corroborates other sources on Mozart's dependence on the keyboard as a compositional tool) is consistent with one about the composition of the overture to *Don Giovanni* four years earlier, as told by Niemetschek:

> Mozart wrote this opera in October 1787 in Prague. It was already finished, rehearsed, and was to be performed two days later; only the overture was still lacking. The anxiety of his friends, which increased every hour, seemed to amuse him; the more nervous they became, the more light-hearted Mozart appeared. At last, on the evening before the day of the first performance, when he had amused himself enough, he went into his room around midnight, began writing, and in a few hours completed the astonishing masterpiece that connoisseurs rank below only the

heavenly overture to Die Zauberflöte. The copyists were only just ready in time for the performance, and the opera orchestra, whose skill Mozart already knew, played it excellently *prima vista*.[36]

In considering the plausibility of such stories we need to keep in mind that the act of writing down the music in its final from was only the last (and for Mozart the most tedious) stage in an often laborious process. Mozart's surviving sketches include a few for the overtures of his later operas (such as Figaro and Die Zauberflöte); these overtures at least, even if Mozart completed them shortly before the premieres, were based on ideas that he had carefully worked out in advance.

Autograph scores: the case of Così fan tutte

So far I have focussed on operas where Mozart's compositional process is relatively well documented by letters or other kinds of evidence, such as the anecdotes just cited. In the case of some of Mozart's operas, we know very little about how Mozart went about composing except what we can glean from those fascinating documents, the autograph scores. Mozart said very little about these scores in his letters. But he did make some interesting remarks about the autograph of Die Entführung when he sent it to his father:

> I'm sending you here the original score and two copies of the libretto. You will see much that has been crossed out. That is because I knew that the score is copied immediately. So I gave my imagination free rein, and before I submitted it for copying made my alterations and cuts here and there. It was performed just as you have it. Here and there the trumpets, timpani, flutes, clarinets, and the Turkish music are missing, because I could not get any paper with so many lines. They are written on extra sheets. The copyist has probably lost them, for he could not find them. The first act, when I was sending it somewhere or other – I forget where, unfortunately fell in the mud, which explains why it is so dirty.[37]

The autograph score of Così fan tutte is particularly valuable in view of the paucity of other documentation concerning its composition.[38] Like Mozart's other operatic autographs, it originally consisted of an unbound pile of bifolia and a few single leaves. It was among the huge treasure trove of autograph scores that Constanze Mozart sold to the publisher Johann Anton André in

January 1800, and was later owned by André's son Gustav (1816–74), from whom the Preußische Staatsbibliothek in Berlin obtained it. At some point it was bound in two volumes, the first containing act 1 and the second act 2. The two volumes were hidden for safekeeping during the Second World War. Either during or shortly after the war the two volumes became separated. Volume 2 returned to Berlin; it is now preserved in the German State Library in Berlin. The location of volume 1 was unknown until it reappeared in the late 1970s in the Biblioteka Jagiellońska, Kraków, in Poland, where it has remained to this day.

While the autograph of act 1 is almost complete, the autograph of act 2 is missing several sections: the duetto with chorus (no. 21), "Secondate aurette amiche"; the orchestrally accompanied recitative "Ei parte . . . senti . . . ah no . . . partir si lasci" before Fiordiligi's rondò (no. 25), "Per pietà, ben mio, perdona"; and the recitative "Come tutto congiura" before the duet no. 29, which, though present in the autograph, is in the hand of a copyist. The recitative "Ah poveretto me," and Don Alfonso's lesson that follows, "Tutti accusan le donne, ed io le scuso" (no. 30) are also missing from the Berlin manuscript; but they survive separately in the Stadt- und Universitätsbibliothek, Frankfurt am Main.

Both major parts of the autograph lack some wind, brass, and timpani parts, especially in the finales, where Mozart's twelve-staff paper did not allow him to notate these parts. He wrote them on separate leaves that have not apparently survived. Vienna's professional copyists seem to have been particularly careless with these extra sheets of autograph material.

The autograph of act 1 consists of 174 leaves ruled with twelve staves. As Alan Tyson showed, all but two of these leaves belong to one or the other of two paper types.[39] Type I paper is characterized by a watermark to which Tyson assigned the number 66; Type II paper by a watermark to which he assigned the number 100.

The autograph of act 2 consists of 138 leaves, also ruled with twelve staves. With the exception of a few isolated bifolia and individual leaves, it uses Type II paper throughout.

From Mozart's use of these two paper types in works written before and after Così fan tutte, Tyson concluded that his use of Type I paper largely preceded his use of Type II paper. Based on that conclusion, he went on to argue that Mozart composed those parts of the opera that he wrote on Type I paper before he composed the parts that he wrote on Type II paper. Thus, most of his early work on the opera (like that of Salieri on *Le donne letterate*) involved the composition of ensembles in act 1 (but not the finale); later work involved the composition of act 2, the finale and most of the arias in act 1, and (probably last of all) the overture.

In two numbers in act 1, the quintet "Di scrivermi ogni giorno" and Ferrando's aria "Un'aura amorosa," Mozart used a mixture of both types of paper, suggesting that he wrote them as he neared the end of his supply of Type I paper.

The autograph also contains evidence of distinct compositional layers within numbers, related to Mozart's practice – documented in the case of *Così fan tutte* by Eybler – of first writing out the vocal parts and bass, so that copyists could produce *parti cantanti* from which the singers could learn their music. Only later did he finish the orchestration. This *modus operandi* is reflected in the autograph, where different colors and shades of ink sometimes allow us to differentiate two or more notational layers.

At the beginning of the sextet "Alla bella Despinetta," for example, Mozart appears to have started by writing down the bass and vocal parts and the first six measures of the first violin (figure 5.2). Later he returned to this page to fill in the texture by writing down the second violin and viola parts, which are notated with a lighter ink and differ also from the other compositional layer in using shorter abbreviations for dynamics (*p:* instead of *pia:*, *f:* instead of *for:*).

In some numbers it may be possible to distinguish three notational layers. For example, in the duet "Al fato dan legge," the two vocal parts and the bass constitute one layer (figure 5.3). Mozart notated the rest of the violin and viola parts in a second layer, with lighter ink and a pen with a wider tip (producing wider beams and slurs). He apparently notated the clarinets, bassoons, and horns in yet a third layer, with ink that in its darkness is somewhere between that of the parts written above and below.

Of course there was no reason for Mozart not to make corrections or other alterations in an already completed layer as he worked on another layer. Thus in "Al fato dan legge" (see figure 5.3) he probably added the dynamic marks in the bass (*cresc:*, *f:*, and *p:*) at the same time as he notated the violin and viola parts.

Fig. 5.2. *Così fan tutte*, act 1, scene 11. The autograph score of the beginning of
the sextet "Alla bella Despinetta" shows the names Dorabella and Fiordiligi
crossed out and their places switched. Mozart used a dark ink in notating the
bass, Alfonso's vocal part, and the first violin part up to m. 6 (at the top of the
page). It was probably after a copyist created the *parte cantante* from the bass and
vocal parts and Joseph Eybler, Mozart's assistant, started rehearsing the singers,
that Mozart returned to the autograph, notating the second violin and viola
parts, and the first violin part after m. 7, with a lighter ink.

Despite Mozart's practice of writing his music down in a series of separate
layers, the autograph of *Così fan tutte* is the product of a composer who worked
out his ideas carefully in advance, in sketches that, in the case of this opera,
have mostly disappeared.[40] This autograph can almost be described as a fair
copy, ready for Wenzel Sukowaty's professional copyists to use as the basis
for the performing score (that is, the score that was used in the theater for
rehearsals and performances).[41] That makes the changes that Mozart did make
in his autograph all the more interesting.

Fig. 5.3. *Così fan tutte*, act 1, scene 4. The autograph score of the duettino "Al fato dan legge" (shown here: mm. 11–21) contains evidence of three notational layers: the bass and the vocal parts of Ferrando and Guilelmo, the violins and violas (at the top of the page), and the woodwinds and horns (in the middle of the page).

One change, or series of changes, has important implications for the history of the opera's early development. In the duet "Ah guarda sorella," the quintet "Sento, o Dio, che questo piede," the terzettino "Soave sia il vento," and the sextet "Alla bella Despinetta" (all assigned by Tyson to the earlier compositional layer), Mozart originally assigned to Dorabella words and music that he later assigned to Fiordiligi, and vice versa (see figure 5.2). Moreover, after composing Guilelmo's aria "Rivolgete a lui lo sguardo" but before deciding to replace it, Mozart changed the stage directions so that Guilelmo, instead of telling Fiordiligi to look at him and Dorabella to look at Ferrando, tells Dorabella to look at him and Fiordiligi to look at Ferrando (figure 5.4).

Ian Woodfield has pointed to these changes as evidence that at some point relatively early in the compositional process (before starting to use Type II

Fig. 5.4. "Rivolgete a lui lo sguardo," excised from *Così fan tutte* a few weeks before the premiere, mm. 1–8 and 19–25. The autograph (of which only the bass and vocal line are reproduced here) documents a change of plan as to the order in which Guilelmo addresses Dorabella and Fiordiligi.

paper), Mozart and Da Ponte changed their minds about the characterization of the sisters.[42] Dorabella (probably originally to have been sung by Ferrarese) was perhaps originally the more heroic of the two, and a more suitable mate for Ferrando; while Fiordiligi was the more playful, and a more suitable mate for Guilelmo. This would help to explain Fiordiligi's first lines of recitative, which seem uncharacteristically frivolous in the mouth of the woman we now know as Fiordiligi:

Mi par che stammattina volentieri	I think this morning
Farei la pazzarella: ho un certo foco,	I'd like to play the fool: I feel a kind of burning,
Un certo pizzicor entro le vene . . .	a kind of itching in my veins . . .
Quando Guilelmo viene . . . se sapessi	When Guilelmo comes . . . if only he knew
Che burla gli vo far!	what tricks I want to play on him!

The original stage directions in Guilelmo's aria suggest the possibility (also proposed by Woodfield) that Da Ponte and Mozart intended at one time to have

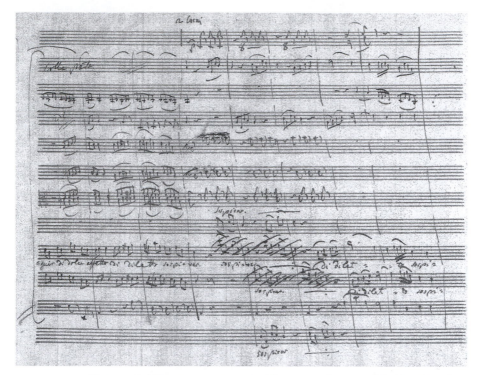

Fig. 5.5. *Così fan tutte*, act 2, scene 12. The autograph score of the duet "Fra gli amplessi in pochi istanti" records Mozart's change of mind about the melodic shape of the canonic passage at mm. 121–123.

the young men, disguised, seduce their own fiancées (as in Goldoni's *Le pescatrici*, a libretto that prefigures Da Ponte's and that he almost certainly knew). If Fiordiligi had allowed herself to fall in love with a disguised Guilelmo (rather than a disguised Ferrando), audiences might have found her betrayal easier to understand, and Guilelmo would certainly have found it easier to forgive.

Of purely musical changes that Mozart made in his autograph score one of the most striking is in the second-act duet "Fra gli amplessi in pochi istanti." In the concluding Andante, where Fiordiligi and the disguised Ferrando celebrate their new relationship and anticipate its sexual consummation, Mozart depicted their embrace with a short canon, which originally began with a phrase, sung twice, descending triadically from high A. He liked this idea, because he repeated the whole canonic passage, now decorated, immediately afterwards (figure 5.5). But later (before writing in the first violin and viola

Fig. 5.6. *Così fan tutte*, act 1, scene 2. In the duet "Ah guarda sorella," mm. 40–43, Mozart originally set the words "Se fiamma, se dardi/Non sembran scoccar" as a series of repeated notes and octave leaps; he later made the melodic line more lyrical (on the otherwise empty staff at the bottom of the page).

parts, which double the vocal lines), he must have realized that the high A at the beginning of the canon undercut the effectiveness of the climactic E three measures later. Mozart crossed out the canon's opening idea and replaced it (on staffs above and below those of Fiordiligi and Ferrando) with a line beginning an octave lower.

Mozart made an equally felicitous revision in the duet "Ah guarda sorella," where Dorabella (originally Fiordiligi) sings the heroic lines "Se fiamma, se dardi/Non sembran scoccar." The vocal line originally involved little more than repetition of tonic E and leaps up and down an octave. It was probably after Mozart and Da Ponte sorted out the characterizations of Dorabella and Fiordiligi that the composer revisited this passage – now assigned to Dorabella – and reshaped it into something more graceful (figure 5.6).

Only rarely did Mozart have second thoughts after committing the *parti cantanti* to paper. An example of where he did so is in Guilelmo's big aria "Rivolgete a lui lo sguardo," which he and Da Ponte eventually decided to replace with the shorter, simpler "Non siate ritrosi."[43] That decision was not reached, apparently, before Mozart fully orchestrated "Rivolgete." In writing the aria down he decided to cut a passage of fifteen measures that he had already notated in the vocal line and bass. Mozart, evidently feeling that the aria was too long for its context in opera, first tried to solve the problem by shortening it. His later decision to replace "Rivolgete" altogether amounted to a recognition that his attempt to fix the aria did not go far enough.

CHAPTER 6

Mozart and his singers

Visiting Munich in 1777, Mozart attended a performance of Piccinni's comic opera *Le pescatrici* in German translation. He sent his father an account that relegates the opera and the composer to an afterthought:

> The prima donna is named [Margarethe] Kaiser; she is the daughter of a cook in the household of a count here. A very pleasant young woman, she looks pretty on the stage; I have not yet seen her up close. She was born here. When I heard her she was acting only for the third time. She has a beautiful voice, not strong but not weak either: very pure, good intonation. Her teacher is Valesi, and from her singing you know that her teacher understands both singing and how to teach it. When she sustains a note over a couple of beats I was astonished at how beautifully she makes the crescendo and decrescendo. She sings the trill slowly, and I am glad about it, since that will make it all the purer and clearer when she wants to make it faster. Besides, a fast trill is always easier. The people here are very happy with her, and I with them . . . I observed Kaiser with my spyglass, and she often drew tears from me. Several times I said "Brava, bravissima!" For I kept thinking that this was only her third appearance on the stage. The piece was entitled *Das Fischermädchen*, a very good translation of Piccinni's opera.[1]

An important part of Mozart's fascination with opera was a fascination with singers – not only their voices, but their stage presence and acting, and their personalities and lives off the stage. From the time that "little Mozart was much taken notice of by Manzoli, the famous singer" (as Barrington put it) in London in 1764–65, he studied, learned from, and sought both personal and professional relations with singers.

Since eighteenth-century composers were expected to shape their operatic music to the abilities of the singers who were to perform it, these composers obviously had to know the singers well. It was also useful for composers to establish personal relations with important singers, who, as we saw in chapter 3, were often engaged before composers in the operatic system that prevailed in eighteenth-century Italy. Singers preferred to sing in operas by composers they liked or respected. Several of Mozart's operas – including *La finta semplice* and *Die Zauberflöte* – may have received some of their initial impetus from singers with whom Mozart was on good terms.

Mozart studied and befriended singers with equal enthusiasm during his first tour of Italy, nowhere more memorably than in Parma, where he and his father met the soprano Lucrezia Aguiari. Mozart wrote to his sister on 24 March 1770:

> In Parma we got to know a singer and heard her perform very beautifully in her own house, namely the famous Bastardella who has (1) a beautiful voice, (2) an elegant throat, (3) an unbelievable range. She sang the following notes and passages in my presence.[2]

Leopold was just as impressed:

> In Parma Signora Lucrezia Aguiari, also known as Bastardina or Bastardella, invited us to dinner and sang three arias for us. I could not believe that she could sing up to C *sopra acuto* [an octave above high C], but my ears convinced me. The passages Wolfgang has written down were in her aria and she sang these, it is true, more softly than her deeper notes,

but as beautifully as an octave stop in an organ. In short, she sang the trills and the passages just as Wolfgang has written them down, note for note. Moreover, she has a good deep alto down to G. She is not beautiful, but not ugly either. She sometimes has a wild look in her eyes, like that of people who are subject to epilepsy, and she limps with one foot. In other respects she has good behavior, a good character, and a good reputation.[3]

As late as 1780 Aguiari's singing served as a standard with which Mozart evaluated female sopranos; the celebrated Gertrud Mara, he wrote, "has not had the good fortune to please me. She does too little to be able to equal a Bastardina (for that is her specialty) and too much to move the heart, like a Weber, or a sensible singer."[4]

When Mozart presented to De Amicis one of the arias she was to sing as Giunia in *Lucio Silla*, he "told her with a smile that if she did not like that aria he had another completely different one, composed especially for her; and that if the second was also not pleasing to her, he could present her with a third."[5] That anecdote is preserved in an account published so long after the fact (in 1817), that one might suspect its accuracy. But Mozart demonstrated much the same flexibility and willingness to please when showing an aria to another famous singer, Raaff, about six years later. In this often quoted passage we can see clearly Mozart's eagerness to satisfy singers (even an aging tenor whose singing and acting had tempted him to laugh, as we saw in chapter 1) and his understanding that to do so was a key to his own success as a composer:

> I was at Raaff's yesterday and brought him an aria that I have composed for him in the last few days. The words are "Se al labbro mio non credi, bella nemica mia," etc. I don't think the text is by Metastasio. He liked the aria very much. One must treat a man like him in a special way. I chose this text with care, because I knew that he already had an aria with these words; so he will sing them more easily and with more pleasure. I said to him that he should tell me candidly if it did not suit him or if he did not like it; I'm willing to change the aria for him as he wishes, or even to make another. "God forbid," he said, "the aria must remain just as it is, for it is very beautiful; but please shorten it a little for me, for I am no longer able to sustain my notes." "Most gladly, as much as you like," I answered. "I made it a somewhat longer on purpose, for one can always leave

something out, but adding something is not so easy." After he had sung the other part, he took off his glasses, looked at me with wide-open eyes, and said: "Beautiful! Beautiful! That is a beautiful *seconda parte*." And he sang it three times. As I was going away he thanked me very politely; and I assured him in response that I would arrange the aria for him in such a way that he would sing it with pleasure. For I love an aria to fit a singer as perfectly as a well-made suit.[6]

Mozart was an astute judge not only of singers' vocal abilities but of their acting as well. His return to Munich in 1780 to finish *Idomeneo* and to bring it to the stage brought him back in contact with Raaff. He expressed pessimism not only about the tenor who was to create the title role, but also about Vincenzo dal Prato, the inexperienced and badly trained musico who was to portray Idamante: "Now a sorry story. I have not, it is true, the honor of knowing the hero dal Prato; but from the description, Ceccarelli is almost better. For in the middle of an aria his breath often gives out; and – take note – he has never been on any stage. And Raaff is a statue. Now imagine the scene in the first act."[7] The scene in question was the one in which Idomeneo meets his son Idamante. When rehearsals revealed the opera to be too long, this was one of the scenes that Mozart decided to shorten.

Professional collaboration

For Mozart, as for many other eighteenth-century composers, the composition of an opera was inseparable from personal contact with the singers who were to perform it. This interaction consisted of private sessions in which the singers learned their arias and ensembles from the composer himself. The sessions often involved give and take between composer and singers. The composer, hearing his music sung for the first time, had a chance to change anything with which he was dissatisfied; the singers had a chance to ask the composer to change passages that they felt did not suit them.

During these informal rehearsals singers often used *parti cantanti* – manuscripts containing only their vocal parts and the accompanying bass lines. While many singers had the keyboard skills and harmonic knowledge to accompany themselves from a *parte cantante*, sometimes the composer's presence was necessary for the singer to have a clear and accurate impression of the music. Michael Kelly, who created a role in Paisiello's *Il re Teodoro in Venezia* in Vienna in 1784, recalled how he misjudged an aria on the basis of the "voice part" alone; it was only when Paisiello played the full accompaniment at the keyboard that Kelly realized his mistake:

> The song in Old Gaffurio's part, which I may say was the lucky star of my professional career, strange as it may appear, I had the folly to refuse to sing, thinking it too trivial for me. I sent it back to Paesiello; he desired to see me – I went – and he played me the beautiful accompaniment for it which he had written, but which was not sent me, I having received only the voice part. When I was going away, this great man gave me a gentle admonition, not to judge of things rashly: a piece of advice not thrown away upon me.[8]

The rehearsals for *Mitridate* began in early November 1770 – little less than two months before the premiere on 26 December – with singers studying their arias, with either the composer or another musician as coach. Leopold Mozart wrote on 10 November of Antonia Bernasconi, who was to create the role of Aspasia: "She . . . is beside herself with delight at the arias Wolfgang has made to her specifications, as is her maestro, Signor Lampugnani, who is rehearsing her part with her and who cannot praise Wolfgang's arias enough. Today, when we visited her, she was studying her first aria with him."[9] In reporting the approval of Bernasconi and her coach, Leopold covered up the fact that Mozart actually drafted two versions of Aspasia's first aria, "Al destin che la minaccia." It was probably only after Bernasconi rejected a setting in G major that he composed the aria in C major that became part of the opera.

A decade after *Mitridate* two other sopranos, the sisters Dorothea and Elisabeth Wendling, who portrayed Ilia and Elettra in *Idomeneo*, were equally pleased with the music Mozart wrote for them. "Madame Dorothea Wendling is *arcicontentissima* with her scena; she wanted to hear it three times in a row," Mozart wrote on 8 November 1780.[10] Exactly what Dorothea heard is unclear; possibly Mozart began his coaching sessions by singing the aria in falsetto while accompanying himself at the keyboard. Elisabeth Wendling, in contrast, expressed her approval by singing Mozart's music herself: "Lisel Wendling has also sung through her two arias half a dozen times – she is very happy."[11] Since *Idomeneo* was originally scheduled for performance in early January, the Wendlings' private rehearsals in the first half of November fit into a rehearsal schedule resembling the one that preceded the premiere of *Mitridate*.

The early rehearsals for singers usually took place in private residences – of the singer (as in the case of Bernasconi's rehearsal with Giovanni Battista Lampugnani), of the composer, or of the impresario or the manager of the theater. During preparations for *Idomeneo* Mozart played host to one singer after another for meetings that were social as well as musical. He wrote on 15 November: "Raaf was with me yesterday. I ran through his first aria for him and he was very happy with it."[12] And a week later he recorded the arrival of Domenico de Panzacchi (who sang Arbace) as it happened: "Herr Raaff visited me yesterday morning and I gave him your regards, which greatly delighted him. He too sends you his compliments. He is indeed a worthy and thoroughly honest man! . . . Come in! Herr Panzachi. He has already visited me three times, and has just invited me to lunch on Sunday."[13] Raaff returned on 30 November: "Yesterday morning Monsieur Raaff came to see me again to hear the aria in the second act. The man is as infatuated with his aria as only a young, ardent man might be with his fair one, for he sings it at night before going to sleep and in the morning when he awakes."[14]

In Vienna during the 1780s, the residence of Count Rosenberg, Emperor Joseph's chamberlain and theatrical manager, served as a site for preliminary rehearsals. Carl Zinzendorf, the theater-loving bureaucrat whose diary constitutes an important source of information about Viennese theater, occasionally witnessed rehearsals in Rosenberg's apartment. "I visited the chamberlain. Benucci, Mandini, Calvesi rehearsed a piece from [Salieri's] *La grotta di Trofonio*."[15] And on another occasion: "I visited the chamberlain where Storace and Coltellini were rehearsing an opera."[16] But Mozart may have preferred to have rehearsals in his own apartment. He wrote to his friend and creditor Michael Puchberg in December 1789, some weeks before the premiere of *Così fan tutte* (the exact date of the letter is unknown): "But Thursday I invite you (and you alone) to my apartment at 10 in the morning for a little opera rehearsal – I'm inviting only you and Haydn."[17]

The establishment of tempos was one of the chief functions of these early rehearsals, tempo being one of the musical parameters most difficult to notate precisely. That composers relied on rehearsals to communicate by gesture and word of mouth the exact tempos they had in mind emerges clearly from those exceptional occasions when a composer was not present for rehearsals, and had to try to communicate his intentions in writing. Some of the instructions in Jommelli's letters to Lisbon give us some sense of what he might have said had he been working with the singers who were to create roles in the operas he wrote for the Portuguese court; but in the end his comments only demonstrate the inadequacy of words. "The tempo of the present aria is fast but always adaptable, however, to accommodate the singer." "This aria . . . depends on the correctness of the tempo for all its good effect." "The tempos of both must be moderate, neither the one too fast nor the other too slow." "My things . . . must be taken precisely at the tempo noted."[18]

Some singers needed help with more than tempos. The musico Dal Prato caused Mozart much trouble: "I bet that fellow will never get through the rehearsals, let alone the opera. The guy is thoroughly unsound . . . When the castrato comes, I have to sing with him, for he has to learn his whole role like a child. He has not a Kreutzer's worth of technique."[19]

Lack of formal training did not necessarily keep singers from achieving great operatic success. The tenor Gioacchino Caribaldi combined a total lack of training in music theory (he could not read music) with a wonderful natural aptitude. Mosel's biography of Salieri contains an anecdote about Caribaldi, for whom the composer wrote an aria shortly before the premiere of *Le donne letterate*. "Two days before the performance of the opera Salieri took the aria . . . to the singer . . . Salieri sang the aria for him, and the singer, delighted with the composition and gifted with an extraordinary memory, learned it by heart the same day."[20]

The case of Antonio Baglioni, Mozart's first Ottavio and Tito

The tenor Antonio Baglioni, one of the few singers for whom Mozart wrote more than one important operatic role, spent most of his career in Guardasoni's opera troupe, which performed mostly in Prague, but also in Leipzig and Warsaw. The length of his involvement with Guardasoni (from 1787 to 1794 or early 1795), the quantity and importance of the roles with which he was entrusted and of the music he sang, and especially the difficulty of the music that Mozart wrote for him, might lead us to conclude that he was a first-rate singer. Yet critical appraisals of Baglioni by his contemporaries were mixed; and he never seems to have reached the highest rank in his profession, either as a *mezzo carattere* tenor – the singer who typically portrayed the young lover in comic operas – or as a tenor in opera seria.

One listener appreciated Baglioni's singing enough to write poetry for him. In Warsaw (where the Guardasoni troupe performed from 1789 to 1791) one Antonio Carpaccio published in 1790 a sonnet addressed to "Signor Baglioni, who sustains with universal applause the *mezzo carattere* role in the Italian opera."[21] A discussion of the Guardasoni company published in 1792 contains more useful praise of what the poet called Baglioni's "armoniosi accenti," singling out a particular *mezzo carattere* role in which he excelled: "Herr Baglioni. First tenor. He certainly earns well deserved applause. His voice has improved: it is rich, pure, and full of expression, so that few theaters can boast of such a tenor. We have not heard his equal in a long time. His main role is Colloardo [*recte*: Calloandro] in [Paisiello's] *La molinara*. Here he brings singing and acting together in the most masterful way."[22]

That approbation was countered by a hostile appraisal of Baglioni in a report on the Italian opera in Prague published in the December 1794 issue of the *Allgemeines europäisches Journal* of Brno. The anonymous article has been plausibly attributed to Niemetschek, partly because it displays a dislike of Italians that was characteristic of him:

> The first tenor, Herr Baglioni. This singer left the [Guardasoni] troupe a year ago, and spent some time in Italy. [The critic refers to Baglioni's appearances in the Teatro San Benedetto in Venice during Fall 1793 and Carnival 1794.] Here he eagerly collected all the bad habits of Italian artists and non-artists, and returned with them to Herr Guardasoni. Not a single note does he sing as the composer wrote it and wanted it, he drowns the most beautiful ideas in his Italian leaps and trills, and passes off as acting a monotonous waving of the hands, so that it is difficult to recognize arias when he sings them. Of course he needs such flourishes to disguise his defective voice, which is more of a *mezzo basso*; but just because Herr Baglioni cannot sing his arias in Mozart's *Così fan tutte*, he should not criticize the arias as badly written. For the great Mozart, whose genius is

always incomprehensible to foolishly babbling Italians, certainly did not
take Herr Baglioni as his standard of measurement when composing![23]

Elsewhere the critic expressed his disapproval of Baglioni simply by ignoring
him, never even mentioning, in his discussions of *Don Giovanni* and *Tito*, the
roles he created.[24]

The contributor to the *Allgemeines europäisches Journal* was not alone in ignoring Baglioni. The few surviving assessments of the first production of *Tito*
are silent on Baglioni's singing. We know from Zinzendorf that Emperor
Leopold II was delighted with Maria Marchetti Fantozzi, who created the role
of Vitellia;[25] but Zinzendorf said nothing about Baglioni. Mozart, informed
by the clarinetist Anton Stadler of the success of the last performance of *Tito*
on 30 September 1791, mentioned to his wife the performances of Marchetti
Fantozzi, Domenico Bedini (as Sesto), Carolina Perini (Annio), and Antonia
Miklaszewicz (Servilia), but not Baglioni in the title role.[26]

All this raises interesting questions, since Mozart wrote some of the finest
and most characteristic music in *Don Giovanni* and *Tito* for Baglioni, who
presumably continued to sing this music (together with that of Ferrando in
Così fan tutte) during the productions of these operas that occurred while he
remained a member of the troupe. If Baglioni really was a mediocre singer –
or if he excelled only in Paisiello's *La molinara* – how could Mozart have written such difficult and beautiful music for him? Did Mozart, in portraying
Ottavio and Tito, write for an imaginary virtuoso in the hope that sometime
in the future those roles would be performed as they should be? Everything that we know of Mozart's relations with singers tells us that he did
not.

Baglioni's career as a professional singer is summarized in the appendix
to this chapter. After making his professional debut in an opera seria (in
Bologna during Spring 1786) Baglioni turned to comic opera. He sang minor
roles – as *secondo tenore* and *secondo mezzo carattere*, and in parts designated as
"seconde parti" – and then rose, in Spring 1787, to the level of *primo mezzo
carattere*, in Parma and Bologna.

Among the operas in which Baglioni sang in the first phase of his career
(that is, before he became a *primo mezzo carattere*) was Gazzaniga's setting
of Bertati's *Don Giovanni o sia Il convitato di pietra*: the second part of a

two-part entertainment presented in Venice during Carnival 1787 – and a work that was to have important repercussions on Baglioni's career. (I mentioned this operatic double bill in chapter 3, in connection with the possibility that Baglioni, when he joined the Guardasoni troupe later in 1787, suggested to his new boss that Bertati's *Don Giovanni* be performed in Prague.)

The libretto published in Venice lists the singers and their roles in the first opera, *Il capriccio drammatico* (in which Baglioni created the role of Valerio) but not in the second. This has led to some disagreement as to what role Baglioni sang in Gazzaniga's *Don Giovanni*. Some state that he took the title role;[27] others that he was the first Duca Ottavio.[28] I believe Ottavio is more likely to have been his role. In librettos printed for some later productions of the double bill, the cast for the second opera is given; in these librettos the singer who portrayed Valerio in *Il capriccio drammatico* portrayed Duca Ottavio in *Don Giovanni*.[29]

This is an important issue, because Gazzaniga's *Don Giovanni* is one of very few surviving operas written before Mozart's for a cast that included Baglioni; most of the other operas in which he created roles are lost. Thus Gazzaniga's opera contains valuable evidence of Baglioni's vocal profile – as long as we can be relatively sure about what role was written for him. The only other opera with a part written for Baglioni that I have been able to identify and examine is Gazzaniga's *L'amore costante*, in which he created the role of Gioher, likewise in Venice during Carnival 1787. *L'amore costante* survives in the form of a manuscript score (possibly an autograph) in the Bibliothèque Nationale, Paris.

Each of Gazzaniga's operas contains one aria for Baglioni. These arias are quite different in character. Gioher's "Se rimiro quel visetto," in two tempos (Andante con moto/Allegretto), is an expression of love set to music in a light, comic style.[30] Duca Ottavio's "Vicin sperai l'istante," the first of at least four arias in B flat written for Baglioni, adopts the heroic language of opera seria. "Se rimiro quel visetto" is completely *parlando*; "Vicin sperai l'istante" has some simple coloratura. But the two arias have the same tessitura and range.

Gazzaniga treated Baglioni as having a tessitura (that is, the part of his range where he did most of his singing and to which the declamation of text was mostly limited) of one octave, from the F below middle C to F above, which he occasionally extended up to G, for a range of a ninth. A composer typically used the opening melody of an aria to display a singer's tessitura, and we can see Gazzaniga doing so in the opening melody of "Se rimiro quel visetto" (where only a few grace notes touch high G) and in the tune at the beginning of the Allegretto (ex. 6.1a and b). He did the same in "Vicin sperai l'istante (ex. 6.2a), later requiring Baglioni to show off his ability to sing coloratura (ex. 6.2b) and exploiting his high G for climactic effect near the end of the aria (ex. 6.2c).

"Sperai vicin l'istante" documents, more fully than "Se rimiro quel visetto," the vocal qualities that Baglioni brought with him to Prague – the raw material from which Mozart crafted the roles of Ottavio and Tito. In writing these roles, Mozart subjected Baglioni to a series of challenges, gradually expanding his tessitura and range and increasing the complexity and difficulty of coloratura. The challenges began with "Il mio tesoro intanto," where Mozart widened Baglioni's tessitura and range slightly by asking him repeatedly to sing G above the staff (starting with the opening melody, ex. 6.3), to delve suddenly down to an isolated D below the staff, and to spin out much longer strands of coloratura than in "Sperai vicin l'istante." As if to compensate for these demands, Mozart wrote the aria in the same key as "Sperai vicin l'istante" and allowed Baglioni to dwell often (at great length, already in the opening melody) on the F at the top of his tessitura, a note that he must have been able to sing with particular ease and beauty.

That Baglioni was a willing participant in this process of vocal develop-ment is suggested by the vocal training he engaged in while in Prague, with enough frequency to exasperate one of his neighbors. The young composer Wenzel Johann Tomaschek, who settled in Prague in 1790, lived next door to Baglioni, and recalled in his memoirs that the tenor's vocal exercises annoyed him greatly.[31] We can get some idea of the challenges posed by Baglioni's exercises by those he published later, after he retired from the stage to become a singing teacher: two volumes entitled *Nuovi esercizi per il canto composti e dedicati al nobile Sig\u1d3f Costantino Maruzzi . . . da Antonio Baglioni* (published by Ricordi in Milan). The notes that accompany some of these exercises convey Baglioni's pedagogical priorities: "per formare la voce ed unire le corde di testa con quella di petto"; "per il trillo"; "per li mordenti e gruppetti"; "per le appoggiature"; "per le terzine"; "per li salti"; "per il

Ex. 6.1   Giuseppe Gazzaniga, *L'amore costante* (Venice, Carnival 1787), "Se rimiro quel visetto"

(a) mm. 14–31

(b) mm. 42–54

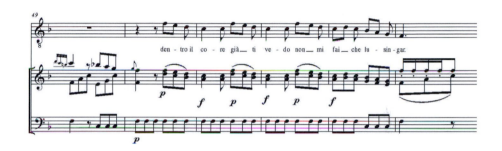

Ex. 6.2 Gazzaniga, *Don Giovanni o sia Il convitato di pietra* (part 2 of *Il capriccio drammatico*, Venice, Carnival 1787), "Vicin sperai l'istante"

(a) mm. 14–20

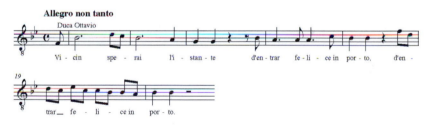

(b) mm. 44–49

Ex. 6.2 (cont.)

(c) mm. 79–85

Ex. 6.3 Mozart, *Don Giovanni*, "Il mio tesoro intanto," mm. 8–29

portamento di voce"; "per l'arpeggio." The other exercises consist mostly of very florid passagework, with elaborate lead-ins and cadenzas that bring to mind the "Italian leaps and trills" that annoyed the critic in the *Allgemeines europäisches Journal*.

   Also crucial to Baglioni's development as a singer was his exposure to opera seria. Although he made his professional debut in an opera seria, he must have found comic opera more congenial to his voice and stage personality. In Prague during the late 1780s the repertory was exclusively comic. But in Warsaw the Guardasoni troupe responded to an interest in serious opera with performances of Pietro Persichini's *Andromeda*, Paisiello's *Pirro*, Cimarosa's *La vergine del sole*, Anfossi's *Zenobia in Palmira*, and opera seria-like oratorios by Paisiello (*La passione di Gesù Cristo*) and Guglielmi (*Debora e Sisara*). Although we do not know in what operas Baglioni appeared in Warsaw, we do know that he sang in the oratorios.[32] He almost certainly sang in some of the serious operas as well.

When Guardasoni returned to Prague in June 1791, a few weeks before sign-
ing a contract in which he promised to present an opera seria in celebration
of the coronation of Leopold II as king of Bohemia, he brought with him not
only a repertory that included some of the serious dramas he had presented in
Warsaw – within a few months of his reestablishment in Prague he presented
Pirro and *Debora e Sisara* – but also a tenor experienced in opera seria and
willing to challenge and shape his own voice.

Mozart, in writing the part of Tito for him, took full advantage of the "new"
Baglioni, whose development as a singer reached its climax in his third aria in
Tito. "Se all'impero" is in the same key as "Vicin sperai l'istante" and "Il mio
tesoro," but its opening melody (ex. 6.4a) announces a tessitura wider and
higher than the one exploited by Gazzaniga a few years earlier. Baglioni was
familiar with a motive in this melody from having sung it in "Il mio tesoro";

Ex. 6.4   Mozart, *La clemenza di Tito*, "Se al impero, amici dei"

(a) mm. 11–22

(b) mm. 98–115

the sustained F in m. 20 of Tito's aria is followed by a sixteenth-note descent from G exactly as in mm. 26–27 of Ottavio's aria. The coloratura later in "Se all'impero" (ex. 6.4b) grows out of this motive; but at the same time it must have pushed Baglioni to his limits of flexibility and range (up to B flat, a minor third higher than Gazzaniga required). Firmly based on Mozart's knowledge of Baglioni's voice and experience, "Se all'impero" was the ultimate test of the tenor's vocal powers and musicianship.

Musical declarations of love

Mozart's relations with singers went far beyond professional collaboration. Opera offered him not only outlets for his musical and dramatic talents, but also opportunities for social interaction. In the theater Mozart found not only admiration and applause, but friendship and love.

Michael Kelly, a member of the Burgtheater's opera buffa company from 1783 to 1787 and creator of the roles of Basilio and Curzio in *Le nozze di Figaro*, was one of many singers who maintained friendly relations with Mozart. He wrote in his memoirs:

> He gave me a cordial invitation to his house, of which I availed myself, and passed a great part of my time there. He always received me with kindness and hospitality. – He was remarkably fond of punch, of which beverage I have seen him take copious draughts. He was also fond of billiards, and had an excellent billiard table in his house. Many and many a game have I played with him, but always came off second best.[33]

When Kelly left Vienna, "I could hardly tear myself away from him; and, at parting, we both shed tears."[34]

Similarly close contact with singers, especially men, prevailed as Mozart wrote *Die Zauberflöte*. He composed much of the opera in the lodgings of the first Sarastro, Franz Gerl, and in the garden of the first Papageno, Schikaneder.[35] Of Gerl, a friend wrote: "He was a good friend of Mozart... They were together daily, and played *Zwicken* [a card game], which Mozart liked very much."[36] The tenor and composer Benedikt Schack created the role of Tamino. According to a musical dictionary published in 1811, "Mozart often came to take Schack for a walk, and while the latter was dressing, Kapellmeister Mozart would sit down at his desk and compose a piece here and there in his operas. Thus in Schack's operas several passages occur that reveal Mozart's hand and genius."[37]

In the letters that Mozart wrote from Mannheim in early 1778 he gave expression to the complex mixture of musical admiration, operatic ambition, friendship, and sexual attraction that characterized his relations with the young soprano Aloysia Weber. Some of these elements were already in place a few months earlier, when he stared admiringly at Margarethe Kaiser through his spyglass. But while circumstances in Munich kept Mozart and Kaiser from coming into personal contact, in Mannheim Mozart's close and warm ties with the Weber family encouraged his admiration for Aloysia's musical talents to develop quickly into a passion that, according to Aloysia, he felt for the rest of his life.[38] Mozart introduced her to his father in a letter of 17 January 1778: "She sings most admirably and has a lovely pure voice. The only thing she lacks is dramatic action; were it not for that, she might be the prima donna on any stage. She is only sixteen . . . She sings most excellently my aria written for De Amicis with those horribly difficult passages."[39]

In the days that followed, Mozart and Aloysia performed together in several recitals. His admiration for her increased: "I have got to know her properly and as a result to discover her great powers."[40] Just as his interest in Mlle. Kaiser in Munich had filled him with eagerness to write a Singspiel, now his feelings for Aloysia made it difficult for him to think of anything except Italian serious opera. Soon he was imagining a future in which he and the young soprano were traveling together in Italy as composer and prima donna (and, though he did not say it to his father) as husband and wife: "As far as her singing is concerned, I would wager my life that she will bring me renown. Even in a short time she has greatly profited by my instruction, and how much greater will the improvement be by then!" He asked his father to initiate contacts with impresarios in Italy: "Do not forget how much I desire to write operas. I envy anyone who is composing one. I could really weep in frustration when I hear or see an aria. But Italian, not German; serious, not comic."[41]

A few days later Mozart's ardor – operatic, romantic, and erotic, and all three inextricably connected – had lost none of its warmth: "In my last letter I forgot to mention Mlle. Weber's greatest merit, which is her superb cantabile singing. Please do not forget about Italy. I commend this poor, but excellent little Mlle. Weber to your interest with all my heart, *caldamente*, as the Italians say. I have given her three of De Amicis's arias, the scena I wrote for Madame Duschek... and four arias from *Il re pastore*."[42] Five years earlier, during the rehearsals for *Lucio Silla*, Leopold had written of De Amicis: "We are very friendly and intimate with her."[43] In giving her arias to Aloysia, Mozart, now twenty-two years old, hoped to establish a different kind of friendship and a different kind of intimacy with his new protégée.

But it is in the music that Mozart wrote for Aloysia – and in the irresistable urge that led him to compose it – that we find the most moving evidence of his feelings for her. He wrote to his father on 28 February 1778:

> For practice I have also set to music the aria "Non so d'onde viene," which has been so beautifully composed by Bach. Just because I know Bach's setting so well and like it so much, and because it is always ringing in my ears, I wished to try and see whether in spite of all this I could not write an aria totally unlike his. And, indeed, mine does not resemble his in the very least. At first I intended it for Raaff; but the beginning seemed too high for his voice. Yet I liked it so much that I would not alter it; and from the orchestral accompaniment, too, it seemed to me better suited to a soprano. So I decided to write it for Mlle. Weber. Well, I put it aside and started off on the words "Se al labbro" for Raaff. But all in vain! I simply couldn't compose for the first aria kept on running in my head. So I returned to it and made up my mind to compose it exactly for Mlle. Weber's voice. It's an Andante sostenuto (preceded by a short recitative); then follows the second part, "Nel seno a destarmi," and then the sostenuto again. When it was finished, I said to Mlle. Weber: "Learn the aria yourself. Sing it as you think it ought to go; then let me hear it and afterwards I will tell you candidly what pleases me and what displeases me." After a couple of days I went to the Webers and she sang it for me, accompanying herself. I was obliged to confess that she sang it exactly as I wished and I should have taught it to her myself. This is now the best aria she has; and it will ensure her success wherever she goes.[44]

Two instruments on which Mozart excelled as a soloist – the piano and the violin – have particularly prominent roles in two of his most beautiful arias. He wrote the scena "Ch'io mi scordi di te," K. 505 (including the aria "Non temer amato bene") for himself as well as for Nancy Storace, who created the role of Susanna in *Figaro*; in the thematic catalogue that he compiled from 1784 on, he described it as "Scena mit Rondò mit Klavier Solo. für Mad.selle

Storace und mich."[45] It is very likely that he also wrote the solo violin part in "L'amerò, sarò costante" in Il re pastore (almost certainly first sung by the musico Consoli) for himself; the year in which he wrote this opera, 1775, was precisely the period when he wrote – and presumably played – most of his violin concertos.[46] ("L'amerò, sarò costante" was probably one of the "four arias from Il re pastore" that he gave Aloysia three years later.) Both it and "Non temer amato bene" are miracles of vocal–instrumental interaction in which the instrumentalist pays respectful and affectionate homage to the singer. Speaking through the violin and the piano, Mozart made his most intimate declarations of love to singers and to the art of singing.

Appendix

Antonio Baglioni's career as a professional singer

From Fall 1787 Baglioni sang in the Guardasoni troupe. Except in a few cases (such as the first production of Don Giovanni and La clemenza di Tito) we do not know in which operas Baglioni sang, and what roles he took (uncertainty compounded by the fact that Guardasoni usually employed two mezzo carattere tenors), but he probably sang in most of the operas listed below.

Year	Season	City	Role	Opera	Composer
1786	Spring	Bologna	Vamiro (secondo tenore[1])	Ariarate (S)*	Tarchi
	Fall	Venice	Pasquinello (secondo mezzo car.[2])	Le donne fanatiche (S)	Gazzaniga
			Sig. Guerini (secondo mezzo car.)	La contessa di Novaluna (S)	Fabrizi
1787	Carnival	Venice	Gioher (1 of 2 "seconde parti"[3])	L'amore costante (S)	Gazzaniga
			Valerio/Duca Ottavio	Il capriccio drammatico/ Don Giovanni (S)	[pasticcio] Gazzaniga
	Spring	Parma[4]	primo mezzo car.	Fra i due litiganti	Sarti
			primo mezzo car. (Roberto[5])	Gli amanti alla prova	Caruso
			primo mezzo car.	La secchia rapita	Salieri (continued)

(Continued)

Year	Season	City	Role	Opera	Composer
	Summer	Bologna[6]	primo mezzo car. (Roberto)	*Gli amanti alla prova*	Caruso
			primo mezzo car. (Balena[7])	*La statua matematica*	Valentini
	14 October	Prague[8]	Basilio?	*Le nozze di Figaro*	Mozart
	29 October		Don Ottavio	*Don Giovanni* (S)	Mozart
	Fall		Giovanni?	*Una cosa rara* (S)	Martín
			Pantaleo?	*Lo sposo senza moglie*	Cimarosa
			Endimione?	*L'arbore di Diana*	Martín
1788	Carnival			[repertory as above]	
	Summer	Leipzig[9]		[repertory unknown]	
	?	Prague	?	*Elisa* (S)	Naumann
	Fall[10]		Atar?	*Axur re d'Ormus* (S)	Salieri
			Don Ottavio?	*Don Giovanni*	Mozart
			Endimione?	*L'arbore di Diana* (S)	Martín
			Basilio?	*Le nozze di Figaro*	Mozart
			Giovanni?	*Una cosa rara*	Martín
			Lindoro?	*Il talismano* (S)	Salieri
1789	Carnival			[repertory as above]	
	?		Ernesto?	*Il mondo della luna* (S)	Paisiello
	?		Gerrardo?	*Il trionfo dell'amore sulla magia* (S)	Schuster
	?	Warsaw[11]	Endimione?	*L'arbore di Diana*	Martín
			Giovanni?	*Una cosa rara* (S)	Martín
			Artemidoro?	*La grotto di Trofonio*	Salieri
			Lindoro?	*Il talismano*	Salieri
			Atar?	*Axur re d'Ormus*	Salieri
			Sandrino?	*Il re Teodoro*	Paisiello
			[no tenor role]	*La serva padrona*	Paisiello
			Giorgino?	*La contadina di spirito*	Paisiello
			Don Ottavio?	*Don Giovanni* (S)	Mozart
			Basilio?	*Le nozze di Figaro*	Mozart
			Giocondo	*L'isola d'amore*	Sacchini
			?	*Il trionfo d'amore*	Schuster
			?	*L'impresario innamorato*[12]	Maestro Guardasino di Littuania (sic!)
			Gianferrante?	*La modista raggiratrice* (S)	Paisiello

(Continued)

Year	Season	City	Role	Opera	Composer
			Orfeo?	Orfeo ed Euridice (S)	Gluck?
1790	Carnival			[repertory as above]	
	?		?	Andromeda (S)	Persichini
	17 January		Pirro?	Pirro (S)	Paisiello
	3 July		Palmoro?	La vergine del sole (S)	Cimarosa
	Fall[13]		Palmoro?	La vergine del sole	Cimarosa
			Aureliano?	Zenobia di Palmira	Anfossi
			Sandrino?	Il re Teodoro in Venezia	Paisiello
			Cav. dell'Oca?	I finti eredi	Sarti
1791	Carnival			[repertory as above]	
	Lent[14]		?	La passione di Gesù Cristo	Paisiello
			Sisara?	Debora e Sisara (S)	Guglielmi
	Spring		?	Andromeda	Persichini
			Basilio?	Le nozze di Figaro	Mozart
	"in tutto l'anno"	Prague[15]	Atar?	Axur re d'Ormus	Salieri
	"in tutto l'anno"		Don Ottavio?	Don Giovanni	Mozart
	29 August		Pirro?	Pirro	Paisiello
	2 September		Don Ottavio?	Don Giovanni	Mozart
	6 September		Tito	La clemenza di Tito (S)	Mozart
	?		Ferrando?	Così fan tutte (S)	Mozart
	?		Calloandro	La molinara (S)	Paisiello
	?		Lindoro?	Nina (S)	Paisiello
	December		Sisara?	Debora e Sisara (S)	Guglielmi
1792	?		Capitano?	La dama soldato (S)	Naumann
	?		Paolino?	Il matrimonio segreto (S)	Cimarosa
	?		Astolfo?	La pastorella nobile (S)	Guglielmi
	Summer	Leipzig[16]	Paolino?	Il matrimonio segreto	Cimarosa
			Ferrando?	Così fan tutte	Mozart
			Astolfo?	La pastorella nobile	Guglielmi
			Capitano?	La dama soldato	Naumann
			Calloandro?	La molinara	Paisiello
			Lindoro?	Il talismano	Salieri
	3 August		Aureliano?	Zenobia di Palmira (S)	Anfossi

(continued)

(Continued)

Year	Season	City	Role	Opera	Composer
	Fall	Prague	Mont'Albore?	Lo spazzacamino principe (S)	Tarchi
1793	?		?	Gli equivoci (S)	Storace
	?		Nocesecca?	La maga Circe (S)	Anfossi
	?		?	L'incanto superato (S)	Süssmayr
	?		Rubicone?	Il mercato di Monfregoso (S)	Zingarelli
	3 August	Leipzig	Pirro?	Pirro (S)	Paisiello
	Fall	Venice	Costanzo	I fratelli rivali (S)	Winter
1794	Carnival		Simoncino	Gabbia dei matti (S)	?
			Clitandro[17]	Belisa (S)	Winter
			Barbadoro	I zingari in fiera (S)	Paisiello
	Fall	Prague	Costanzo or Silvio	I fratelli rivali (S)	Winter
			Cleante?	Le confusioni della somiglianza (S)	Portogallo
			Duca?	Giulietta e Pierotto (S)	Weigl
	3 December[18]		Tito?	La clemenza di Tito	Mozart
1795	?		Clitandro?	Belisa (S)	Winter
	?		?	Il trionfo del bel sesso (S)	Winter
	September[19]		?	Lo specchio d'Arcadia	Süssmayr
1796	10 April[20]	Vienna	Silvio	I fratelli rivali	Winter
	6 May		Lelio	La pietra simpatica	Palma
	7 August		Ramiro	Il moro (S)	Salieri
	11 December		Polidoro	L'astuta in amore	Fioravanti
1797	12 March[21]		Lelio	La pieta simpatica	Palma

*S = Sartori, I libretti italiani

CHAPTER 7

Rehearsal, revision, and promotion

Operatic composers of Mozart's time usually helped singers learn their parts and supervised rehearsals; librettists often oversaw the staging. Composers notated music and librettists wrote stage directions with the assumption that they would have plenty of opportunity to supplement these with oral instructions, with gestures, and with the sound of the keyboard instrument at which the composer or his assistant sat during rehearsals.

The schedule of rehearsals depended on the kind of operatic production. Operas commissioned by contract, and planned for a particular season, had to be rehearsed on a strict schedule; if the opera destined for performance at the beginning of Carnival was not ready, there was nothing that could take its place. Operas composed for a repertory system like that of the Burgtheater in Vienna could be rehearsed with more flexibility, because any of several operas in the repertory could always be performed in place of a new opera whose premiere was delayed.

Contracts issued within the Italian seasonal system stipulated when singers and composers were to arrive in the city in which they were to present an opera – allowing sufficient time, usually from one to two months, for rehearsals. In the case of *Mitridate* rehearsals took place methodically, at an almost leisurely pace. Two years later, however, the very late arrival of a principal singer, the tenor who was to create the title role in *Lucio Silla*, threw Mozart's composing schedule off, and consequently the rehearsals had to be rushed.

Dialogue and staging

As the date of an opera's premiere approached, informal sessions (discussed in chapter 6) involving the composer and individual singers gave way to a series of formal rehearsals involving increasingly large numbers of people. For *Mitridate* the managers of the Regio Ducal Teatro in Milan seem to have followed a rehearsal schedule similar to the one drawn up in Turin exactly ten years later for Martín y Soler's *Andromaca*, the first opera for Carnival 1781:

11 December	recitative
13	recitative
14	music
17	music
19	music
21	music and dress rehearsal for scenery ["generale scenario"]
23	dress rehearsal for music
24	dress rehearsal for ballet
26	first performance[1]

The first two of these rehearsals involved the assembled cast practicing the dialogue in simple recitative and, in doing so, making sure the text copied by the composer into his autograph score and copied again by professional copyists in the *parti cantanti* matched the text of the libretto. The first recitative rehearsal for *Mitridate* took place a few days earlier than the analogous rehearsal for Martín's opera. Leopold Mozart wrote on 8 December 1770:

> The second recitative rehearsal is today . . . The first rehearsal went so well that only once did someone take up a pen to change a single letter, and that was to change *della* to *dalla*. This does the copyist credit and astonished everyone, in that usually (as everyone says) an amazing number of words and notes have to be altered everywhere. I hope it will be the same with the instrumental rehearsals, which, by the time you receive this letter, will perhaps have already begun.[2]

Once the composer, librettist, and performers had agreed on a text, they proceeded to the staging – the placing of actors on stage in relation to the audience and to each other, and the physical and verbal interaction of the actors. We have very little solid information about how Mozart and his contemporaries handled these things. But for an amusing glimpse at this important part of operatic production we can turn to a comic opera entitled *La prova di un'opera seria* (The rehearsal of an opera seria), performed in Milan in 1805 with music by Francesco Gnecco. The librettist Grilletto begins the staging of an important scene by first explaining the dramatic situation to the assembled cast:

Please bear with me! The action represents Hector's condemnation of the queen. At the fatal announcement she almost faints. Semira supports her, and the extras stand all around her. You stand here (*to Corilla, placing her at the center*). You here (*to Violante, positioning her as Corilla's support*). You there (*to Federico, placing him to one side*). You others round about (*to the chorus, positioning them around Corilla*). And you there pretend to be the first musico (*to Fastidio, positioning him near Corilla*). Now let's begin. Maestro![3]

Notice that the maestro's – that is, the composer's – responsibility here was limited to supplying the instrumental accompaniment, presumably at the keyboard.

The several librettists that Mozart worked with must have done much the same as Grilletto. However great Mozart's interest in the staging of his operas, he seems to have always expected and wanted a stage director at his side as a new opera approached performance; and that stage director was usually the librettist or the house poet. That Da Ponte played an active role in the staging of the operas he wrote with Mozart is suggested by his taking the trouble to go to Prague and stay there for several days during the rehearsals for *Don Giovanni* in October 1787. The delay of that opera's first performance, combined with pressing responsibilities in Vienna, forced Da Ponte to leave Prague before *Don Giovanni* came to the stage: "I spent a week there directing the actors who were to create it; but before it appeared on the stage, I had to hurry back to Vienna because of a fiery letter I received from Salieri, wherein he informed me, truly or not, that *Assur* had to be ready at once for the marriage of [Archduke] Franz, and that the emperor had ordered him to call me home."[4]

For the staging of his next opera for Prague, *Tito*, Mozart again worked with his librettist. Although we do not know when Mazzolà arrived in Prague, we do know that he was there during the coronation festivities, because his departure from the Bohemian capital is recorded in a local newspaper on 13 September 1791, a week after the premiere of *Tito*.[5] He almost certainly came to Prague to supervise the staging of the drama whose text he had revised for Mozart.

Ensembles

In the composition and rehearsal of arias Mozart willingly gave his singers an important role in the creative process; but in ensembles he claimed more authority. He drew a distinction between arias and ensembles when Raaff asked for changes in "Andrò ramingo e solo," the great quartet in *Idomeneo*, as he explained to his father:

> I have just had some trouble with him over the quartet. The more I imagine this quartet on stage, the more effective I consider it; and it has pleased all those who have heard it played on the Clavier. Raaff alone thinks it will produce no effect. When we were alone he said to me: "Non c'è da spianar la voce." It is too limited. As if in a quartet one should not speak more than sing. That kind of thing he does not understand at all. I said only: "My dear friend, if I knew of one single note which ought to be altered in this quartet, I would do so at once. But so far there is nothing in my opera with which I am so pleased as with this quartet; and when you have once heard it as a whole, you will talk differently. I have taken great pains to serve you well in your two arias; I shall do the same with your third one – and shall hope to succeed. But as far as trios and quartets are concerned, the composer must have a free hand." Whereupon he said that he was satisfied.[6]

Leopold, in response, agreed fully with his son: "I need not say anything about the quartets, and so forth, for which declamation and action are far more essential than great singing ability or his everlasting 'spianar la voce.' In this case action and diction are the necessary qualities."[7]

Yet a few years later, in rehearsals for *Figaro*, Mozart found himself on the other side of a similar discussion. Kelly argued for a speechlike delivery of his part, that of the stuttering judge Curzio, in the sextet "Riconosci in questo amplesso," which he remembered as "Mozart's favourite piece of the whole opera." Mozart, claiming his free hand as the composer of ensembles, insisted at first on a more purely musical singing of the kind that Raaff had wanted to display in "Andrò ramingo e solo":

> All through the piece [i.e. the opera] I was to stutter; but in the sestetto, Mozart requested I would not, for if I did, I should spoil his music. I told him, that although it might appear very presumptuous in a lad like me to differ with him on this point, I did; and was sure, the way in which I intended to introduce the stuttering, would not interfere with the other parts, but produce an effect; besides, it certainly was not in nature, that I should stutter all through the part, and when I came to the sestetto, speak plain; and after that piece of music was over, return to stuttering; and, I

added, (apologising at the same time, for my apparent want of deference and respect in placing my opinion in opposition to that of the great Mozart,) that unless I was allowed to perform the part as I wished, I would not perform it at all.

Mozart at last consented that I should have my own way, but doubted the success of the experiment. Crowded houses proved that nothing ever on the stage produced a more powerful effect; the audience were convulsed with laughter, in which Mozart himself joined. The Emperor repeatedly cried out Bravo! and the piece was loudly applauded and encored. When the opera was over, Mozart came on the stage to me, and shaking me by both hands, said, "Bravo! young man, I feel obliged to you; and acknowledge you to have been in the right, and myself in the wrong."[8]

Rehearsals with orchestra

The first orchestral rehearsal sometimes involved an orchestra much smaller than the one that would later assemble for the final rehearsals and the performances. One function of this scaled-down orchestral run-through was, again, proofreading – to make sure the parts had been accurately copied from the autograph score, as Leopold wrote of preparations for *Mitridate*: "On the 12th [of December, exactly two weeks before the premiere] was the first rehearsal with instruments, but only with sixteen players, in order to see if everything has been copied correctly. On the 17th will be the first rehearsal with the full orchestra."[9]

Sixteen players: perhaps two first violins, two second violins, one viola, one cello, one double bass, two flutes, two oboes, two trumpets, two horns, and Mozart at the keyboard.

Similar run-throughs for *Idomeneo* took place ten years later, but because of the score's complexity, they were spread out over two days. Mozart wrote: "The rehearsal [of act 1] went off extremely well. There were only six violins in all, but we had the necessary wind-instruments . . . A week from today we are to have another rehearsal, when we will have twelve violinists for the first act (for which the parts will be duplicated in the meantime), and the second act will be rehearsed like the first on the previous occasion."[10]

The second orchestral rehearsal of *Idomeneo* (and probably the first as well) took place in the residence of Count Seeau, the manager of the theater. But as more instrumentalists were brought in, the orchestra had to be moved, as Mozart wrote on 19 December: "Next Saturday both acts [1 and 2] are to be rehearsed again, but in a large hall at court, which I have long wished for, because there is not nearly enough room at Count Seeau's."[11]

The rehearsals for *Mitridate* similarly moved to a large hall – the court ballroom – before moving to the theater, in order to accommodate a very big orchestra. Writing on 22 December, four days before the premiere, Leopold gave what seems to be a complete schedule of the four final rehearsals: "On the 19th was the first rehearsal on stage; the one before, on the 17th, was in the Redoutensaal. Thank God it went very well. Yesterday evening we had a rehearsal of the recitatives, today after Ave Maria there will be a second rehearsal on stage, and on Monday [24 December] the dress rehearsal will take place."[12]

In scheduling the first rehearsal of *Mitridate* in the theater only a week before the premiere, the management may have been conforming to a widespread convention. Twenty years later, the first performance of *Così fan tutte* took place in Vienna's Burgtheater on 26 January 1790. Six days earlier, on 20 January, Mozart wrote to Michael Puchberg: "We are having the first instrumental rehearsal in the theater tomorrow. Haydn is coming with me. If your business allows you to do so and if you care to hear the rehearsal, all you need do is to be so kind as to turn up at my quarters at ten o'clock tomorrow morning and then we will all go there together."[13]

One kind of music to which Mozart probably directed a great deal of attention during orchestral rehearsals was orchestrally accompanied recitative, the notation of which involved special conventions that may not have been familiar to all instrumentalists. Haydn acknowledged the challenges posed by accompanied recitative when, unable to attend rehearsals for a cantata, he sent instructions for its performance:

> In the accompanied recitatives, you must observe that the accompaniment should not enter until the singer has quite finished his text, even though the score often shows the contrary. For instance, at the beginning where the word "metamorphosis" is repeated, and the orchestra comes in at "-phosis," you must nevertheless wait until the last syllable is finished and then enter quickly; for it would be ridiculous if you would fiddle away the word from the singer's mouth, and understand only the words "quae

metamo . . . " But I leave this to the keyboard player, and all the others
must follow him.[14]

Under the normal circumstances of operatic production, the keyboard player
would have been the composer himself.

Operatic orchestras

The orchestras that came together during the course of rehearsals for Mozart's
operas varied widely in quality and size. One of smallest and best was the
orchestra in Prague that presented the first productions of *Don Giovanni* and
La clemenza di Tito, of which Niemetschek wrote:

> The opera orchestra is relatively scantily staffed (it has only three first and
> second violins, three violas, the basses and the appropriate wind
> instruments) but, according to the opinions of Mozart and other famous
> composers who know it, it can be reckoned among the finest in Germany.
> It does not count famous concerto soloists or virtuosi among its members,
> but all its members are skilled and thorough, many are first-rate artists,
> fired by a sense of honor, who through renunciation of personal priority
> and a long period of continuous playing together, produce a remarkably
> unified whole that seems to come forth from a single soul. It has often,
> without any rehearsal, performed the most difficult pieces of Mozart to his
> complete satisfaction. One need only look at the instrumental parts of *Don
> Juan*, which Mozart wrote for this orchestra, to agree with my opinion.[15]

The orchestra of the Theater auf der Wieden for which Mozart wrote *Die
Zauberflöte* was probably about the same size as that of Prague's Nostitz Theater. A musical almanac of 1796 describes Schikaneder's orchestra as having
three first violins, three second violins, two violas, one cello, two double
basses, and pairs of oboes, flutes, clarinets, bassoons, horns, trumpets, and
timpani.[16]

The largest orchestra for which Mozart composed was the one that accompanied his Milanese operas. Of *Mitridate* Leopold Mozart wrote proudly on
15 December 1770: "On the 17th will be the first rehearsal with the whole
orchestra, which consists of fourteen first and fourteen second violins (thus
twenty-eight violins), two Clavier, six double basses, two cellos, two bassoons, six violas, two oboes and two flutes (who, where there are no flutes,

always play as four oboes), four horns, and two trumpets, etc. – sixty players in all."[17] Charles Burney, who attended a performance in the Regio Ducal Teatro a few months earlier, found the orchestra remarkably big, even for so large a theater: "The band was very numerous and orchestra large in proportion to the house."[18]

Mozart's other operatic orchestras fell, in size, somewhere in between these extremes. The orchestra of Vienna's Burgtheater changed little during the decade in which Mozart had contact with it. During the theatrical year 1782–83, when Die Entführung reached the stage, the orchestra consisted of six first violins, six second violins, four violas, three cellos, three double basses, and pairs of oboes, flutes, clarinets, and bassoons.[19] Of four horns listed in payment records, probably two were expected to play trumpet when necessary. The management engaged a timpanist and other percussionists (such as those needed in the Turkish music in Die Entführung) only for operas that required them. The orchestra that accompanied the Viennese version of Don Giovanni during the theatrical year 1788–89 differed only in having three double basses instead of four, in explicitly dividing the brass group into two horns and two trumpets, and in having a permanent timpanist. The Burgtheater had no permanent trombonists during the 1780s and there is no record of any being hired especially to play in Don Giovanni. That, together with the absence of trombone parts from the Burgtheater's performance score of Don Giovanni, suggests strongly that early Viennese performances of Mozart's opera, under the composer's supervision, did not involve trombones.

It was probably in reference to the Burgtheater orchestra that a Swiss visitor to Vienna, Johann Kaspar Riesbeck, wrote this account, published in 1783:

> The number of real virtuosi [in Vienna] is small; but as far as orchestral musicians are concerned, one could hardly hear anything in the world more beautiful. I have already heard about thirty or forty instruments play together; and they all produce a tone so correct, pure, and clear that one might believe one were hearing a single, supernaturally powerful instrument. One stroke of the bow brings all the violins to life, one breath all the wind instruments. An Englishman next to whom I sat thought it amazing that through an entire opera one could hear, I won't say a single dissonance, but none of those things that normally occur in a large orchestra, such as a too hasty entrance, a note held too long, or an

instrument bowed or blown too loud. He was enchanted by the purity and correctness of the harmony; and yet he had just come from Italy.[20]

The orchestra that took part in the performance of *Idomeneo* was limited in size by the space available in Munich's Cuvilliés Theater (illustrated in chapter 8). Although the electoral court at Munich employed enough musicians to form a large orchestra, Mozart referred to the band that was to accompany *Idomeneo* as "the whole orchestra (that is, as much of it as can fit in the opera house)."[21] The twelve violins that took part in some later rehearsals – and presumably also the performances – of *Idomeneo* made that orchestra very similar in size to that of the Burgtheater.

Rehearsal as public relations campaign

Operatic rehearsals often took place against a backdrop of what Mozart and his contemporaries called "cabals" – vaguely defined mixtures (partly real, partly imagined) of malicious gossip and conspiratorial efforts to undermine an opera's success. The Mozarts, father as well as son, learned from their experience with *La finta semplice* in Vienna in 1768 to be particularly sensitive to the slightest hint of a cabal.

That fiasco was still fresh in Leopold's mind during the rehearsals for *Mitridate*:

> Before the first rehearsal with the small orchestra took place, there were plenty of people who satirically proclaimed – so to speak prophesied – the music in advance as something immature and wretched, because they thought it would be impossible that such a young boy, and, what is more, a German, could write an Italian opera, and, although they recognized him as a great virtuoso, that he could sufficiently understand and apply the *chiaro ed oscuro* that is necessary for the theater.[22]

Nothing much had changed for Leopold when, fifteen years later, he wrote to his daughter:

> Today your brother's opera *Le nozze di Figaro* will be staged for the first time. It will be remarkable if it succeeds, for I know that extraordinary cabals have been mounted against him. Salieri and his followers have set heaven and earth in motion yet again to defeat him. M. and Mme. Duschek

have already said to me that your brother has so many cabals against him because he has gained such a great reputation through his special talents and cleverness.[23]

In view of Leopold's fear and hatred of cabals, it is amusing to see him, occasionally, acting as an enthusiastic member of a cabal himself, denigrating the operas performed in conjunction with Wolfgang's while representing himself as a model of fairmindedness. On *Ascanio in Alba* and Hasse's *Ruggiero* in Milan during October 1771: "It really distresses me very greatly, but Wolfgang's serenata has killed Hasse's opera more than I can say in detail."[24] And when *La finta giardiniera* was about to be performed in Munich in 1775, Leopold happily anticipated (in a letter quoted in chapter 3) that Wolfgang's opera would put Tozzi's *Orfeo ed Euridice* in the shade.

Mozart feared cabals as much as his father. Inviting Puchberg to a rehearsal of *Così fan tutte*, in December 1789, he wrote: "I shall tell you when we meet about Salieri's plots, which, however, have completely failed already."[25]

An important function of orchestral rehearsals, at least as perceived by Leopold and Wolfgang, was to counteract the effect of any and all cabals by impressing the singers, the orchestra, and the select audience that witnessed the rehearsals with the quality of the music. The good impression that orchestral rehearsals made would, they hoped, encourage the musicians to perform with as much energy and committment as possible, while favorable reports of the opera, quickly spreading by word of mouth far beyond the theater, would increase the size and excitement of the audience and enhance the composer's reputation. Thus the rehearsals served as a kind of publicity campaign directed at both the performers and the potential audience.

Conversely, a badly organized rehearsal, or a rehearsal for which the singers were not fully prepared, might lead to disaster. This seems to have happened with *La finta semplice*, as Leopold stated in the appeal that he made to Emperor Joseph II after the opera was cancelled:

It rarely happens that an opera comes out perfectly at the first rehearsal, without changes being made here and there. Exactly for this reason the practice is to begin at the *Flügl* [i.e. a wing-shaped harpsichord or piano] alone, and until the singers know their parts, and especially the finales, never to rehearse with all the instruments. Yet here just the opposite happened. The roles were not studied enough, there was no rehearsal of the singers at the Clavier, the finales were not studied in ensemble, and yet the first act was tried out with all the instruments, in order to give the thing a poor and confused appearance right from the beginning. No one who was present will call that a rehearsal without becoming embarrassed.[26]

Memories of that rehearsal may have haunted Mozart and his father for years afterward.

About two and a half years later the first rehearsal of *Mitridate* with a reduced orchestra had precisely the opposite effect. According to Leopold, it silenced those who had been spreading derogatory rumors:

> Since the evening of the first small rehearsal [that is, the first rehearsal with reduced orchestra] all these people have been silent and have not uttered a syllable . . . The singers are very happy and indeed delighted, and especially the prima donna and the primo uomo, who are overjoyed with their duet. The primo uomo has said that if this duet does not succeed, he will let himself be castrated again. Basta! Everything now depends on the public's caprice.[27]

Of the first orchestral rehearsal of *Idomeneo* (act 1 only), Mozart wrote triumphantly of the delight and surprise that the music stirred up in both the very small audience and the pared-down orchestra:

> But indeed I never expected anything else, for I assure you I went to that rehearsal with as easy a mind as if I were going to a lunch party somewhere. Count Sensheim said to me: "I assure you that though I expected a great deal from you, I really did not expect that." The Cannabichs and all who frequent their house are really true friends of mine. When I walked home with Cannabich to his house after the rehearsal (for we still had much to talk over with the Count), Madame Cannabich came out to meet us and embraced me, delighted that the rehearsal had gone off so well. For Ramm and Lang had gone to her house, simply beside themselves with joy . . . Ramm said to me – now when you meet him, you will call him a true German – for he tells you to your face exactly what he thinks: "I must honestly confess that no music has ever made such an impression on me, and I can assure you that I thought fifty times of your father and of what his delight will be when he hears this opera."[28]

Mozart was equally proud of how the next rehearsal with orchestra went: "The second rehearsal [on 16 December] was as successful as the first. The orchestra and the whole audience discovered to their delight that the second act was actually more expressive and original than the first."[29]

The elector witnessed part of what was probably the third orchestral rehearsal, causing two numbers to be played out of order:

> The most recent rehearsal was splendid. It took place in a big room at court. The elector was there too . . . After the first act the elector called out to me quite loudly, Bravo! When I went up to kiss his hand he said: "This opera will be charming and cannot fail to do you honor." As he was not sure whether he could remain much longer, we had to perform the aria with obbligatos for wind instruments and the thunderstorm at the beginning of Act II, when he again expressed his approval in the kindest manner and said with a laugh: "Who would believe that such great things could be hidden in so small a head?"[30]

No doubt aided by Mozart and Leopold, word of the success of the rehearsals traveled quickly. Leopold wrote from Salzburg on 25 December: "Throughout the city people are talking about the excellence of your opera."[31]

Although Mozart valued the publicity that originated with rehearsal audiences, sometimes the audience was too large. Shortly before the premiere of *Lucio Silla* he wrote: "The rehearsal tomorrow is at the theater, but Signor Castiglione, the impresario, has begged me not to tell anyone about it; otherwise a whole crowd of people will be coming in, and we do not want this."[32]

Leopold wrote at some length (again in reference to *Idomeneo*) of another function of the orchestral rehearsals – to win over not just the orchestra's admiration but its good will. The instrumentalists needed to feel well disposed toward a composer, according to Leopold, to play their best:

> But try to keep the whole orchestra in good humor; flatter them, and, by praising them, keep yourself in their good graces. For I know your style of composition – it requires unusually close attention from the players of every instrument; and to keep the orchestra at such a level of diligence and alertness for at least three hours is no joke. Every musician, even the most inferior violist, is deeply touched by personal praise and becomes much more zealous and attentive, and that kind of courtesy costs nothing but a word or two. However – you know all this yourself – I am just

mentioning it, because during rehearsals there are few chances for this, and so one forgets; and because only when the opera is staged do you really need the friendship and the enthusiasm of the whole orchestra.[33]

Mozart absorbed his father's advice. Niemetschek gives us a glimpse of him cultivating the friendship and goodwill of a local musician, the keyboard player and orchestral director Jan Křitel Kuchař, during rehearsals for *Don Giovanni*. Kuchař specialized in the production of keyboard reductions of Mozart's operas. In the case of *Don Giovanni* he was probably at work on a keyboard score even before the opera's premiere, benefitting from unusually close access to the composer (and probably to his autograph score).[34] The anecdote came from Kuchař himself:

> Once (it was after the first rehearsal of his *Don Giovanni*) Mozart went for a walk with the then orchestra director and Kapellmeister Herr Kucharz. In the course of their private conversation the talk turned to *Don Juan*. Mozart said: "What do you think of the music of *Don Juan*? Will it please as much as *Figaro*? It is quite a different kind of opera."
>
> *Kuch.*: How could you have any doubt? The music is beautiful, original, profound.
>
> *Moz.*: Your confidence reassures me, coming as it does from a connoisseur. But I have not spared myself trouble and labor in order to produce something extraordinary for Prague.[35]

Evidence of Mozart's efforts to please Kuchař (whose name, in Czech, means "cook") can be found even in the score of *Don Giovanni*. In the dinner scene near the end of the opera, where Don Giovanni's wind ensemble plays music from comic operas by Sarti, Martín y Soler, and Mozart, Leporello sings the quotation from Mozart's "Non più andrai" to the repeated words "Si eccellente è il vostro cuoco" (Your cook is so excellent). The audience at the premiere of *Don Giovanni* in Prague must have understood this as a comic tribute to Kuchař, who was even then cooking up a keyboard reduction of the opera.[36]

Rehearsals for *Figaro*

Michael Kelly, whose recollections of a rehearsal of "Riconosci in questo amplesso" I quoted earlier, left a vivid description of an orchestral rehearsal

that demonstrates that in Vienna too one of the functions of rehearsal was
to display the quality of the music to the performers. Mozart's praise of the
great singer who was to create the role of Figaro, Francesco Benucci, shows
again that he had learned his father's lesson about winning the performers'
goodwill:

> I remember at the first rehearsal of the full band, Mozart was on the stage
> with his crimson pelisse and gold-laced cocked hat, giving the time of the
> music to the orchestra. Figaro's song, "Non più andrai, farfallone
> amoroso," Bennuci gave, with the greatest animation and power of voice.
>   I was standing close to Mozart, who, *sotto voce*, was repeating, Bravo!
> Bravo! Bennuci; and when Bennuci came to the fine passage, "Cherubino,
> alla vittoria, alla gloria militar," which he gave out with Stentorian lungs,
> the effect was electricity itself, for the whole of the performers on the
> stage, and those in the orchestra, as if actuated by one feeling of delight,
> vociferated Bravo! Bravo! Maestro. Viva, viva grande Mozart. Those in the
> orchestra I thought would never have ceased applauding, by beating the
> bows of their violins against the music desks. The little man
> acknowledged, by repeated obeisances, his thanks for the distinguished
> mark of enthusiastic applause bestowed upon him.[37]

But if this first orchestral rehearsal won over the singers and instrumentalists, the dress rehearsal played an even more important role in keeping an
important part of the opera from being cancelled against Mozart's wishes.
In Da Ponte's account of the affair, Rosenberg ordered that the ballet music
from the finale of act 3 be omitted from the opera, probably because the
Italian troupe at the time did not include professional dancers; hiring them
would involve extra expense. The dialogue between theater director and librettist, undoubtedly partly invented by Da Ponte, nicely conveys the emotional
tension that must have prevailed as *Figaro* neared performance:

> "So, the *signor poeta* has used a ballet in *Figaro*?"
> "Yes, Excellency."
> "The *signor poeta* does not know that the emperor does not want ballets in
>   his theater?"
> "No, Excellency."
> "In that case, *Signor poeta*, I am telling you now."

"Yes, Excellency."

"And I will tell you further, *Signor poeta*, that you must take it out." He repeated this "*Signor poeta*" in a significant tone that gave it the meaning of "Signor Jack-ass" or something of the sort. But my "Excellency" had its innuendo too.

"No, Excellency."

"Have you the libretto with you?"

"Yes, Excellency."

"Where is the scene with the ballet?"

"Here it is, Excellency."

"This is the way we do things." Saying which he took two sheets from the libretto, laid them carefully on the fire and returned the libretto to me. "You see, *Signor poeta*, that I can do anything." And he honored me with a second dismissal.

I hurried to Mozzart, who on hearing the bad news from me, was desperate. He wanted to go to the count, to give Bussani [the singer who had called Rosenberg's attention to the ballet] a beating, to appeal to Caesar, to withdraw the score. It was a task for me to calm him. I finally begged him to give me just two days' time, and to leave everything to me.

The dress rehearsal of the opera was to be held that same day. I went in person to tell the sovereign, and he promised to attend at the hour set. And in fact he came, and with him half the aristocracy of Vienna. The Abbé [Casti, Da Ponte's rival] likewise came with him.

The first act went off amid general applause, but at the end [of act 3] comes a pantomimic scene between the Count and Susanna, during which the orchestra plays and the dance takes place. But the way His Excellency Know-it-all had adapted the scene, all one could see was the Count and Susanna gesticulating and the orchestra being silent, it all looked like a puppet show. "What's all this?" exclaimed the emperor to Casti, who was sitting behind him.

"You must ask the poet that!" replied the Abbé, with a malicious smile. So I was summoned, but instead of replying to the question put to me, I handed him my manuscript, in which I had restored the scene. The sovereign glanced through it, and asked why the dance was not being performed. My silence gave him to understand there was some intrigue behind it all. He turned to the count, asked him to explain; and he, spluttering, said that the ballet had been left out because the opera troupe had no dancers.

"Are there not dancers," he asked, "in the other theaters?" The answer was that there were.

"Very well, let Da Ponte have as many as he needs."

In less than half an hour twenty-four dancers arrived. At the end of the second [recte: third] act the scene that had been suppressed was rehearsed; and the emperor shouted: "Now it's all right!"[38]

Cuts and other revisions

The dress rehearsal of Figaro helped keep it intact; but that was probably an exceptional occurrence. Late rehearsals often involved cuts, painful for the composer and performers alike. It was only when an opera began to take shape on stage that it could be perceived as a whole, its theatrical viability most accurately evaluated, and excessive length recognized and remedied.

The great length of Idomeneo in particular emerged during the late rehearsals as a signficant problem. It was only on 19 December, after two orchestral rehearsals, that Mozart started to make cuts. First he looked for places to trim the dialogue in recitative, writing to his father: "The scene between father and son in Act 1 and the first scene in Act 2 between Idomeneo and Arbace are both too long. They will certainly bore the audience, especially since in the first scene both the actors are bad, and in the second, one of them is; besides, they only contain a narrative of what the spectators have already seen with their own eyes."[39] These cuts helped, but in the end they were not enough. In order to tighten Idomeneo still further Mozart consented to the omission of a great aria for Raaff, "Torna la pace al core." Both Mozart and Raaff must have found it painful to abandon this beautiful music. But Mozart was willing to sacrifice musical beauty in the interests of the overall theatrical effectiveness of Idomeneo.[40]

Mozart's autograph scores do not usually reflect the changes his operas underwent during the later rehearsals. This is because the score used in these rehearsals, and in the performances that followed, was not the autograph but a copy made from it by professional copyists. Some of the performing scores from the original productions of Mozart's operas survive, and these contain valuable evidence about how the operas evolved during rehearsals and early performances.

The performing score for *Così fan tutte*, preserved in the Austrian National Library under the call number OA 146, is the principal source for most of the music missing from the autograph. It also serves as the most reliable record of changes made to the opera during rehearsals and performances, some by Mozart or with his approval.

One such change – surprising to modern audiences who treasure the music involved – was the replacement of the canon in the second-act finale by a new, thirteen-measure passage. OA 146 contains both the canon (on pages formerly stitched together with thread, indicating that they were once omitted from performance) and the new passage. On the basis of the paper on which the new passage was copied, Alan Tyson concluded that the copying was done around 1804–05. He suggested that Mozart's autograph of the thirteen-measure passage had originally been part of the performing score, only replaced by a copy when it was recognized as an autograph in 1804.[41]

OA 146 documents many other cuts, carefully itemized and analyzed by Dexter Edge, who believes that several of them can be associated with the first run of performances in 1790 (and therefore made with Mozart's approval, or at least his knowledge).[42] The overture, both finales, Ferrando's aria "Ah lo veggio," and much dialogue in simple recitative were subject to cuts, suggesting that in bringing *Così fan tutte* to the stage Mozart had to go through the painful process so well documented in the letters he wrote from Munich during the rehearsals of *Idomeneo*. The decision to replace "Rivolgete a lui lo sguardo" with "Non siate ritrosi" came early, in December 1789; there is no trace of "Rivolgete" in OA 146. But it was probably only as the opera took shape on stage and as the first performances revealed its effect on audiences that Mozart recognized some of the other places where the opera might be improved by shortening.

In other operas, late rehearsals occasionally led to the last-minute insertion of new material. The singer Sebastian Mayer, second husband of the singer who created the role of the Queen of the Night in *Die Zauberflöte* and himself a portrayer of Sarastro from 1793, told an anecdote about the rehearsals of that opera:

> Mozart had originally written the duet where Papageno and Papagena first see each other quite differently from the way in which we now hear it. Both

originally cried out "Papageno!" "Papagena!" a few times in amazement. But when Schikaneder heard this, he came down into the orchestra. "Hey, Mozart! That's no good, the music must express greater astonishment. They must both stare dumbly at each other, then Papageno must begin to stammer: 'Pa-papapa-pa-pa'; Papagena must repeat that until both of them finally get the whole name out." Mozart followed the advice, and in this form the duet always had to be repeated.

Further, when the priests were assembling in the second act, this happened as late as the dress rehearsal without any musical accompaniment, but Schikaneder asked that a solemn march be composed for it. Mozart is reported to have then said to the musicians: "Give me your music folders!" and to have at once written this splendid march into their parts.[43]

That Mozart wrote the march directly into the manuscript parts from which the instrumentalists were reading is highly unlikely. But his own thematic catalogue confirms that he composed the march very late. He listed it and the overture (in an entry separate from that of the opera as a whole) under the date 28 September, two days before the premiere. Thus Mayer was almost certainly correct that Mozart wrote the march in response to a need perceived during one of the last rehearsals.

Extra rehearsals and postponed premieres

Mozart's growing musical sophistication and ambition produced operas that from the mid 1770s on seem to have almost without exception required more rehearsal than normal, which often resulted in delayed performances. The difficulty of Mozart's operatic music seems to have first emerged as a significant issue during rehearsals of *La finta giardiniera* in Munich during December 1775. Leopold wrote on 28 December:

> At ten in the morning was the first rehearsal of Wolfgang's opera, which was so well received that the first performance has been postponed until January 5th, so the singers may learn their parts better and thus, knowing the music perfectly, may act with greater confidence and not spoil the opera, which would have been a rushed affair if performed on 29 December. As a musical composition it is amazingly popular, and so it will be performed on 5 January. Now everything depends on the

production in the theater, which I hope will go well, for the actors are not unfavorable to us.[44]

Leopold may have been putting the best face on a bad situation here: the singers, though well disposed toward Wolfgang, were apparently having trouble learning their music.[45] Having been postponed to 5 January, *La finta giardiniera* was postponed again; Leopold's letters are silent on the reason for the delay. Mozart's opera reached the stage only on 13 January.

Mozart's tendency to procrastinate combined with the extraordinary complexity of *Idomeneo* to produce another delayed premiere during the Munich Carnival of 1781. Likewise with *Figaro*, which Mozart was already working hard to complete in November 1785, perhaps hoping for a first performance during Carnival 1786. After that plan was abandoned, a completely new schedule called for a premiere on 28 April 1786, further postponed until 1 May.[46] In Prague *Don Giovanni* was originally planned for performance on 14 October 1787. But because the production was not yet ready, a performance of *Figaro* had to be substituted. Mozart wrote to his friend Gottfried von Jacquin on 15 October:

> You probably think that my opera is over by now. If so, you are a little mistaken. In the first place, the stage personnel here are not as smart as those in Vienna, when it comes to mastering an opera of this kind in a very short time. Secondly, I found on my arrival that so few preparations and arrangements had been made that it would have been absolutely impossible to produce it on the 14th, that is, yesterday. So yesterday my *Figaro* was performed in a fully lighted theater and I myself conducted.[47]

Mozart deserves some of the blame for the delay, since his arrival in Prague less than two weeks before the scheduled premiere did not allow nearly enough time to rehearse a big, complex opera like *Don Giovanni*, even for the most skillful and experienced singers.

The premiere was postponed until 24 October, but the illness of a singer caused another delay, as Mozart explained to Jacquin:

> As the company is small, the impresario is in a perpetual state of anxiety and has to spare his people as much as possible, lest some unexpected indisposition should plunge him into the most awkward of all situations, that of not being able to produce any show whatsoever! So everything

dawdles along here because the singers, who are lazy, refuse to rehearse on opera days and the manager, who is anxious and timid, will not force them.[48]

Improvisation: vocal embellishments and comic business

Singers not only learned their music in rehearsals, but also began to embellish it, working out with the composer what parts of the vocal line were susceptible to improvised ornamentation and what parts were to be sung as written. Such improvisation was a crucial part of eighteenth-century performance practice. A critic writing of a performance of Sarti's *Giulio Sabino* in London in 1788 was unimpressed with Sarti's music but found much to admire in the performance of the musico Marchesi. The score, he said, "is not very striking nor moving. However some part of it has much merit, and what made it appear most brilliant last Saturday was the appearance in it of Signor Marchesi. Though it must always be understood that the modulations, flights, and variations which he utters are his own, and not the master's."[49]

The problem of where to embellish, and how much, must have risen frequently in rehearsals. Much depended, of course, on the dramatic situation, on the singer's skills, on the character of the vocal line and of the accompaniment, and on the tastes of the composer.

One of the few bits of evidence about Mozart's views on improvised embellishment is an anecdote about the rehearsals for *Die Zauberflöte*. Carl Joseph Schikaneder, the librettist's nephew, reported many years later that Gerl, who created the role of Sarastro, ornamented the vocal line of "In diesen heil'gen Hallen" when singing the second strophe (which is, in so far as Mozart notated it, exactly the same as the first strophe). The composer shouted to his friend: "Stop, Gerl! If I had wanted it that way, that's the way I would have written it. Sing it as it stands."[50]

The story attractively evokes a picture of Mozart in rehearsal, but we should not interpret it to mean that Mozart always insisted on singers performing his music exactly as he wrote it. He may have sometimes welcomed or demanded improvisation, even elsewhere in *Die Zauberflöte*.

One type of aria to which improvisation was particularly suited was the rondò, recognized by singers, composers, and audiences alike as an aria of special significance. Usually near the end of an opera, it offered the prima donna or primo uomo a climactic moment of soloist display. The rondò typically begins with a slow section in the form A–B–A, A being a simple, unadorned melody. Many composers made the second A-section exactly the same as the first, as if inviting improvised embellishment from the great virtuoso for whom it was written. But Mozart sometimes varied the second A-section himself. For example, in "Al desio di chi t'adora," which Mozart wrote for Ferrarese (in the role of Susanna) to sing in the 1789 Viennese production of *Figaro*, he gave melody A on its second appearance a new accompaniment of pizzicato strings. The orchestral novelty must have distracted the listener's attention away from Ferrarese and discouraged her from introducing embellishments other than the few simple ones that Mozart himself added.

A few months later, when Ferrarese created the role of Fiordiligi in *Così fan tutte*, she encountered a similar situation with her next rondò, "Per pietà, ben mio, perdona." This time Mozart not only supplied a new accompaniment for the second A-section (with horns playing remarkably active interjections) but also embellished Ferrarese's vocal line, again restraining the prima donna's impulse to improvise.

But sometimes Mozart gave his singers more leeway. He wrote the role of Sesto in *La clemenza di Tito* for a musico, Domenico Bedini, who had sung for many years in Italy's leading theaters. In "Deh per questo istante solo," the rondò he wrote for Bedini, the A-section returns completely unchanged. Bedini may have insisted on keeping for himself the privilege of ornamenting his melody; or perhaps Mozart, under pressure of time, had the good sense to entrust this important aspect of the performance to his talented and experienced musico.

That Mozart normally relied on the taste and creativity of his singers is suggested by comments he made about an unusually inexperienced singer, the young musico who created the role of Idamante: "To my *molto amato castrato* Dal Prato I will have to teach the whole opera. He is incapable of improvising a cadenza [*Eingang*] worthy of the name; and such an uneven voice!"[51] Mozart's coaching presumably included the composition of cadenzas and other embellishments for Dal Prato to memorize.

The dialogue and action in eighteenth-century comic opera sometimes allowed for improvisation, which Mozart appreciated and encouraged, at least on some occasions. Luigi Bassi, who created the role of Don Giovanni, compared later performances of the supper scene with that of the original production: "This is all nothing, it lacks the liveliness, the freedom, that the great master wanted in this scene. In Guardasoni's company we never sang the scene the same from one performance to the next, we did not keep the beat exactly, and instead used our wit, always new things and paying attention only to the orchestra; everything *parlando* and almost improvised – that is how Mozart wanted it."[52] Mozart probably used rehearsals to set down the parameters within which such business took place.

Jan Nepomuk Štěpánek, director of the Estates Theater in Prague during the 1820s, recorded in 1825 an anecdote about a rehearsal of *Don Giovanni* that almost certainly took place after Da Ponte had returned to Vienna. In it, we can catch a glimpse of Mozart as stage director:

> At the first rehearsal of this opera in the theater, Signora Bondini, as Zerlina, seized by Don Giovanni at the end of act 1, was unable to scream properly and at the right moment, even after several repetitions. Mozart left the orchestra, went on stage, and directed that the scene be repeated yet again. At the moment in question, he seized the actress so abruptly and forcefully that she screamed in terror. "That's the way," he said approvingly. "That's how to scream."[53]

Between dress rehearsal and performance

Don Giovanni, despite the delays, a singer's illness, and Da Ponte's absence, eventually reached the stage on 29 October 1787. The effectiveness of the rehearsals and of Mozart's ingratiating himself with local musicians like Kuchař in generating good publicity is illustrated by a short report in a Prague newspaper anticipating the first performance:

> Prague, 29 October. The director of the Italian opera company here yesterday issued news of the opera *Don Juan, or Debauchery Punished*, formerly intended for the visit of the exalted Tuscan guests. It has the Court Theater poet, the Abbé Da Ponte, for its author, and is to be performed for the first time today, the 29th. All look forward with pleasure to the excellent composition of the great maestro Mozart.[54]

Fig. 7.1. Playbill for the first performance of *Le nozze di Figaro*.

As for what Mozart might have felt once the rehearsals were over and the moment of performance finally approached, we can extrapolate from Salieri's reminiscences of his feelings and actions in the hours before the premiere of his very first opera, when he was nineteen years old:

> On the day before the first performance of the opera was the dress rehearsal; in the evening of the same day I went to the theater with heart pounding, to hear my work announced: "Tomorrow the Italian opera troupe will have the honor to perform a new opera entitled *Le donne letterate*, poem by Herr Gaston Boccherini, music by Herr Anton Salieri, the first work of both." Several members of the audience applauded, which gave me sweet comfort and seemed to be a good omen. The following morning, as soon as I could think that the playbills had been posted at street-corners, I went out to see my name in print for the first time, which gave me great pleasure. Not content to see it once, as if afraid it might have been left out of the other playbills, I ran through the whole city to read it everywhere.[55]

Fig. 7.2. Playbill for the first performance of *Così fan tutte*.

The Italian system of operatic production, in which during a typical Carnival season the first opera was performed twenty to thirty times in a row before being replaced by the second opera involving all or most of the same singers, required no more than a single poster for the whole season, with the titles of the operas and ballets and the names of the singers, dancers, choreographers, and composers who had been engaged for the season. But the theatrical system in operation in Vienna, with its unpredictable schedule and gradually evolving repertory, required daily announcements in the theaters and posters, changed daily, throughout the city. The position of *Ansager* (announcer) was a permanent one on the court theater staff. The playbills that Salieri admired at Vienna's street corners advertized performances not only at the court theaters but also at the suburban theaters that arose in the wake of Emperor Joseph's liberalization of theatrical regulations in the mid 1770s. Posters announcing the first performances of *Figaro* (figure 7.1), *Così fan tutte* (figure 7.2), and *Die Zauberflöte* (figure 7.3) were valid for one day only; they all refer to the performance as taking place *heute* (today). The poster for *Die Zauberflöte* uses

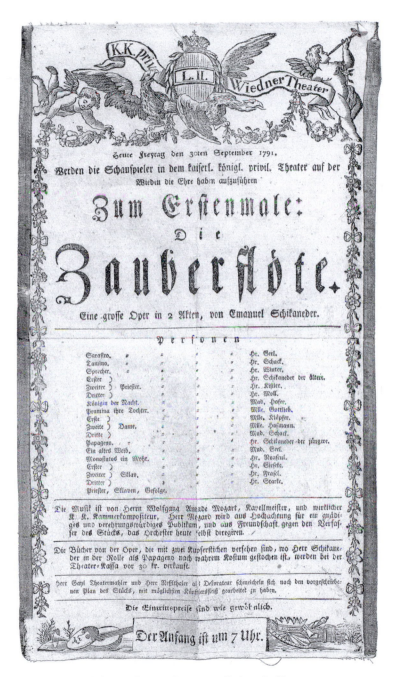

Fig. 7.3. Playbill for the first performance of *Die Zauberflöte*.

much the same wording as did the man announcing the premiere of *Le donne letterate* two decades earlier: "Today, Friday 30 September 1791, the actors of the Imperial Royal Privileged Theater auf der Wieden will have the honor to perform, for the first time, *Die Zauberflöte*, a grand opera in two acts by Emanuel Schikaneder . . . The music is by Herr Wolfgang Amade Mozart."

CHAPTER 8

Theaters and stage design

Mozart may not have intended all his operas for theaters. He probably wrote *Bastien und Bastienne* for performance in Franz Anton von Mesmer's country house near Vienna.[1] The only eyewitness account of the first (and possibly only) performance of *Il re pastore* calls it a "serenade" – a term suggesting (together with the likelihood that no libretto was printed for the production) that the performance in Salzburg on 23 April 1775 was not a full theatrical staging. But he wrote most of his operas for well-equipped theaters, shaping each work according to the size, shape, and acoustics of a particular auditorium and the scenic apparatus offered by a particular stage.

Because Mozart's operatic activity was largely limited to four cities, the number of theaters for which he composed was relatively small. He wrote operas for six theaters, three of which presented the premieres of two or more operas. The Regio Ducal Teatro in Milan staged *Mitridate*, *Ascanio in Alba*, and *Lucio Silla*. Munich's Theater am Salvatorplatz (or Salvatortheater) was the intended venue for *La finta giardiniera*; but whether the much-delayed premiere of that opera took place there or in the Redoutensaal is subject to debate.[2] The Electoral Theater in Munich (the Cuvilliés Theater) presented *Idomeneo*; the Burgtheater in Vienna *Die Entführung aus dem Serail*, *Figaro*, the Viennese version of *Don Giovanni*, and *Così fan tutte*; the Theater auf der Wieden in the suburbs *Die Zauberflöte*; and the Nostitz Theater in Prague (also known as the National Theater and the Theater of the Estates) *Don Giovanni* in its original version and *La clemenza di Tito*.

The oldest of Mozart's theaters was the Salvatortheater in Munich, completed in 1654 and remodelled in 1685; it was torn down at the end of the eighteenth century. No seventeenth- or eighteenth-century plan of the theater as a whole seems to exist. Two prints show how it looked in the 1680s. The back of the auditorium (figure 8.1) had a semicircular plan, with four tiers: stadium-style seating on the lowest level and three galleries above. The

Fig. 8.1. Theater am Salvatorplatz (Salvatortheater), Munich, as it appeared in 1686. Engraving by Michael Wening after Domenico Mauro. Deutsches Theatermuseum, Munich.

proscenium (figure 8.2) was richly adorned with sculptures; whether it maintained this appearance into the 1770s is unknown.

The other five theaters for which Mozart wrote operas were all built in the eighteenth century, and in the order (more or less) in which Mozart used them. Giovan Domenico Barbieri designed the Regio Ducal Teatro in Milan, inaugurated in 1717 (figures 2.2 and 8.3).[3] From 1751 to 1753 François Cuvilliés the Elder built for the elector of Bavaria a theater (figure 8.4) that in the libretto for *Idomeneo* is called the Teatro Nuovo di Corte (to distinguish it from the Teatro Vecchio, the Salvatortheater).[4] Between 1747 and 1759 Nicolas Jadot transformed an indoor tennis court connected to the imperial palace in Vienna into the Burgtheater (figure 8.5).[5] Much more modern when Mozart wrote operas for them were the Nostitz Theater, built by Anton Hafenecker in 1783 (figure 8.6), and the Theater auf der Wieden, built by Andreas Zach in 1787.[6] Plans of these theaters reproduced at the

Fig. 8.2. Theater am Salvatorplatz, Munich. Proscenium framing a design by Domenico and Gasparo Mauro for a nocturnal scene in Agostino Steffani's *Servio Tullio* (1686). Deutsches Theatermuseum, Munich.

same scale and placed side by side convey an idea of their relative size and shape (figure 8.7).

The Regio Ducal Teatro burned down in 1776. The Theater auf der Wieden was demolished shortly after Schikaneder's troupe moved to the new Theater an der Wien in 1801; the Burgtheater was torn down in 1888. The Cuvilliés Theater survived until the Second World War, when Allied bombs destroyed the Residenz of which it was a part. Before the bombing the theater's wooden interior was taken apart and stored for safekeeping outside Munich. It was reassembled in a different part of the rebuilt Residenz in the mid 1950s. Neither the stage nor the stage machinery is original. Only one of Mozart's theaters, the Nostitz Theater, survives, but not in its eighteenth-century state; it underwent radical remodeling in the nineteenth century. Most of the theaters were already subject to remodeling in the eighteenth century; the few

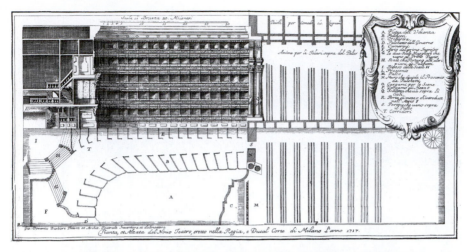

Fig. 8.3. Longitudinal section and plan of the Regio Ducal Teatro, Milan. Engraving after drawings by Giovanni Domenico Barbieri. From Serviliano Latuada, *Descrizione di Milano*, Milan, 1738.

surviving depictions and descriptions of them do not allow us to follow those changes with much precision. Nevertheless, in what follows I have tried to describe the theaters, in so far as the sources permit, as they were when they presented Mozart's operas for the first time.

Auditoriums

At least two of Mozart's eighteenth-century auditoriums were U-shaped in plan: the Regio Ducal Teatro (figure 8.7a) and the Nostitz Theater (figure 8.7d). The Theater auf der Wieden, in a plan dated 1789, appears to have been roughly rectangular (figure 8.7e); but since that plan does not show how its two tiers of boxes were integrated into the structure, we cannot draw from it definite conclusions about the shape of the auditorium. Judging from the placement of benches in the parterre (which resembles the arrangement in the Nostitz Theater), it may well have been U-shaped. The Cuvilliés Theater had a bell-shaped auditorium, but with a lip that curved out only slighly at the proscenium (figure 8.7b). The Burgtheater had the shape of an elongated horseshoe (figure 8.7c). The auditoriums ranged in length (measured from the front of the boxes at the back of the auditorium to the

Fig. 8.4. Interior of the Cuvilliés Theater, Munich. Although this watercolor by Gustav Seeberger (1867) shows the action, in accordance with nineteenth-century taste, taking place entirely behind the proscenium, it nevertheless conveys the size and shape of the theater in which *Idomeneo* was first performed. Stadtmuseum, Munich.

front of the stage) from about 20.6 m in the Regio Ducal Teatro to about 12 m in the Cuvilliés Theater. They ranged in maximum width (that is, the maximum distance from the front of the boxes on one side of the auditorium to the front of the boxes on the other side) from about 15.3 m in the Regio Ducal Teatro to about 10.6 m in the Burgtheater.[7]

The floor (the parterre) of most of the auditoriums was flat; the parterre of the Cuvilliés Theater, exceptionally, sloped quite steeply toward the stage (figure 8.8). In the Cuvilliés Theater, the Burgtheater, the Nostitz Theater, and the Theater auf der Wieden the parterre was divided into the *parterre noble* (directly in front of the stage, and reserved for members of the nobility) and the second parterre (behind the *parterre noble*, and open to members of the middle class).

Fig. 8.5. Part of the Michaelerplatz, Vienna, with the Burgtheater on the right, dwarfed by the Imperial Riding School. Detail of an engraving by Carl Schütz (1783).

From the parterre rose vertically several tiers of boxes. By far the largest number of boxes was in the Regio Ducal Teatro, with five tiers, each containing thirty-six boxes (180 boxes in all); this number was expanded, probably in 1771, by the conversion of the proscenium walls into an additional column of boxes on each side of the stage (two new boxes in each tier, one on the left and one on the right).[8] Burney attended a performance in the Regio Ducal Teatro in

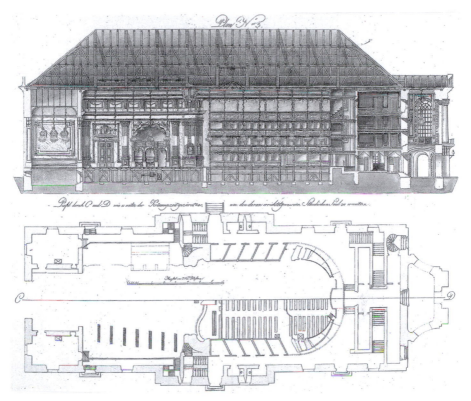

Fig. 8.6. Longitudinal section and plan of the Nostitz Theater, Prague,
Engraving by Philipp and Franz Heger.

July 1770, just a few months before the production of *Mitridate*; he found it
"very large and splendid."[9] The Cuvilliés Theater had four tiers, containing
about sixty-four boxes. The Burgtheater had four tiers, but not all with boxes.
The first tier contained twenty-six boxes, plus a big court box at the back of the
auditorium; the second tier contained twenty-eight boxes. In addition there
were four boxes on the ground floor, for a total of at least fifty-eight boxes.[10]
In the Nostitz Theater three tiers contained fifty-two boxes;[11] but those boxes,
to judge from the plans reproduced here, were considerably bigger than those
in Mozart's other theaters; above was an open gallery. The Theater auf der
Wieden had only two tiers of boxes when *Die Zauberflöte* was first performed
there in 1791 (figure 8.9); another tier was added in 1794.

a

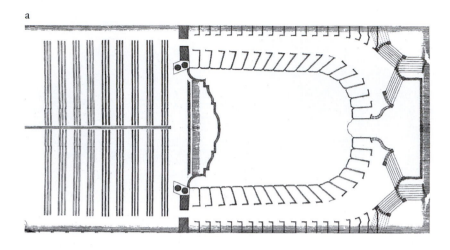

b

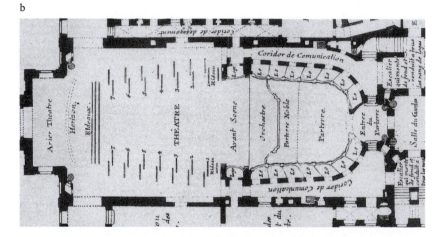

Fig. 8.7. Plans of five theaters for which Mozart wrote operas, reproduced at the same scale: (a) Regio Ducal Teatro, Milan. Since the original plan (see figure 8.3) shows only half of the theater, the other half has been added digitally.
(b) Cuvilliés-Theater, Munich. Detail of a plan by François Cuvilliés the Elder. From Steinmetz and Lachner, *Das Alte Residenztheater zu München*, 14.
(c) Burgtheater, Vienna. Detail of a plan by J. Hilldebrandt (1779). From Cole, "Mozart and Two Theaters in Josephinian Vienna," 129. (d) Nostitz Theater, Prague. Detail of the plan by Philipp and Franz Heger reproduced in figure 8.6.
(e) Theater auf der Wieden, Vienna. Detail of a plan by Andreas Zach (1789). From Cole, "Mozart and Two Theaters in Josephinian Vienna," 133.

c

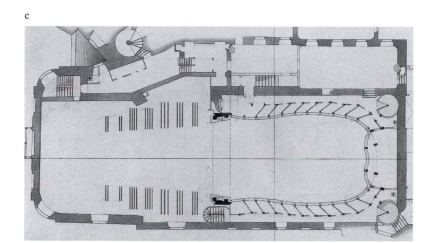

d

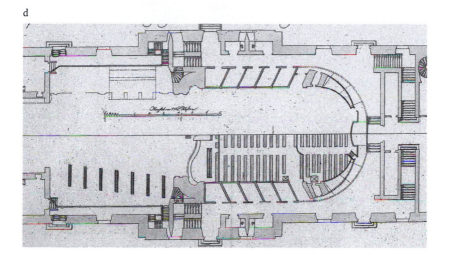

e

SCALE

10 meters

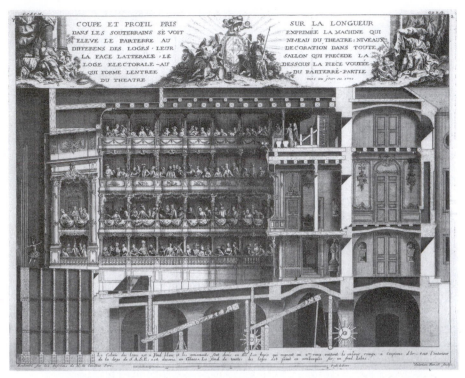

Fig. 8.8. Longitudinal section of the Cuvilliés Theater, Munich. Engraving by Valerian Funck after a drawing by François Cuvilliés, from *Ecole de l'architecture bavaroise*, Munich, 1771.

The orchestra sat at the front of the auditorium, at the same level as the spectators seated on benches in the parterre, and separated from the spectators by a low partition that allowed the audience to see and hear the players clearly. No pits or overhanging stages – nineteenth-century inventions – muffled the sound of Mozart's orchestras. The size of some of the orchestras that accompanied his operas, as discussed briefly in chapter 7, corresponded to some extent with the size of the theaters in which they played. By far the largest of Mozart's operatic orchestras (numbering sixty players in the case of *Mitridate*) played in his biggest theater, the Regio Ducal Teatro. One of the smallest of his orchestras, that of the Theater auf der Wieden, played in one of his smallest theaters. Yet his second-largest theater, the Nostitz Theater,

Fig. 8.9. Emanuel Schikaneder as Lubano in *Der Stein der Weisen*, act 1, scene 14, as performed in the Theater auf der Wieden. Title page of the *Allmanach für Theaterfreunde auf das Jahr 1791*.

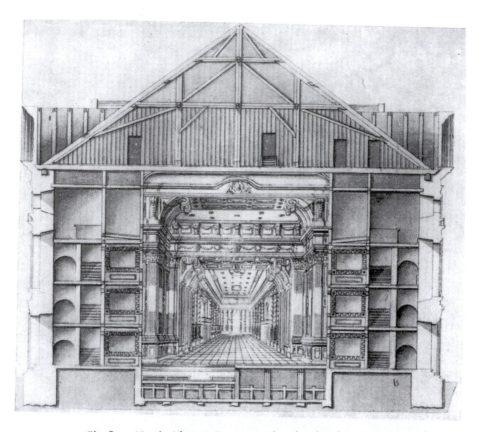

Fig. 8.10. Nostitz Theater, Prague. Section showing the proscenium and stage, as decorated for the ball on 12 September 1791 celebrating the coronation of Maria Luisa, wife of Emperor Leopold II, as queen of Bohemia (for a view of the same stage full of dancers, see figure 2.3). Engraving by Philipp and Franz Heger.

was home to an orchestra roughly the same size as the one that played in the Theater auf der Wieden.

The stage was higher than the floor of the auditorium, keeping the orchestra from blocking the view of the audience in the parterre. But in two of Mozart's theaters, the Cuvilliés Theater and the Nostitz Theater, machinery below the floor allowed it to be lifted to the level of the stage so that the entire theater could be used for balls (such as those shown in figures 2.3 and 2.4) and other festivities. The longitudinal section of the Cuvilliés Theater shows the floor in its lowest position, with the winches and levers used to raise it. (On some occasions, presumably, the floor was raised halfway, to a horizontal position.) A longitudinal section of the Nostitz Theater (figure 8.6) shows the floor of the auditorium raised to its full height. A latitudinal section presenting a view of the stage (figure 8.10) shows the floor raised on one side and lowered on the other.

Stages

The stage and backstage areas in most of Mozart's theaters together made up a roughly rectangular space considerably wider than the auditorium. The Burgtheater, fitted into a building earlier used for other purposes, had to make do with an irregularly shaped backstage area. In the plan of the Theater auf der Wieden reproduced here (figure 8.7e) the backstage area appears to be no wider than the auditorium; but the omission of the boxes from this plan probably makes the auditorium look wider than it actually was.

The part of the stage actually visible to the audience during a performance consisted of two overlapping areas: the forestage or acting stage in front, and the scenic stage behind.[12] The forestage was the area between the front of the stage (which in eighteenth-century theaters often extended well beyond the front of the proscenium arch) and an imaginary line corresponding roughly with the back of the proscenium arch. In the plan of the Cuvilliés Theater the forestage is labelled *Avant Scène*. In this area, directly behind the footlights, most of the acting and solo singing occurred. Performers on the forestage could easily see and hear the orchestra in front of them, and could be easily seen and heard from the auditorium. The engraving by Marc'Antonio dal Re reproduced here as figure 2.6 dramatically evokes the closeness – even the intimacy – of singer, orchestra, and audience that the forestage made possible.

The scenic stage consisted of an area that, in plan, had the shape of an isosceles trapezoid, in which the back of the forestage defined the longer of the two parallel sides, a painted backdrop defined the shorter parallel side, and a series of painted wing flats on parallel grooves defined the two sides. These sides, by converging, conveyed to the audience an illusion that the stage was longer than it actually was, thereby producing the effect of great size and distance (*vastità*) that, according to eighteenth-century theorists, was one of the main goals of stage design.[13] In the longitudinal section of the Cuvilliés Theater (see figure 8.8) a dancer stands in the area of overlap between the scenic stage (to his left, where the first wing flats are visible) and the forestage (to his right).

In most of Mozart's theaters the length of forestage and scenic stage together exceeded the length of the auditorium (including the space occupied by the orchestra). Exceptional in this respect was the Theater auf der Wieden, where the plan of 1789 (figure 8.7e) shows the stage to have been noticeably shorter than the auditorium.

The grooves for the wing flats were arranged in banks of two or more so that at a scene change each flat, pulled back until it was out of the audience's sight, could be replaced almost simultaneously by another at more or less the same distance from the audience. The Theater auf der Wieden had five or six banks of grooves on each side of the stage;[14] the Cuvilliés Theater, the Nostitz Theater, and the Burgtheater seven banks of grooves; the Regio Ducal Teatro nine.

Drops could be lowered from several places above the scenic stage, depending on the depth of the stage needed in any particular set. Hanging from above the stage, in front of the drop, was a series of horizontal borders that together defined the top of the stage picture and hid the machinery used to raise and lower the backdrop and borders.

Candles or oil lamps along the front of the stage (footlights) and fixed to the backs of the wing flats filled the stage with warm, shimmering light.

All this the audience admired through the proscenium arch, which – together with the floor of the stage – constituted a frame that, in several of Mozart's theaters, was almost exactly square. In the Regio Ducal Teatro, however, the width of the proscenium – about 15 m – exceeded its height.

Stage design

Stage design was a product of complex collaboration involving the librettist, the house poet, the designer of the scenery, painters, carpenters, and a mechanic in charge of changing the wings, backdrops, and borders at exactly the right moment. The composer too was often involved in aspects of stage design. Changes of scene sometimes needed to be accompanied by music. The composer had to take into account the acoustical differences between short sets (with a backdrop close to the audience reflecting the sound outward, thus favoring solo voices and quiet accompaniments) and long sets (which absorbed more sound but also provided room on stage for many singers, including chorus). Many aspects of Mozart's operas can be explained with reference to the system of stage design for which they were conceived.

Mozart began his operatic career with exposure to scenery by some of the most famous Italian scenic artists. The brothers Fabrizio and Bernardino Galliari of Turin served as resident stage designers for the Regio Ducal Teatro of Milan during the 1770s.[15] They provided the sets for *Mitridate*, *Ascanio in Alba*, and *Lucio Silla*. As was usually the case in Italy, the librettos printed for the productions of these operas mention the scenographers by name, with the implication that theater managers and audiences alike considered their work an important part of the operas to which they contributed.

That does not mean, however, that all the Galliari sets used in Mozart's operas were new. Librettists – perhaps by force of habit, or more likely under the pressure of impresarios to keep expenses as low as possible – often made use of the same or very similar settings in different operas, allowing and even encouraging impresarios to reuse sets. Librettos occasionally announced that sets for a particular production were "completely new" – leaving the impression that without such a boast there was a good chance that the sets were not new. Most theaters probably maintained a supply of stock scenery that could be used whenever a dramatic situation allowed it. Even within the material that the Galliari brothers used in Mozart's Milanese operas, they had a chance to reuse sets. Part or all of the scenery that they had prepared for Gasparini's setting of *Mitridate* (performed in Turin during Carnival 1768) could have served the same purpose in Mozart's setting of the same libretto.[16] Although the Galliari prepared several drawings in connection with the staging of Mozart's *Lucio Silla*,[17] at least two of its scenes could easily have used sets from *Mitridate*. Act 2 of *Mitridate* opens with a view of "Appartamenti." The second set in act 1 of *Lucio Silla* represents "Giunia's apartment." The first set in act 3 of *Mitridate* depicts a "Hanging Garden." So does the second set in act 2 of *Lucio Silla*.

During his decade in Vienna Mozart experienced scenographic extremes. On the one hand, the Burgtheater apparently depended largely on stock scenery, and made little effort to surprise and delight its audience with purely visual effects. On the other hand, the Theater auf der Wieden – despite its relatively small stage and relatively few banks of grooves for wing flats – specialized in the marvels of stage design.

The Burgtheater during the 1780s had no theatrical painters on its permanent staff.[18] In 1784 the Bohemian stage designer Joseph Platzer earned 1150 Gulden for "decorations painted at imperial expense" for the Burgtheater.[19] The size of that fee – substantially more than the annual salaries of Salieri as music director and of Da Ponte as house poet – suggests that the project was a big one. Platzer added two more sets to the Burgtheater's inventory in 1786.[20] Platzer's sets, together with whatever scenic material already existed in the court theater storage rooms, probably constituted the stock scenery used during the rest of the 1780s.

That scenery was not a high priority for Emperor Joseph II and his theater director Rosenberg (once they had accumulated a full supply of stock sets) is suggested by a production that Joseph personally arranged. When the musico Marchesi visited Vienna during the summer of 1785, Joseph mounted a staging of Sarti's *Giulio Sabino* in the Kärntnertortheater with Marchesi in the title role and Caterina Cavalieri as Epponina. An engraving of the opera's climactic dungeon scene seems to have captured faithfully what audiences actually saw in the Kärntnertortheater (figure 8.11). Marchesi, Cavalieri, and two child actors stand near the front of the scenic stage. The expected backdrop, wing flats, and overhead borders are all here, but they are conspicuously uninteresting, and contribute little to the scene's emotional or aesthetic content. An engraving published in 1785 (thus more or less contemporary with the production of *Giulio Sabino* in Vienna) depicts almost identical wing flats during the performance (probably in the Burgtheater) of a play or an opera (figure 8.12).

In 1792, after a major theatrical reorganization by Emperor Leopold II had greatly increased the variety and expense of scenery in both the Burgtheater and Kärntnertortheater, Rosenberg criticized the new handling of stage design as wasteful, and he defended his own (and Joseph's) more parsimonious approach:

> As far as scenery in concerned, a false economy results from having a painter on the permanent payroll and allowing him to appraise his work and to be paid at his own discretion, for he can pay badly the painters

Fig. 8.11. Luigi Marchesi and Caterina Cavalieri in Sarti's *Giulio Sabino* in the Kärntnertortheater (August 1785). Raccolta Bertarelli, Milan

engaged by him, and take for himself half of the agreed-upon price. A more economical approach would involve bargaining with freelance painters and choosing the lowest bid submitted by them. Moreover, these numerous sets [produced under Leopold II] not only did financial harm – for to make these new sets all the old ones in the warehouse were painted over and those in the Kärntnertortheater used up, so that good old pieces like *L'arbore di Diana*, *La grotta di Trofonio*, and *Il re Teodoro* can no longer be given – but also spoiled the public, which expects new sets almost every week.[21]

In the absence of a permanently employed theatrical painter, composers and librettists in Vienna may have fended for themselves. As early as 1770, when Salieri was preparing for the performance of his first opera, he was involved in scenery: "I wrote night and day, I ran to the rehearsals, I went

Fig. 8.12. Interior of a theater, probably the Burgtheater, Vienna. Engraving by
Mansfeld from *Bildergalerie weltlicher Misbräuche*, Vienna, 1785

through the vocal parts with the singers, I corrected the copies, together with the poet I took care of the scenery and costumes."[22] In taking care of the scenery, Salieri and Boccherini presumably put together suitable sets from stock material. Four years later, in 1774, Salieri was again working with scenery, this time during preparations for *La calamita de' cuori*. A theatrical journal reported: "An unusual circumstance is to be noted, that during the last rehearsal the music director supervised the scenery and the acting on stage, while the theatrical poet was in the orchestra distributing the music."[23]

Such anecdotes suggest to our imagination the amusing image of Mozart and Da Ponte choosing, from among the Burgtheater's stock scenery, the sets for *Figaro*, *Don Giovanni*, and *Così fan tutte*. For *Figaro* they could have had recourse to some of the sets used in Sarti's *Fra i due litiganti il terzo gode*, performed often in the Burgtheater since 1783. Sarti's opera, whose plot strikingly anticipates that of *Figaro*, takes place in "a country house on the Count's estate"; *Figaro* takes place "in the castle of Count Almaviva." The second act of *Fra i due litiganti* begins in the "Anticamera della Contessa"; the second act of *Figaro* takes place in a "Camera ricca, con alcova e tre porte" within the Countess's apartment. Salieri's *La fiera di Venezia*, first performed in Vienna in 1772 and revived in 1785, reaches its climax in the finale of act 2, with a set described by the librettist Boccherini as a "Magnifica sala illuminata per il Ballo." Elsewhere I have suggested that Salieri's ballroom scene, as performed in 1785, helped to inspire Don Giovanni's "gran festa di ballo" two years later.[24] When Mozart presented *Don Giovanni* in Vienna in 1788, the idea of reusing Salieri's ballroom set might easily have occurred to those preparing the production of Mozart's opera. The same set could have been used yet again at the end of *Così fan tutte*, where Da Ponte called for "Sala ricchissima illuminata. Orchestra in fondo."

Did Mozart and Da Ponte plan certain scenes with the intention of reusing existing scenery? The setting in act 2 of *Così fan tutte* "Garden on the seashore ... A boat adorned with flowers, with a group of instrumentalists" might have been prohibitively expensive to make from scratch. But with some minor adjustments the first set in *Die Entführung*, along with some of its props, might have worked well: "A plaza in front of the pasha's palace on the seashore ... The pasha and Constanze arrive in a pleasure boat. Another boat carrying Janissary musicians lands ahead of them. They arrange themselves on the shore."

Sets for *La clemenza di Tito*

The impresario Domenico Guardasoni promised in his contract with the Estates of Bohemia (quoted in chapter 3) that the coronation opera he was to present less than two months later would include two new sets. The libretto printed for the first production of *Tito* says nothing explicit about new sets, but it implies that Guardasoni went beyond his contractual obligation. The prefatory material refers to four sets, attributing them to specific artists: "The first three *decorazioni* are by Sig. Pietro Travaglia, presently in the employ of His Highness Prince Esterazi. The fourth is by Sig. Preisig of Coblenz."[25] This announcement appears at first sight to be inconsistent with the libretto itself, which calls for more than four sets. But what if it refers only to newly designed sets? The libretto supports this interpretation by enclosing several of its scenic descriptions in parentheses, as if to indicate that these sets were to be realized with stock scenery. The only descriptions of scenery *not* in parentheses are the following four:

1   "Part of the Roman Forum magnificently adorned with arches, obelisks, and trophies; facing [the audience], a view of the outside of the Capitol and a magnificent road leading up to it" (act 1, scenes 4–5).
2   "The Capitol as before" but probably without the Forum in the foreground (act 1, scenes 11–13).
3   "A great chamber destined for public audiences. Throne, seat, and table" (act 2, scenes 5–15).
4   "Magnificent space that leads into a vast amphitheater, from which one can see through several arches the interior. Already visible in the arena are the conspirators condemned to the wild beasts" (act 2, scenes 16–17).

The first three of these settings probably correspond to the three attributed in the libretto to Travaglia, a scenographer who designed the scenery for many of Haydn's operas; the fourth is probably the one designed by the otherwise unknown Preisig.

Sergio Durante has recently identified among Travaglia's drawings two that he has argued persuasively constitute preliminary sketches for his designs for

Mozart's opera.[26] Below one of the drawings (figure 8.13) Travaglia wrote: "Sala terena destinata per le publiche udienze." That inscription closely resembles a scenic description in *Tito*. For the third of the sets listed above (act 2, scenes 5–15) the Prague libretto calls for "Gran sala destinata alle pubbliche udienze." Durante has identified another drawing as a preparatory sketch for the second set in act 1 – corresponding to the first of the sets listed above. If Durante is correct (the drawing contains no corroborating inscription), the Forum is in the foreground and middleground, and the Capitol, at the top of the stairs, in the background (figure 8.14). Both designs appear to involve cutout drops: that is, drops partially cut away to reveal complete drops further back (the Capitol in act 1, the amphitheater in act 2). Travaglia depicted only one half of each design, with the implication that the full set would be symmetrical. A realization of Travaglia's sketch for the "Sala terena" placed within the Nostitz Theater's proscenium gives a sense of the original visual context for one of Mozart's most memorable scenes (the confrontation of Tito and Sesto in act 2, scene 10) and four of his greatest arias: Sesto's "Deh per questo istante solo," Tito's "Se all'impero, amici dei," Servilia's "S'altro che lagrime," and Vitellia's "Non più di fiori" (figure 8.15).

Long sets and short sets

Descriptions of scenery in eighteenth-century librettos sometimes contain hints about the size of the sets librettists had in mind. Adjectives such as *aperto*, *spazioso*, and *magnifico* encouraged audiences to expect long sets; so did phrases like "nel fondo della scena" (at the back of the stage). Such nouns as *camera*, *gabinetto*, and *Zimmer* and the adjectives *corto* and *kurz* raised expectations of short sets. This dichotomy is somewhat artificial. Many theaters allowed for the hanging of drops at various points between the front and the back of the scenic stage. Furthermore, with a cutout drop the scenic designer combined features of a short set and a long one (visible through the perforation). More important than the actual length of a set was whether it was longer or shorter than those that preceded and followed it.[27]

One way that librettists communicated to set designers and opera lovers that they envisioned a long set was to give a long, detailed description in the libretto. For example, De Gamerra, the librettist of *Lucio Silla*, described

Fig. 8.13. "Sala terena destinata per le publiche udienze." Stage design by Pietro Travaglia, recently identified as one of the designs he prepared for Mozart's *La clemenza di Tito*. This sketch depicts only the left half of the stage. National Library, Budapest.

Fig. 8.14. Stage design by Pietro Travaglia, possibly intended for *La clemenza di Tito*, act 1, scenes 4–5 and 11–14. This sketch depicts only the left half of the stage. National Library, Budapest.

the opening set of that opera as "A solitary enclosure strewn with trees and ruins of crumbling edifices. Bank of the Tiber. In the distance a view of the Monte Quirinale, with a little temple on its crest." This description, and in particular the phrase "In the distance," refers almost certainly to a long set.

Fig. 8.15. Travaglia's drawing of a "Sala terena destinata per le publiche udienze" (as shown in its original state in figure 8.13) completed digitally and by hand by Michael Lorenz and the author and placed within the proscenium of the Nostitz Theater (as depicted in the engraving shown in figure 8.10.)

One of Fabrizio Galliari's surviving scenic drawings is a sketch for precisely this set (figure 8.16).[28] To show how painters and carpenters might have transformed such a sketch into a long set, I have divided the elements of the drawing among six flats (three for each side of the stage) (figure 8.17); the craftsmen of the Regio Ducal Teatro, with nine banks of grooves on each side of the stage, probably used more flats. Another sketch for *Lucio Silla* by

Fig. 8.16. Fabrizio Galliari, stage design for act 1 of *Lucio Silla*. Pinacoteca di Brera, Milan.

Fig. 8.17. Speculative distribution of the elements of Fabrizio Galliari's set design among six wing flats.

Galliari (for the "Magnificent entrance hall where the monuments to Roman heroes are located and [which] leads to an underground chamber") seems to require a cutout drop (figure 8.18) framing a set long enough to accommodate the chorus that plays an important role in the scene.

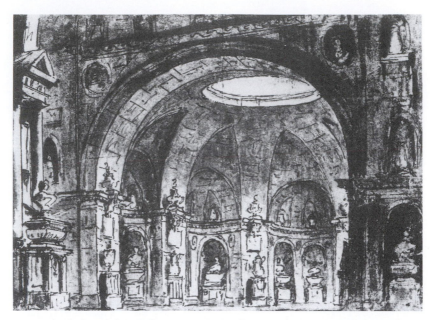

Fig. 8.18. Fabrizio Galliari, stage design for act 1 of *Lucio Silla*. Pinacoteca di Brera, Milan.

Long sets generally involved more people than short sets. *La clemenza di Tito* has several fine examples of long sets in which the chorus plays a crucial role.[29] In act 1, for example, the second set, presenting a view of "Part of the Roman Forum magnificently adorned with arches," must have been big enough to hold a great many people, including Publio, Roman senators, delegates of subject provinces, lictors, the Praetorian Guard, and a large crowd. As if the chorus "Serbate o dei custodi" were not enough by itself to give musical grandeur to the scene, Mozart composed a march that accompanies the change of scene (from the set representing Vitellia's apartment, undoubtedly short) and gives time for all the people to assemble on stage.

Librettists and stage designers tended to avoid two long sets in a row. They preferred to alternate long sets and short ones, allowing stagehands to use the time that passed during a short set to prepare for the following long set. In *Don Giovanni*, for example, Da Ponte's scenic descriptions suggest that he and Mozart conceived the whole opera as a succession of alternating long and short sets:

Act 1
1) Garden [outside of Donna Anna's house] [short]
2) Street [long]
3) Garden [outside of Don Giovanni's house] [short]
4) A hall illuminated and prepared for a great ball [long]

Act 2
1) Street [long]
2) A dark entrance hall in Donna Anna's house [short]
3) An enclosed area representing a cemetery; various equestrian statues; statue of the Commendatore [long]
4) A dark room [short]
5) A hall [long][30]

To cite just one example of how a short set allows for the following long set to be prepared behind a backdrop: all that happens in the "dark room," the opera's penultimate set, is a brief conversation between Donna Anna and Don Ottavio that provides some context for Anna's rondò "Non mi dir, bell' idol mio."[31] Da Ponte and Mozart probably intended the singers who portray Anna and Ottavio to play this scene entirely on the forestage, with a backdrop at or near the front of the scenic stage. The short set not only focusses the audience's attention on the prima donna at this crucial moment and places her voice in the most favorable possible acoustical context, but gives the stage crew time to remove the props from the previous set (the equestrian statues and the statue of the Commendatore) and to prepare the spectacular final set, which involves a new prop: "a table prepared for eating."[32] In addition to arranging that, the stage manager needs time to bring on stage the musicians who are to play the dinner music, to set up the trap door through which Don Giovanni will descend to hell, to prepare the device for the fire that will accompany his descent, and to make sure that the off-stage chorus of demons is ready to sing. To an audience that knows the opera, the knowledge that all of this is happening backstage while Donna Anna is singing her rondò on the forestage gives her great aria an extra edge of excitement.

Of the sets in which *Don Giovanni* was first performed we can get some idea from Platzer's surviving drawings and from engravings of some of his stage designs made in the early nineteenth century by Norbert Bittner. In 1783, the year in which the Nostitz Theater was finished, Platzer painted twelve stage

Fig. 8.19. Luigi Bassi, who created the role of Don Giovanni in Prague.
Engraving by Medard Thoenert.

sets for the new theater. Like those he made a year later in Vienna, these sets
probably served as stock scenery during the next several years. *Don Giovanni*,
when it reached the stage in 1787, probably used some of Platzer's sets.[33]
An engraving that depicts Luigi Bassi, the original Don Giovanni, singing a
serenade (figure 8.19) places him in a public square resembling the urban
scene depicted in one of Platzer's stage designs (figure 8.20), suggesting that

Fig. 8.20. Stage design by Joseph Platzer, from Norbert Bittner,
*Theaterdecorationen nach den Original Skizzen des K. K. Hoftheatermahlers Josef Platzer
radirt und verlegt von Norbert Bittner*, Vienna, 1816.

this was the set used to represent the "strada" in acts 1 and 2 of *Don Giovanni*.[34]
By superimposing the portrait of Bassi on Platzer's set and placing it within
the proscenium of the Nostitz Theater (figure 8.21) we get some idea of how
this scene might have appeared to audiences in Prague.

The unusually rich scenic resources available at the Theater auf der Wieden
did not free its librettists, composers, and scenographers from the usefulness
and convenience of alternating long and short sets. On the poster advertizing the first performance of *Die Zauberflöte* (see figure 7.3) is the following
statement: "Herr Gayl, theatrical painter, and Herr Neßthaler, set designer,
flatter themselves that they have followed the prescribed plan of the work with
all possible artistic diligence." This "prescribed plan" survives, at least in part,
in Schikaneder's libretto, which contains descriptions of every set. Twice in
the second act Schikaneder used the adjective *kurz*, as if explicitly signaling to

Fig. 8.21. Medard Thoenert's engraving of Luigi Bassi in the role of Don Giovanni superimposed on Norbert Bittner's engraving of a stage design by Joseph Platzer and placed within the proscenium of the Nostitz Theater (as depicted in the engraving shown in figure 8.10).

Gayl and Neßthaler the use of short sets. This enables us to understand act 2, with only a little guesswork, as a succession of long and short sets – in which marches and choruses appear only in the long sets:

1) Palm grove; march, chorus [long]
2) A short vestibule of the temple
3) A pleasant garden [long]

4) A hall in which the flying machine can go [short]
5) The vault of pyramids; chorus [long]
6) A short garden
7) Two great mountains; march, chorus [long]
8) The former garden [short]
9) A sun; chorus [long]

This sequence of sets differed from those in Mozart's other operas not so much in the technical means by which it was produced but in the number, variety, and originality of images it presented.

Two engravings of a scene in an opera performed about a year before *Die Zauberflöte*, in the same theater and with many of the same singers, convey a sense of how these singers and the audience in the Theater auf der Wieden interacted with the theater's scenic effects. Act 1 of *Der Stein der Weisen*, with a libretto by Schikaneder and music by several composers, including Mozart, involves just two sets.[35] The long set with which the act begins returns at the end. The libretto describes it as follows:

> An Arcadian landscape. In the background a bower with five entrances and as many hanging chandeliers, adorned with flowers and ribbons. In the center stands a pyramid, engraved with different figures in gold, lit by many chandeliers. At the base of the pyramid are the steps where the shepherds lay their offerings. The men stand to the left, the maidens to the right all along the stage, beneath green boughs, also hung with chandeliers.[36]

The second set (for scenes 7–14) is "A short forest" – "short" probably meaning, as in the stage directions for *Die Zauberflöte*, that this set did not use the stage's full length – "with Lubano's shepherd's hut in Indian style." It is here that the evil spirit Eutifronte (played by Franz Gerl, the first Sarastro) abducts Lubanara, Lubano's young bride (played by Barbara Gerl, the first Papagena). By way of a trap door they descend into the earth while Lubano (played by Schikaneder) berates Eutifronte, as illustrated in a contemporary print (figure 8.22).[37] When Lubanara and Eutifronte disappear, Lubano sticks his head in the hole; on withdrawing it, he finds that he has gained a pair of golden antlers. He stands up, exclaiming: "Oh ye gods! What is this? I've been bewitched!" This is the moment recorded in the engraving (reproduced as figure 8.9) of part of the stage and part of the auditorium of the Theater

Fig. 8.22. Emanuel Schikaneder as Lubano, Barbara Gerl as Lubanara, and Franz
Gerl as Eutifronte in *Der Stein der Weisen*, act 1, scene 14. The libretto describes the
set as a "Kurzer Wald." From the *Allmanach für Theaterfreunde auf das Jahr 1791*.

auf der Wieden. Schikaneder stands on the forestage. Behind the three-
dimensional hut are three wings and a backdrop depicting the forest.[38]
Together, these engravings can serve as the basis for a speculative plan of the
Kurzer Wald as depicted in the Theater auf der Wieden in 1790 (figure 8.23): a

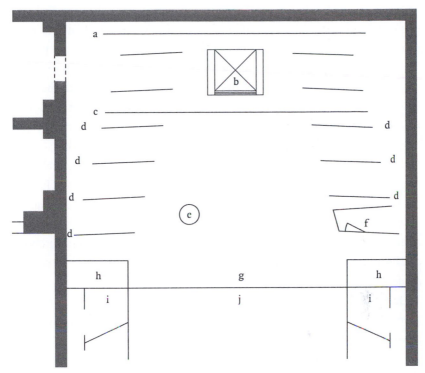

Fig. 8.23. Speculative reconstruction of the stage of the Theater auf der Wieden, as arranged for *Der Stein der Weisen*, act 1, scenes 7–14 ("Kurzer Wald"):
(a) backdrop depicting a bower (not visible during scenes 7–14)
(b) pyramid with steps in front (not visible during scenes 7–14)
(c) backdrop depicting trees
(d) wings depicting trees
(e) trap door
(f) hut with practicable door and three windows, one practicable
(g) forestage
(h) proscenium
(i) first boxes on left and right
(j) orchestra.

medium-length set that conceals, behind it, some elements of a more spectacular longer set.

Act 1 of *Mitridate* shows Mozart adapting his orchestration to acoustics that changed with the position of the backdrop. The opera begins in "A square in Nymphaea with a view in the distance from the city gate. Sifare with a retinue of officers and soldiers and Arbate with the City Fathers, one of whom carries the keys of the city on a tray." The Galliari brothers probably realized Cigna-Santi's description with a long set (note the phrase "in the distance" again) or a shorter set using a cutout drop that depicted the city gate. The next set is described as "Temple of Venus with the altar lit and adorned with myrtle and roses. Farnace, Aspasia, Farnace's soldiers all around and priests near the altar." Although the large number of people on stage here precluded a drop at the front of the scenic stage, this set was almost certainly shorter than the one before it. Mozart used the big orchestra of the Regio Ducal Teatro quite differently in these scenes. He scored heavily the two arias sung in the opening set, especially Aspasia's *aria di bravura* "Al destin che la minaccia," in which trumpets, oboes, and horns have prominent roles. In the temple scene, in contrast, the trumpets are silent, while the oboes and horns play together in only one aria; two other arias are scored for strings alone.

During the temple scene, stagehands behind the backdrop were probably preparing the next set, which the librettist Cigna-Santi seems to have conceived to use as much space and as many people as possible. The backdrop depicting the Temple of Venus rose to reveal:

> A seaport, with two fleets anchored on opposite sides of the channel. In the distance a view of the city of Nymphaea. To the sound of joyful music another squadron of vessels sails in. Mitridate and Ismene land from the largest ship. He is followed by the Royal Guard and she by an escort of Parthians. Arbate with his retinue receives them on the beach. Then the troops disembark and form up on the shore.

Mozart enhanced the pleasure this set excited, and responded to the new acoustics it offered, exactly as he did twenty years later when composing the first act of *La clemenza di Tito*. He wrote a grand march, with trumpets and drums, that accompanies the entrance of the ruler and of the crowds that greet him.

CHAPTER 9

The audience

"The theater is a little republic," wrote the pamphleteer Ange Goudar in one of his many published letters on Italian opera and ballet, this one dated 1774.[1] He expressed an idea that lay at the heart of the way people thought about the theater in the age of enlightened absolutism. The concept of the theater as microcosm of the state shaped much of eighteenth-century discussion of theatrical patronage, and it influenced the actions of patrons and their beneficiaries alike. From this concept extended a web of symbolic associations: metaphorical connections that bound the stage, the audience, and the ruler.

The powerful symbolism of the theater arose from and contributed to its unique importance in the social and political life of eighteenth-century Europe. The theater offered many cities their main center of social interaction, a place where all elements of society (society being understood in its restricted sense of that minority of the population with the education and the leisure to be interested in the theater and the money to afford it) could meet to be entertained, to see their ruler, and to chat with friends and acquaintances. "Why does one go to the theater today?" asks Love in Saverio Bettinelli's *Dialoghi d'Amore*, first published in 1788. Melpomene, the muse of tragedy, answers: "Just between us, one goes there out of habit, to see and be seen; the women to look each other over, the men to flirt with them. If there were no boxes and theaters women would no longer know each other or how to dress. It is the only remaining social tie, the passions finding it to their advantage there."[2]

This does not mean that the audience mingled indiscriminately in the theater. Far from it: the theater reflected and reinforced the hierarchical structure of the society it served. The ruler and his family, the nobility, the citizens: each group had its well-defined place in the theater. We have seen how the theaters of Munich, Vienna, and Prague for which Mozart wrote operas reserved the front of the parterre for the nobility. John Rosselli has described the typical auditorium in late eighteenth- and early nineteenth-century Italian theaters:

> There was no doubt in any leading theatre, whatever its structure of
> ownership, which were the 'noble' areas. The seating arrangements were
> hierarchical in the most visible way. The second tier of boxes (out of four,
> five, or six) was always the most aristocratic: except in commercial ports
> like Trieste and Leghorn it was largely occupied by nobles, at least in the
> fashionable season. The first or the third tier in some theatres enjoyed
> equal standing with the second. More often both were a little lower in
> esteem and price; in the leading or second-rank theatres boxholders' lists
> show a mixture of nobles and professional men . . . The status of the tier
> or tiers above the third was lower still but varied with the theatre. It was
> not unknown to find the odd (presumably impoverished) noble in a
> top-tier box. Taking out the partitions in this top tier to make a gallery was
> a signal that the lower classes – however defined – were being let in. Two
> leading theaters most heavily dominated by aristocratic boxholders were
> late in making this change: the Carolino, Palermo, did it in 1830; La
> Fenice, Venice, not till 1878.[3]

The ruler in the theater

An eighteenth-century audience in the presence of its ruler typically divided
its attention between the stage and the ruler's box. If the ruler applauded so
did his people. Frederick the Great, having returned to Berlin from a military
campaign in Silesia, ordered Carl Heinrich Graun's *Rodelinda* to be performed.
A member of the audience wrote an account of the performance that captures
something of the complex dynamics of such an occasion:

> [The overture] was such a masterpiece of full, pure harmony . . . that it
> seemed as if the Muses and the Graces had united to draw our Frederick
> out of his own heroic sphere and to themselves, where he could be held
> back from the rude cares of war. The bewitching voices of the singers, the
> naturalness and beauty of the action – everything was captivating to eye
> and ear. The whole spectacle, brought to such artistic perfection and
> executed with such skill, was received by the monarch with high approval,
> and the public went forth from the theater lost in enchantment.[4]

Just as the audience's perception of the performance was intertwined with the
ruler's reaction to it, so the audience could sense the ruler's mood and judge

his character by what they saw in the theater. Count Firmian, Mozart's most important Italian patron, ruled Lombardy as Austrian plenipotentiary minister during the 1760s, a decade in which, according to the Milanese intellectual Pietro Verri, "we were entirely dominated by despicable bureaucrats with a violent disposition," while Firmian, remote and uncaring, left the Milanese to their own devices. But Verri hoped for better things from Firmian when Archduke Ferdinand became governor in 1772. Verri's optimism was based on what he saw in the theater: "Count Firmian no longer lives so solitary a life ... In the theater one sees him in a few boxes. This is a good thing. He will see the Milanese as they are, not as they have been painted to him; he will gain even more affection, which he merits, and, for his part, he will grow more sociable with us."[5]

Nowhere was the symbolic power of the theater, and musical theater in particular, more strongly felt than in Vienna. Burney, visiting the Hapsburg capital in 1772, formed his impression of young Emperor Joseph II from what he saw in the theater. His memories of Joseph in the theater merged imperceptibly into comments on the emperor's character and his actions outside the theater. The interest that Burney showed in Joseph's reaction to the opera (Salieri's comedy *Il barone di Rocca Antica*) seems to imply that the opera was a success if it pleased the ruler:

> The Emperor, the arch-duke Maximilian, his brother [for whom Mozart
> would write *Il re pastore* three years later], and his two sisters, the
> Arch-duchesses, Marianne, and Mary Elizabeth, were all at this burletta.
> The box, in which they sate, was very little distinguished from the rest;
> they came in and went out with few attendants, and without parade. The
> Emperor is of a manly fine figure, and has a spirited and pleasing
> countenance; he often changes his place at the opera, to converse with
> different persons, and frequently walks about the street without guards,
> seeming to shun, as much as possible, all kinds of unnecessary pomp. His
> imperial majesty was extremely attentive during the performance of the
> opera, and applauded the Baglione several times very much.[6]

Joseph's operatic tastes naturally influenced those of his subjects. He revealed his preference for comedy over tragedy on the operatic stage in an exchange of letters with Prince Wenzel Anton Kaunitz, state chancellor, regarding an impending visit to Vienna of the grand duke and duchess of Russia in

1781 – the visit for which *Die Entführung aus dem Serail* was conceived. Kaunitz wrote that one of Joseph's goals should be to give the Russian dignitaries "a clear idea of the power of this monarchy":

> To this end it seems to me that, as with all occasions of this importance, *chi più spende, meno spende*; that both for this reason and to make their stay in Vienna as pleasant as possible it would be most useful to present the court and the city with as much éclat as possible. The first of these things can only be done by Your Majesty summoning from Italy, for example, two or three of the best voices to give a magnificent Italian opera seria, as well as the best possible ballet troupe with the younger Vestris and Mlle. Hennel.[7]

Joseph, in line with his tendency to avoid "all kinds of unnecessary pomp," rejected Kaunitz's advice and made his opinion of the genre clear: "In regard to opera seria from Italy it is too late to arrange something good; and anyway it is such a boring spectacle that I do not think I will ever use it. But I will see if there is the means here [Versailles] to arrange something passable in ballet that is worth the expense and the trouble."[8] Throughout the decade in which he reigned alone, coinciding closely with Mozart's decade in Vienna, opera seria was very rarely performed in the Habsburg capital.

The performance that took place before the ruler and his hierarchically arranged subjects, whether it took place in Berlin, Milan, or Vienna, reflected the generosity of the ruler whose subsidies helped produce it, and whose regulations and tastes shaped it. An audience that applauded a lavish production made possible by the generosity of its ruler applauded the ruler himself. In doing so, the audience accepted and celebrated the ruler and the political system that kept him in power.

Social interaction

When eighteenth-century audiences were not watching their rulers, they were very often watching, and talking with, one another. The spectacle that they witnessed in the theater took place not only on stage but all around them. The poet Francesco Zacchiroli, describing Milan's La Scala during Carnival 1780, conveyed the theater's appearance and atmosphere during a performance of Mysliveček's *Armida*; the audience must have been largely the same as those that had witnessed the performances of Mozart's *Mitridate*, *Ascanio in Alba*, and

Lucio Silla in the same city a few years earlier. Zacchiroli began with a sketch of the boxes from which "young women presented to your gaze an amazing number of heavenly faces" (reminiscent of the description in Rousseau's *Confessions* of the theater at Fontainebleau, and of the women, "as beautiful as angels," who admired his *Le Devin du village*). There follows a catalogue of the feminine beauties that adorn the theater, rather like an excerpt from Don Giovanni's *non picciol libro*: "In those happy tiers can be found something to satisfy every taste. There, together, the lively brunette and the tender blond; there, the wary lady of twenty who pleases, and knows it; and the simple girl of fifteen who please all the more, the less she realizes that she pleases. There, Hellenic features breathing delicacy; there, Roman features full of majesty." The women were not alone:

> In that box you see two fortunate lovers, so oppressed by the weight of their happiness that they have not the power to utter a syllable. Oh, how their eyes tell all to those who know the language! There, in the neighboring box, others who are quarreling *sotto voce*; they are reproving each others' infidelities, obstinately denied because they are true; each threatens to abandon the other, and they end with new protestations of love and with new oaths of constancy and fidelity . . . Each angle, of the theater, in short, presents in turn new points of view, infinitely varied by cheerfulness, laughter, pleasure, jokes, and love. Delightful points of view to whoever has a heart in his breast![9]

The behavior of the Milanese, and of Zacchiroli in observing it, was closely related to the frequency with which individual members of the audience attended the theater. During the Carnival season in Italy the first of two operas was normally performed night after night until it was replaced, somewhere near the middle of Carnival, by the second opera. Members of the audience, many of whom rented boxes for the entire season, came to the theater again and again. Modern opera lovers give all their attention to the stage not only because most of them intend to see a production only once but also because the darkness of the auditorium keeps them from seeing anything but the stage. Eighteenth-century opera lovers gave only part of their attention to the stage because they knew that what they missed one evening they could see or hear on some other occasion and because the auditorium as well as the stage was lit up during the entire evening.

Mozart in the audience

Composers, singers, and other musicians worked within this theatrical culture without much complaint. They seem to have taken it for granted that they would rarely have the audience's undivided attention for long. Mozart, indeed, took part in the socializing himself. Although he claimed that it was unusual for him to talk during an opera, he did so at a performance of Paisiello's *Le gare generose* in Prague during January 1787: "In regard to the performance of this opera I can say nothing definite because I chattered a lot."[10]

Contracts and custom required Mozart, like other composers, to direct the first three performances of his operas at the keyboard. But after these performances had given him and his performers a chance to work out some of the problems they had not solved during rehearsals, his responsibilities for the opera were largely over. Another musician – generally the theater's resident maestro di cappella or his assistant – took over the composer's place at the keyboard. (Or in the case of those Italian orchestras with two keyboard players, the resident maestro took the composer's place while his assistant sat at a second keyboard.) In the case of *Figaro* and the Viennese version of *Don Giovanni*, Salieri's assistant Weigl directed subsequent performances.

The end of Mozart's responsibility at the keyboard left him free to enjoy his handiwork from various parts of the auditorium, during performances that sometimes, as happened with *Mitridate*, evolved into social occasions. Leopold wrote:

> Since the third performance we have been listeners and spectators, sometimes in the parterre and sometimes in the boxes or palchi, where everyone is eager to speak with Signor Maestro and see him up close. During the whole performance we walk about here and there, wherever we like. For the maestro is obliged to direct the opera in the orchestra only for three evenings, when Maestro Lampugnani accompanies at the second keyboard. Now that Wolfgang is no longer playing, Lampugnani plays the first Clavier and Maestro Melchior Chiesa the second.[11]

Leopold took pride in this changing of the guard, when his son gave up the labors of an ordinary musician and mingled with the nobility in their boxes:

> If about fifteen or eighteen years ago, when Lampugnani in England and Melchior Chiesa in Italy had already composed so much, and I had seen

their opera arias and overtures, someone had said to me that these masters would take part in the performance of my son's music and, when he left the keyboard, would have to sit down and accompany his music, I would have rebuked him as a fool fit for the madhouse.[12]

Twenty years later Mozart enjoyed similar freedom to move about the auditorium and to socialize during performances of *Die Zauberflöte*. As he wrote to his wife on 8–9 October 1791, this brought him into unpleasant contact with a member of the audience who responded boorishly to the opera:

> the know-it-all showed himself to be such a *Bavarian* that I could not remain or I would have had to call him an ass. Unfortunately I was there just when the second act began, that is, at the solemn scene. He laughed at everything. At first I was patient enough to try drawing his attention to a few passages. But he laughed at everything. That was too much for me. I called him *Papageno* and went away. But I don't think the idiot understood my remark. So I went into another box where *Flamm* and his wife happened to be. There everything was pleasant and I stayed to the end.

Mozart's freedom to roam during later performances of *Die Zauberflöte* allowed him to experience the acoustic qualities of different parts of the auditorium: "You cannot believe how charming the music sounds when you hear it from a box close to the orchestra – much better than from the gallery. As soon as you return you must try it."[13]

The audience and the stage

Perhaps because they felt no obligation to keep their eyes and ears constantly focussed on the stage, eighteenth-century audiences could occasionally react to an opera, or to parts of an opera, with an intensity of aesthetic and emotional involvement unmatched by most modern-day audiences.

Kelly, the tenor whose reminiscences of the rehearsals for *Figaro* we followed in chapter 7, spent several years in Italy before joining the Viennese opera buffa troupe; there he learned much about audiences and the passions that opera could arouse in them:

> The Romans assume that they are the most sapient critics in the world; they are, certainly, the most severe ones; – they have no medium, – all is

delight or disgust. If asked whether a performance or a piece has been successful, the answer, if favourable, is, "è andato al settimo cielo," – "it has ascended to the seventh heaven." If it has failed, they say, "è andato all'abbisso del inferno," – "it has sunk to the abyss of hell." The severest critics are the Abbés, who sit in the first row of the pit, each armed with a lighted wax taper in one hand, and a book of the opera in the other; and should any poor devil of a singer miss a word, they call out "bravo, bestia," – "bravo, you beast!"

In Rome, according to Kelly, composers had to be especially careful of avoiding suspicion of plagiarism:

It is customary for the composer of an opera, to preside at the piano-forte the first three nights of its performance, and a precious time he has of it in Rome. Should any passage in the music strike the audience as similar to one of another composer, they cry, "Bravo, il ladro," – "bravo, you thief"; or, "bravo, Paesiello! bravo, Sacchini!" if they suppose the passage stolen from them, "the curse of God light on him who first put a pen into your hand to write music!" This I heard said, in the Teatro Aliberti, to the celebrated composer Gazzaniga, who was obliged to sit patiently at the piano-forte to hear the flattering commendation.

Cimarosa, who was their idol as a composer, was once so unfortunate as to make use of a movement in a comic opera, at the Teatro della Valle, which reminded them of one of his own, in an opera composed by him for the preceding carnival. An Abbé started up, and said, "Bravo, Cimarosa! you are welcome from Naples; by your music of to-night, it is clear you have neither left your trunk behind you, nor your old music; you are an excellent cook in hashing up old dishes!"[14]

In Naples an opera could be whistled off the stage, according to Giacomo Ferrari, who studied composition with Paisiello during the 1780s. He wrote of the premiere of Guglielmi's comic opera *Adalinda*:

Guglielmi was skillful in dramatic music, but lazy, avaricious, and without self-respect. In each opera he wrote two or three pieces in their entirety, then he had the *parti cantanti* of the arias and ensembles orchestrated by his students and by the copyists of Naples. At the first performance the composer of this opera was whistled as he deserved, to the point where, in the middle of the second act, the discontent became so widespread that the curtain had to be lowered and everyone was happy to go home.[15]

But on other occasions in Naples a single exceptionally beautiful number by Guglielmi – typically an ensemble – could make an entire evening a success. Of *Enea e Lavinia* Ferrari wrote: "A magnificent trio sustained the whole opera."[16] Similarly, in Guglielmi's *La pastorella nobile*, "that cunning old lazy-bones wrote a superb quintet in the first act and a *duetto da piazza* in the third act that sustained the whole opera."[17]

I quoted earlier Zacchiroli's description of the boxes at La Scala during a performance of Mysliveček's *Armida*. He and the rest of the audience could, when they wanted to, give extremely close attention to what was happening on stage. His letter continues with a remarkable account of the performance by Marchesi of Sarti's rondò, "Mia speranza io pur vorrei," which the musico had inserted in Mysliveček's opera because he had earlier achieved great success with it in the opera for which it was written, *Achille in Sciro*:

> Oh, dear friend, if only you had seen the rapid revolution that occurred throughout the theater when Marchesi entered to sing this miraculous rondeau! No one batted an eye, hardly did anyone dare to take a breath, and if we could have gone without breathing, we would have done so. Every soul flies attentive to the ears, all the other senses are suspended, so that that of hearing has no distractions. Already the voice – supple, obedient, harmonious – masters the most rebellious combinations of sounds, seizes from nature all those beauties that lie hidden from art and that, after Marchesi, will perhaps be never found again. Ah! I feel it here . . . here in my heart: that enchanting voice, always sweet, delightful, varied, now with high notes that imitate and even surpass the song of the nightingale, now with deep notes that imitate the majesty of the organ . . . I do not remember anything else: nature in its entirety does not exist for me in that moment; an indefinable spell of pleasure, of delight penetrates to the depths of my heart, charms by emotions, inebriates my senses, puts reason to sleep. All my sensations are concentrated on this heavenly song . . . my heart swells . . . I cannot resist the flood of pleasure that drowns me . . . I sigh repeatedly; I end with sobs, with tears, and with applause. The whole theater responds to my sensibility: every listener is overcome by the same delightful delirium and by a pleasure that in its sovereign power borders on pain. No one begins to breathe until Marchesi, in withdrawing from the stage, destroys the lovely illusion.[18]

Burney, attending an opera in the Regio Ducal Teatro of Milan in 1770, found the audience similarly capable of sudden, intense interest in what was happening on stage: "There was an abominable noise except during 2 or 3 arias and a duet, with which every body was in raptures. During this last, the applause continued till the performers returned to repeat it. This is the method of *encoring* an air here."[19]

Audiences in Vienna were not so opinionated, outspoken, and passionate as those in Rome, Naples, and Milan. But they too could reject a new opera; and they were unlikely to be swayed by a single number, no matter how beautiful. Mosel blamed the failure of Salieri's *Daliso e Delmita*, performed in Vienna in 1776, on incompetent staging. His account shows that Viennese audiences paid close attention (at least on some occasions) not only to the staging but to the words being sung in an Italian opera:

> The first scene presents a rural amphitheater in which people are assembled to watch young shepherds wrestling. After the dress rehearsal, when everything went well, the scene designer had the idea, without telling the poet or the composer a word about it, to paint spectators into the ranks of the amphitheater, among the trees with which the entire stage was embellished. In other circumstances this would have produced a useful illusion of extras representing the people. But when the contest ended, and after the victor was crowned, everyone left the stage except the community's chief, who stayed behind with his two daughters, to whom he wants to reveal a secret, and begins with the words "Or che siam soli, o figlie . . . " [Now that we are alone, oh daughters . . .]. The audience, who saw all the painted figures among the shrubbery, not only began to laugh, but laughed louder and louder as they noticed that the singers, who could not guess why the audience was laughing, looked around for some explanation for this interruption, but were unable to find one.
>
> Such accidents rarely happen alone. In the second act Daliso, Delmita's beloved, appeared on stage in armor, with visor down, ready to do battle with the monster to whom Delmita, according to the country's law, must be sacrificed. Daliso wants to reveal his identity to Delmita, who flees in terror, with these words: "Non fuggir, non temer, son'io Daliso" [Flee not, fear not; it is I, Daliso]. At this point he was supposed to open his visor, but he was not able to do so, and at each fruitless attempt the audience laughed louder.

At the end, after the monster was slain, the city of Athens, illuminated, was supposed to be visible in the distance. But the signal was given too late, and when the audience heard one of the characters on stage say

Vedete come allo spendor	See how, in the splendor
Di mille faci e mille	of thousands of torches,
Festeggia Atene. . .	Athens celebrates. . .

without seeing any of it, laughter rang out a third time; and it grew to its loudest when the illumination first began to appear at the same moment as the curtain fell.

So everything conspired to turn this opera seria into an opera buffa. At the end Salieri himself laughed too, especially since he had never expected much of this opera, which he set to music only after repeated, urgent requests and which was sung by members of the comic opera troupe.[20]

Mozart's Viennese audience personified: Carl Zinzendorf

The repertory system in effect in the court theaters of Mozart's Vienna offered audiences a gradually changing group of operas, each of which (with the exception of the most egregious failures) was performed at least six or seven times, and often many more than that. This gave Viennese theater-goers, many of whom rented boxes for six-month terms, plenty of opportunity to get to know operas gradually as they spent evenings dividing their attention, like audiences in Italy, between the stage and the auditorium.

The Viennese opera lover known best to us is Count Zinzendorf, a government official who attended the theater very often during his entire residence in Vienna, from the early 1760s to his death in 1813. (We have already encountered him at operatic rehearsals in the residence of Count Rosenberg and at the premiere of *La clemenza di Tito* in Prague.) The frequency of Zinzendorf's theater-going was probably not unusual. He often named the friends and acquaintances he saw in the theater, from which we know that they too attended the theater often. What is remarkable about Zinzendorf is that he kept a diary in which he recorded his theatrical activity and his opinions of singers and of the operas in which they sang. This diary, now preserved in Vienna's Haus-, Hof- und Staatsarchiv, tells us much about the tastes and behavior of the Viennese audience. Although he attended the premieres of

Die Entführung, Der Schauspieldirektor, Figaro, the Viennese version of Don Giovanni, Così fan tutte, and La clemenza di Tito, as well as later performances of these operas and of Die Zauberflöte, Zinzendorf's brief comments on Mozart's operas are less interesting than the picture that his theatrical commentary as a whole gives us of the audiences for whom Mozart wrote these operas.[21]

Zinzendorf, like his Italian contemporaries, sometimes came to the theater to meet friends or to discuss government business with colleagues. On 12 October 1787, after attending the twenty-third performance of Stephen Storace's Gli sposi malcontenti, he wrote: "Pretty music. I chatted with M. de Reischach." A few days later, on 17 October, he took in the eighth performance of Paisiello's Le due contesse: "Archduchess Marie was there with the Princess of Württemberg. Prince Lobkowitz came to chat about current events." Zinzendorf had seen at least eight performances of Figaro (in its first run in 1786 and its revival in 1789) when he wrote, on 19 September 1789: "In the evening to the opera. Le nozze di Figaro. Prince Lobkowitz in our box complained of the swelling of his belly."

Occasionally Zinzendorf spoke with the emperor, who was clearly no less willing to talk during a performance than Zinzendorf. He wrote on 7 May 1784:

> To the opera. Il vecchio geloso. Music by Alessandri. I had hardly spent any time with Mme. d'Oeynhausen when the emperor had me summoned, and I passed the whole time of the opera in his box. Blushing to the whites of my eyes, I told him of the contents of my report on the Commission on Serf Labor . . . He was happy with the opera, which is extremely comic, but nothing in it touched me.

Sometimes Zinzendorf's conversation, like this one with the emperor, turned to the opera being performed. On 3 December 1772, at a performance of Salieri's La secchia rapita, he chatted with the British ambassador: "M. Keith, next to whom I sat, made me pay attention to the music of La secchia rapita, a little Italian opera in which the serious is wonderfully combined with the comic. The music is by Salieri; the end of the first act admirable."[22]

A confirmed bachelor, Zinzendorf also used the theater to meet the women, several of them married, with whom he was in love. Louise von Diede, Baroness Fürstenstein, the wife of a Danish diplomat, kept Zinzendorf from paying much attention to Paisiello's Il re Teodoro in Venezia on 26 December

1785: "At 7 o'clock to the opera. *Il re Teodoro*. Louise, who was in our box, seemed very pretty to me." When he attended the premiere of *Figaro* on 1 May 1786 he was so preoccupied by Louise's impending departure from Vienna that the opera gave him no pleasure: "At 7 o'clock in the evening the opera *Le nozze di Figaro*, the poetry by Da Ponte, the music by Mozhardt. Louise was in my box, the opera bored me." But soon he was directing his romantic yearnings in the direction of another noblewoman, Countess Maria Josepha Auersperg (née Lobkowitz). "I came late to the opera," he wrote on 6 November 1786. "*Il trionfo delle donne*. Mme. d'Auersperg came even later. We remained in the box until we were alone, and I gave her my arm when she entered her carriage." More than a year later he was still enamored of the same women. He wrote on 17 December 1787: "In the evening to the opera *L'arbore di Diana*. I was delighted to find Mme. Auersberg there." The countess was still distracting Zinzendorf from operatic pleasures on 5 November 1789: "To the theater. *Le nozze di Figaro*. Tormented as a madman not to find Mad.^e A. there."

The count's theater-going included many brief appearances, probably involving just a quick look at the audience and the stage. "A moment at the opera *Giannina e Bernadone*," he wrote on 26 January 1786, in reference to Cimarosa's *Giannina e Bernardone*, which he had already seen at least four times. And on 25 September 1789: "An instant at the opera. *Axur*. Then I went home to read." He had already attended at least twenty-two performances of Salieri's opera.

During the summer, excessive heat often bothered Zinzendorf. "I went to the theater late," he wrote on 29 June 1785. "It was terribly hot. The music of *Gli sposi malcontenti*, though beautiful, did not interest me as much as talking with Madame Fekete about our good Therese." A heatwave in August 1791 (when Mozart was rushing to finish *La clemenza di Tito*) kept Zinzendorf from deriving much pleasure from opera. Attending a performance of Cimarosa's *Le trame deluse* on 15 August, he went to sleep because of the heat.

When not distracted by Emperor Joseph, colleagues, the presence or absence of lady-friends, and summer heat, Zinzendorf paid serious and experienced attention to what was happening on stage, the singers who were performing there, their costumes, the dramas they were representing and the music they were singing. Occasionally he took in an opera, and formed a full, coherent judgment of it, in a single evening; more often he developed his knowledge of an opera, and his opinion of it, over the course of several performances. For example, he attended two performances of Sebastiano Nasolini's *Teseo a Stige* before writing, on 2 January 1792, of a third performance during which "I saw the end of it, which I had not seen before."

Emperor Joseph's preference for comic over serious opera was reflected in Zinzendorf's tastes. Already in 1770 he found little to like in a revival of Gluck's *Alceste*, calling it, on 21 October, "a very lugubrious opera by Calzabigi . . . The choruses have nothing striking about them and the libretto is unendingly sad."[23] More than twenty years later his tastes had changed little. When Joseph's successor Leopold established an opera seria troupe in the court theaters in 1791, the inaugural opera by Nasolini left Zinzendorf cold: "24 November: the empress's birthday. In the evening to the theater. Opera seria. *Teseo a Stige*. The subject very lugubrious, music not striking, the scenery beautiful, no voices that distinguish themselves except that of the tenor." It was only some weeks later that he revealed (as quoted above) that at the premiere he had not stayed to the end of Nasolini's opera.

Zinzendorf often judged an opera's music and libretto separately. He found good music much more often than good stories and interesting characters. After an early performance of Salieri's *La fiera di Venezia*, on 2 February 1772, he wrote: "*La fiera di Venezia* bored me, there is nothing there except very pretty music."[24] Of a new opera by Weigl he wrote on 14 November 1788: "In the evening to the opera. *Il pazzo per forza*. Some beautiful pieces of music, but a wretched libretto." He dismissed Guglielmi's *La quaquera spiritosa* (first performed on 13 August 1790) as "unbelievable subject matter, but pretty music." He similarly rejected everything about Salieri's *Il mondo alla rovescia*, which takes place on an island in which women act as men and vice versa, except the music: "Stupid opera," he wrote on 13 January 1795, "the men dressed as women, the women as men. Beautiful music."[25]

Like the audiences in Rome that Kelly remembered, Zinzendorf enjoyed accusing composers of plagiarism. He wrote of an opera by Giacomo Rust that he heard on 25 October 1784: "The opera *Il marito indolente*, very mediocre music by Rust, full of thefts." Salieri's music for *Il ricco d'un giorno*, when Zinzendorf heard it on 6 December 1784, was "stolen from everywhere." And on 12 July 1786 he dismissed Righini's *Demogorgone* as "music plundered as usual." (With Righini, the charge of plagiarism was hardly new. Already in

1781 Mozart had written to his father: "He composes very charmingly and he is not by any means superficial; but he is a monstrous thief. He offers his stolen goods in such superfluity, in such profusion, that people can hardly digest them."[26])

The Viennese repertory system allowed opera lovers to get to know very well the singers, many of whom stayed in Vienna for several years. As the repertory and the opera company's personnel gradually evolved, the audience could have the pleasure of seeing familiar singers in new roles and of seeing new singers take over and reinterpret familiar roles. Zinzendorf brought an excellent memory to such games. When Joseph's opera buffa troupe made its debut on 22 April 1783, with a performance of Salieri's *La scuola de' gelosi*, he was immediately struck by the beauty and charm of Nancy Storace, the soprano who was later to create Mozart's Susanna, and by the comedic and vocal skills of Francesco Benucci, for whom Mozart was later to write the roles of Figaro and Guilelmo. But Zinzendorf's pleasure was tempered a little by his memory of an earlier production of *La scuola de' gelosi*, in Trieste during Carnival 1780, when he had particularly enjoyed the singing of the tenor Vincenzo Calvesi. Seeing the same opera in Vienna three years later, he missed Calvesi's voice: "Mlle. Storace, l'Inglesina, has a pretty, voluptuous figure, a beautiful throat, and she looks good disguised as a gypsy. She and Busanni sang the duet 'Quel visino è da ritratto,' but Bussani not as well as Calvesi in Trieste. The buffo Venucci [sic] very good; the romantic lead Bussani less so. The audience very happy." Similarly, in 1795, when Sarti's *Fra i due litiganti* was revived many years after Storace and Benucci had shared the Viennese stage for the last time, Zinzendorf judged a new pair of singers by what he remembered of how their characters had been portrayed much earlier: "Mandini and La Sessi sang the notes Benucci and Storace used to sing; but what a difference!"[27]

Sometimes one singer was enough to make an evening at the theater worthwhile. The count was very fond of Storace, several times mentioning her as the only positive element of a performance. "In the evening to the opera," he wrote of a performance of *La scuola de' gelosi* on 19 May 1783. "I was enchanted by it. The way La Storace sang 'Troveremmo' and 'Grande il mondo,' etc., and 'Un vezzo in donna bella e la folia' pleased me immensely." "To the opera. *Fra i due litiganti* etc. La Storace played her part like an angel," he wrote on

14 December 1783. But Storace's subsequent vocal difficulties allowed Zinzendorf to admire other singers. On 26 July 1784 he attended Guglielmi's *Le vicende d'amore*: "La Storace very hoarse. La Cavalieri sang perfectly."

Later in the decade another soprano won Zinzendorf's favor. Of Adriana Ferrarese, Mozart's Fiordiligi (frontispiece), he wrote on 13 October 1788: "Mme. Ferraresi made her debut in the role of Diana in *L'arbore di Diana*. She sings ravishingly. Her acting was not bad, but she was badly dressed, especially in that the cloak she wore had a veil that impeded her movement." A few days later, on 17 October, he had no reservations about the new prima donna: "La Ferraresi enchanted me. *L'arbore di Diana*." When Martín y Soler's *Una cosa rara* was revived on 7 January 1789, Viennese audiences had a chance to see Ferrarese in a role written for Storace: "To the opera. *Una cosa rara*, which lasted until after 10 o'clock. La Ferraresi acquitted herself not badly in La Storace's role." In another revival later that same year, of *Figaro*, with Ferrarese in the role of Susanna, Mozart helped her erase memories of Storace's Susanna by replacing the garden aria with a rondò, "Al desio di chi t'adora." Zinzendorf liked the result. He wrote on 7 May 1790, after he had seen the new production at least eight times: "The duo of the two women and La Ferraresi's rondò continue to please."

Another soprano who charmed Zinzendorf – and consequently dominated his perception of the operas in which she appeared – was Irene Tomeoni, who made her debut on 26 April 1791 in an opera by Guglielmi: "In the evening to the opera. *La bella pescatrice*. The new actress, Irene Tomeoni Dutillieu, is immensely pleasing. She has gaity, petulance, and an agreeable voice. She is especially charming in her *déshabillé de pecheuse*."

A fondness for singers on stage sometimes led Zinzendorf to follow their lives off the stage as well. Suspecting that Storace was having an affair with Benucci, he noticed when the soprano left the theater with a man other than Benucci: "In the evening to the opera *Trofonio*," he wrote on 16 February 1787, referring to Salieri's *La grotta di Trofonio*. "Benucci being hoarse, it was not well done. La Storace is being unfaithful to him and left with Lord Barnard."

Zinzendorf seldom commented on scenery; when he did so, it was probably in response to sets that played a particularly important role in an opera. Salieri's operas seem to have demanded more elaborate scenery than most productions in the court theaters. Although he accused Salieri of having plagiarized the music of Il ricco d'un giorno, Zinzendorf was impressed by the opera's visual evocation of its Venetian setting: "Beautiful scenery. An illuminated gondola." Another opera that takes place in Venice, Salieri's La fiera di Venezia, also earned praise for its scenery. First performed in 1772 and revived by Joseph's opera buffa troupe in 1785, it demanded a series of sets depicting various familiar views of Venice. Zinzendorf wrote on 7 October 1785: "The sets are pretty, and the finale of the second act very amusing, Salieri's music varied. La Coltellini played her role like an angel." (Perhaps Salieri's two Venetian operas made use of some of the same scenery.) He found Salieri's Axur re d'Ormus, first performed in celebration of the marriage of Archduke Francis and Elizabeth of Württemberg, very dull; but the scenery attracted his attention and approval: "The sets are new, some beautiful," he wrote on 8 January 1788. "The fourth act begins with an illuminated garden, with an abundance of waterfalls. A room illuminated by lanterns, then with chandeliers."

When an opera fully interested him, and when his interest in the prima donna did not distract him from the rest of the cast, Zinzendorf could give a carefully balanced assessment of its strengths and weaknesses, while always focusing his attention on individual singers. Citing individual scenes, even specific phrases from the libretto, he remained, at the same time, conscious of the opera's overall effect, and the contribution to that effect made by costumes and scenery. Here, for example, is Zinzendorf's response to the premiere of Salieri's La grotta di Trofonio on 12 October 1785:

> The music charming, the costumes extraordinary. La Storace in her philosopher's cloak was pretty, and Calvesi looked perfectly well. La Coltellini did wonderfully in her role. Benucci dressed as an old philosopher. But the plot is without inspiration, without art. No decorations: always the garden, always the grotto, always transformations. In the fifth scene it was Mandini and La Coltellini who excelled. The ninth scene, between the two of them, very fine: "calamità e felicità." Bussani did only moderately well in his role. At the beginning of the finale of act 1 La Storace sang well: "È un piacer col caro amante."

Zinzendorf was equally attentive, and much happier, at the first Viennese performance of Sarti's Fra i due litiganti. His opinion of Sarti's opera was greatly enhanced by Storace, who had made her Viennese debut on 22 April

1783. Her voice, face, and body still had the charm of novelty on 28 May, when she portrayed Dorina in Sarti's opera. But he admired other members of the cast as well and jotted down the first words of several numbers that he particularly liked, even referring to a page in the libretto with which he followed the performance:

> I heard with perfect pleasure the new opera *Fra due litiganti il terzo gode*. La Storace played her part like an angel. Her beautiful eyes, her white neck, her lovely throat, her youthful mouth have a charming effect. Sarti's music is delectable. La Teuberin's aria "Io voglio un sposino" had to be repeated. Okelli [i.e. Kelly], in the role of Masotto, sang "In amor si vuol finezza" very prettily. The sixth scene, with Dorina, Mingone, and Titta, is charming. "Non fidar amor mi dice." Mandini played the part of Mingone wonderfully. Venucci, as Titta, sings to Livietta "Dunque aspettate o cara (p. 38). La Storace and Okelli in scene 12. Needlework in her hand, she sings "Che bella cosa egli e far' all'amore." And the finale is superb. The fifth scene of the second act, the duo and the quartetto charming. The reconciliation of the count and countess through Masotto's efforts. The eighth scene, La Storace, "Oh che orrore!" The finale of the second act: three instruments accompany first separately, then together. Act 3, scene 4, when Dorina tricks Titta, who kisses her hand. In short, it is a charming opera.[28]

In such accounts, unfortunately rare, Zinzendorf revealed himself a thoughtful and experienced man of the theater: the kind of opera lover whom Mozart may have had in mind when he wrote his operas.

CHAPTER 10

Performance and reception

Brilliantly lit with hundreds of candles, filled with people wearing brightly colored suits and dresses of rich cloth, the eighteenth-century theater presented an image of opulence and festivity in which a member of the audience could find sources of pleasure and entertainment in every direction.

The spectacle offered by the performance of a new opera often included drama taking place not only on stage but in the audience: conflicts between parties supporting various singers, composers, theatrical genres, and nationalities. The cabals operating within the operatic troupe sometimes spilled out into the audience. Thus the conflicts that threatened rehearsals continued during performances. "Can you believe," Mozart asked his father, referring to the second performance of *Die Entführung aus dem Serail*, "that yesterday there was an even stronger cabal than on the first evening? The whole first act was hissed. But they could not prevent the loud shouts of 'bravo' during the arias."[1] Another kind of intrigue added excitement to the first performance of *Lucio Silla*. According to Leopold, rivalry between the prima donna De Amicis and the primo uomo Rauzzini caused the latter to arrange a royal claque, which kept De Amicis from singing her best: "She was jealous because as soon as the primo uomo came on the stage the archduchess clapped her hands. This was a castrato's trick, for he had arranged that the archduchess be told that he would not be able to sing because of nervousness, in order that he might thus ensure that the court would encourage and applaud him."[2]

Into a similar atmosphere, highly charged with carnivalesque pleasure and passionate partisanship, young Salieri entered as he made his way to the keyboard to conduct the premiere of his first opera in Vienna during Carnival 1770:

> In vain would I attempt to describe the joyful restlessness that I felt that
> day as the hour of performance approached; but when it arrived joy turned
> to fear, my face began to burn, and it blushed scarlet; and thus I went

213

with uncertain steps to the Clavier. When I entered the orchestra there was applause, which brought my courage back. I greeted the audience, sat down with a certain ease at the *Spinett*, and the opera began.[3]

We can imagine, with Leopold's help, the thrill that his son must have felt as he directed the premiere of *Mitridate* a few months later. He wrote on 15 December 1770: "On St. Stephen's Day, a good hour after Ave Maria, you can picture to yourselves Maestro Amadeo at the Clavier in the orchestra, and me in a box above, a spectator and a listener, and wish him a successful performance and say a few paternosters for him."[4] And a week later: "You can picture to yourselves Wolfgang in a scarlet suit, trimmed with gold braid and lined with sky-blue satin. The tailor is starting to make it today. He will wear this suit during the first three days when he sits at the Clavier."[5]

The applause that greeted Salieri on his arrival at the keyboard was probably a normal part of an opera's premiere; more unusual were the enthusiastic cheers that, according to a Prague newspaper, welcomed Mozart at the first performance of *Don Giovanni*: "On Monday the 29th the eagerly awaited opera of Maestro Mozart, *Don Giovanni, or das steinerne Gastmahl*, was given by the Italian opera company. Connoisseurs and musicians say nothing like it has ever been performed in Prague. Herr Mozard conducted in person; when he entered the orchestra he was received with three cheers, which also happened when he left it."[6] How many performances of *Don Giovanni* Mozart conducted in Prague in 1787 we do not know, but it was presumably at least four, since the proceeds from that fourth performance were his.

Four years later Mozart returned to Prague for the last time. While completing *Tito* and leading rehearsals of it, he found time to conduct a performance of *Don Giovanni* as well. In the audience was Franz Alexander von Kleist, in whose account of the occasion Mozart was no longer a teenager in a scarlet coat – and the applause and cheers were no longer directed at him:

Never have I left an opera house so richly rewarded as today, when I saw so many people, notable in such different ways, in one place. The emperor and his family were to come to the opera today, and the entire route from the castle to the opera house swarmed with people anxious to see an emperor on his way to the play. In the house all the boxes and the stalls were filled with people, and when the emperor finally arrived, he was received with threefold hand-clapping and cries of "Vivat!" . . . The emperor seemed pleased with his welcome and bowed to the spectators a few times . . .

"Away with these people!" – with a gesture a little man in a green coat, whose eye proclaims what his modest appearance would conceal, bids me attend to more attractive matters. It is Mozart, whose opera Don Juan is to be given today, whose joy it is to see for himself the transports into which his glorious harmonies put the audience's hearts. Who in the whole house can be more proud and glad than he? Who can derive more satisfaction from his own self than he? In vain would monarchs exhaust their treasures, in vain ancestral pride its riches: these cannot buy one spark of the feeling with which Art rewards her darling![7]

The tradition that required Mozart to direct from the keyboard the first performances of Mitridate and Don Giovanni was also honored in Vienna, where we know from Weigl's reminiscences that Mozart directed the first three performances of Figaro and the Viennese version of Don Giovanni. The Hungarian poet Franz Kazinczy wrote of an early performance of Figaro: "Storace, the beautiful singer, enchanted eye, ear, and soul. Mozart directed the orchestra, playing his fortepiano, but the joy this music causes is so far removed from all sensuality that one cannot speak of it. Where could words be found that are worthy to describe such a joy?"[8] The poster announcing the premiere of Die Zauberflöte (see figure 7.3) made a special point of Mozart's role as conductor, probably because it was unusual for the Theater auf der Wieden to present a new work by a single composer: "Herr Mozard, out of respect for a gracious and honorable public, and out of friendship for the author of the play, will today direct the orchestra himself." According to Seyfried, "Süßmayr, the faithful Pylades, sat to his right, diligently turning the pages of the score."[9]

Mozart as operatic conductor

Mozart brought to his conducting an extraordinary ear, described by Niemetschek: "His hearing was so fine, he perceived differences in pitch so exactly and correctly, that he noticed the smallest mistake or discord even in the largest orchestra, and was able to point to the person or instrument at fault."[10] That sensitivity sometimes led to frustration, which he could not always conceal. Constanze Mozart, interviewed by Mary and Vincent Novello in 1829, remembered a performance of Die Entführung led by her husband: "Occasionally [he] would stamp with his foot when impatient, or things did not go correctly in the orchestra. [I was] with him at the opera Il Seraglio when they took the time of one of the Movements too fast – he became quite impatient and called out to the Orchestra without seeming to fear or to be aware of the presence of the audience."[11] Mozart's impatience probably resulted, in part, from the difficulty of communicating his ideas to musicians (singers as well as orchestra) faced with more complex music than they were accustomed to.

Singers were not able to meet every challenge of Mozart's vocal writing during rehearsals of Die Entführung, and during the second performance, as Mozart told his father, the trio at the end of act 1 ("Marsch, marsch, marsch") fell apart: "Bad luck caused Fischer [in the role of Osmin] to make a mistake, which made Dauer (Pedrillo) go wrong too; and Adamberger alone could not set everything right, so that the whole effect was lost, and this time it was not repeated. I was in such a rage (as was Adamberger) that I lost control and said at once that I would not let the opera be given again without having a short rehearsal for the singers."[12]

The complexity of Mozart's operatic music came up again in an article about the first few performances of Le nozze di Figaro (to be quoted in full later in this chapter), which acknowledged: "It is true that the first performance did not go as well as possible, owing to the difficulty of the composition."[13]

The music lovers of Prague took pride in the ability of its musicians to handle Mozart's music. The Prager Oberpostamtszeitung reported on 12 December 1786 that the opera orchestra in Prague accompanied Figaro with particular skill: "Connoisseurs who have seen the opera in Vienna would like to assert that the performance here went off much better; and very likely because the wind instruments, on which the Bohemians are well known to be the finest masters, have a great deal to do in the whole piece; particular pleasure was given by the interchanges of the horns and the trumpets."[14]

But even the Prague orchestra made some mistakes during the first performance of Don Giovanni; here Mozart had to take some of the blame because he completed the overture so shortly before the performance that the orchestra had to read it at sight. The double bassist Swoboda recalled much later that

Mozart congratulated the orchestra for its sight-reading: "Bravo, bravo, das war ausgezeichnet!" And after the performance he congratulated the players again, "even if several notes fell under the music stands."[15] The Prague musicians' exceptional skill and their admiration of and good will toward the composer allowed them to overcome the music's difficulty and the shortness of rehearsal time, according to a local newspaper report: "The opera is, moreover, extremely difficult to perform, and everyone admired the good performance given in spite of this after such a short period of rehearsal. Everybody, on the stage and in the orchestra, strained every nerve to thank Mozard by rewarding him with a good performance."[16]

In the case of Mozart's early Italian operas, Leopold probably encouraged him to keep his music as straightfoward as possible, so as to avoid any possibility that the opera might be rejected as unplayable. The premieres of *Mitridate* and *Ascanio in Alba* went smoothly, and both operas were well received. Leopold's amusing account of the first performance of *Lucio Silla*, in contrast, reads like a catalogue of all the things that could go wrong on such an occasion, none of which could be blamed on Wolfgang's music or conducting:

> The opera went well, although on the first evening several very annoying things happened. The first was that the performance, which should generally begin one hour after the Angelus, started three hours after the Angelus, that is, about eight o'clock by German time, and did not finish until around two o'clock after midnight. The archduke rose from his midday meal only just before the Angelus, and then he had to write with his own hand five letters or New Year's greetings to Their Majesties the emperor and empress, and – take note – he writes very slowly.
>
> Imagine: the whole theater was so full by half past five that no-one else could get in. The singers are nervous on the first night at having to perform before such a distinguished audience. For three hours the anxious singers, the orchestra, and the audience (many of the latter standing) had to wait impatiently in the heat for the opera to begin.
>
> Next, the tenor, whom we had to take as a last resort, is a church singer from Lodi who has never before acted in such an important theater, who has only performed as *primo tenore* in Lodi a couple of times, and finally was only engaged a week before the performance. At the point where in her first aria the prima donna expected from him an angry gesture, he exaggerated his anger so much that he looked as if he was

about to box her ears and strike her on the nose with his fist. This made
the audience laugh. Signora De Amicis, in the enthusiasm of her singing,
did not notice at first why they were laughing; she was disconcerted and
didn't realize at first who was being laughed at, and did not sing well the
whole first evening.[17]

Emperor Leopold II, Archduke Ferdinand's older brother, caused an equally
unpleasant and disruptive delay two decades later at the premiere of another
opera seria, *La clemenza di Tito*, as we will see below.

Mozart seems to have generally taken it for granted that the original productions of his operas, having been supervised by him during rehearsals and
the first few performances, would proceed successfully, and without major
changes, even without his presence at the keyboard. Only once did he express
reluctance to leave an opera in the hands of another conductor. He happily wrote to his mother of the success of the first performance of *La finta
giardiniera*, but his satisfaction must have been tempered by suspicion that if
he gave up his place at the keyboard, his opera might undergo some significant
change:

> As for our trip home, it will not happen soon, and Mamma must not wish
> for it, for she knows how much good it does me to breathe freely. We shall
> come home soon enough. An urgent and necessary reason is that next
> Friday my opera is being given again and it is most essential that I should
> be at the performance. Otherwise it would be quite unrecognizable – for
> the situation here is very strange.[18]

These enigmatic remarks have caused Daniel Heartz to speculate that "Mozart
had difficulty imposing his music on the singers. Perhaps they even tried to
substitute some of Anfossi's setting. At least it indicates that discipline was
a problem."[19] Another possibility is that Mozart feared the comic improvisation that opera buffa performers often brought to their roles. Still quite
inexperienced with opera buffa, Mozart might have rejected the liberties taken
spontaneously by comic singers – liberties that by the time of *Don Giovanni* he
had come to appreciate.

Reception

Every time a composer presented a new opera, the possibility of failure was
real, the number of things that could go wrong practically limitless. Several

operas given in Vienna during the 1780s and early 1790s were withdrawn after a handful of performances: Guglielmi's La quacquera spiritosa (two performances[20]), Paisiello's La finta amante (two performances; "it bored me by the stupidity of the subject and the unpleasantness of Manservisi's acting," wrote Zinzendorf [21]), Weigl's La caffettiera bizzarra (three performances; Zinzendorf called it "a very stupid opera"), Joseph Barta's Il mercato di Malmantile (three performances; Zinzendorf found "the music bad . . . and the play badly acted") and Gazzaniga's Il finto cieco ("performed three times and then put to sleep," as Da Ponte, its librettist, put it in his memoirs), and Righini's L'incontro inaspettato (four performances; "stupid book, detestable music," wrote Zinzendorf). Evidently the management of the court theaters considered these operas hopeless flops and abandoned them as soon as possible.

At the opposite end of the spectrum of opinion with which Viennese audiences received operatic premieres was the unmitigated delight that Zinzendorf expressed (in a diary entry quoted in chapter 9) after the first Viennese performance of Sarti's Fra i due litiganti. The audience as a whole agreed with Zinzendorf. Sarti's opera remained in the repertory for six years, performed sixty-three times.

None of Mozart's Burgtheater operas received nearly that many performances, but none of them was a flop either. Die Entführung had a good initial run – cut short by Joseph's discontinuation of Singspiel in 1783 – of fourteen performances; reconstituted in 1786, the Singspiel troupe treated Die Entführung as a mainstay, giving it it twenty-four times. Despite mixed reactions to the premieres of Figaro and the Viennese version of Don Giovanni, the former received nine performances during its first run and was revived for twenty-nine more in 1789–91; and the latter was given twelve times in 1788. Così fan tutte appeared at first to have the potential to repeat the success of Die Entführung. Zinzendorf wrote: "Mozart's music is charming and the plot is rather amusing."[22] Così fan tutte was given five times to large audiences during Carnival 1790 and five more times during the following spring and summer. If Emperor Leopold II had not initiated his transformation of the Viennese operatic repertory in 1791, Così fan tutte would have probably been performed frequently that year (but then again, Mozart might not have abandoned the court theaters for the Theater auf der Wieden and written Die Zauberflöte).

A clear statement by Mozart himself of what he considered to be the characteristics of a successful premiere is in a letter he wrote to his mother from Munich on 14 January 1775 about *La finta giardiniera*:

> God be praised! My opera was performed yesterday, the 13th, for the first time and was such a success that it is impossible for me to describe the applause to Mamma. In the first place, the whole theater was so packed that a great many people were turned away. Then after each aria there was a terrific noise, clapping of hands and cries of "Viva Maestro." Her Highness the Electress and the Dowager Electress (who were sitting opposite me) also called out "Bravo" to me. After the opera was over and during the pause when there is usually silence until the ballet begins, people kept on clapping all the time and shouting "Bravo"; now stopping, now beginning again and so on.[23]

Mozart may have exaggerated the enthusiasm of his audience.[24] But three indicators of success mentioned here – a crowded theater, applause and cries of approval from the audience as a whole, and applause from the ruling family in whose theater the opera was being performed – recur frequently in accounts of the premieres of Mozart's operas by the composer himself, his father, and others. Another important indicator of success, not mentioned by Mozart in his letter about *La finta giardiniera*, was the repetition of musical numbers that the audience found particularly pleasing. Yet another, closely related to the size of the audience, was the amount of income generated for the theater by ticket sales.

By these standards, most of Mozart's operas had successful premieres, starting with *Mitridate*, of which Leopold Mozart wrote happily:

> God be praised! The first performance of the opera took place on the 26th [December 1770] and won general applause; and two things that have never yet happened in Milan occurred on that evening. First of all, contrary to the custom of a first night, an aria of the prima donna was repeated, though usually at a first performance the audience never call out "fuora." Secondly, after all the arias, with the exception of a few at the end, there was extraordinary applause and cries of "Viva il Maestro! Viva il Maestrino!"
>
> On the 27th two arias of the prima donna were repeated. As it was Thursday and there was Friday to follow, the management had to try to cut down the encores.[25]

This was the not the last time, as we will see, that the success of Mozart's music caused officials in charge of a theater to limit the number of pieces repeated during a performance.

Leopold's report is corroborated by a brief notice in the *Gazzetta di Milano*:

> Last Wednesday the Teatro Regio Ducal reopened with the performance of the drama entitled *Mitridate re di Ponto*, which has met with the public's satisfaction as much for the tasteful stage designs as for the excellence of the music and the ability of the actors. Some of the arias sung by Signora Antonia Bernasconi vividly express the passions and touch the heart. The young maestro di cappella, who has not yet reached the age of fifteen, studies the beauty of nature and shows it to us adorned with the rarest of musical graces.[26]

Mozart wrote to his sister, mentioning another indicator of the opera's popularity: "The opera, God be praised, is a success, for every evening the theater is full, much to the astonishment of everyone, for many people say that since they have been in Milan they have never seen such crowds at a first opera."[27] By "first opera" Mozart meant the first of the two operas scheduled to be performed during the Carnival season.

A crowded theater and calls for encores also welcomed *Die Entführung*. The second performance, although marred by singers' mistakes, earned "loud shouts of 'bravo'":

> In the second act both duets were repeated as on the first night, and in addition Belmonte's rondo 'Wenn der Freude Tränen fliessen.' The theater was almost more crowded than on the first night and on the preceding day no reserved seats were to be had, either in the stalls or in the third circle, and not a single box. My opera has brought in 1200 Gulden in the two days.[28]

A premiere in July ran the risk that summer heat, of which Zinzendorf so often complained, might keep audiences away from the theater. But *Die Entführung* overcame this threat. Mozart wrote on 27 July 1782: "My opera was given yesterday for the third time . . . and won the greatest applause; and again, in spite of the frightful heat, the theater was packed."[29]

Not everyone in the audience was pleased with *Die Entführung*. Some – Mozart, typically, believed them to belong to a well-organized cabal – hissed during some of the early performances. That may have led Zinzendorf, always conscious of how the rest of the audience was responding to an opera, to a largely negative reaction: "In the evening to the theater. *Die Entführung aus dem Serail*, an opera the music of which is pilfered from various others. Fischer acted well. Adamberger is a statue."[30] Zinzendorf liked to accuse operatic composers of plagiarism, as we saw in chapter 9; but this was the only time he was silly enough to accuse Mozart of such a misdeed.

Figaro in Vienna and Prague

The repetition of ensembles and arias demanded by Mozart's admirers at performances of *Die Entführung* and the consequent lengthening of operatic performances resumed with *Figaro*, which received a mixed reaction much like that of *Die Entführung*. More than two months after the premiere, on 11 July 1786, the *Wiener Realzeitung* devoted to *Figaro* a review that, given the rarity with which that journal discussed opera, tacitly acknowledged the importance of the opera and its composer:

> On Monday, 1 May, was performed at the Imperial Royal National Court Theater (for the first time) *La Nozze di Figaro. Die Hochzeit des Figaro.* An Italian Singspiel in four acts. The music is by Herr Kapellmeister Mozart.
>
> "What is not allowed to be said these days, is sung" one may say with *Figaro* [in a footnote: "In *The Barber of Seville*"]. This piece, which was prohibited in Paris and not allowed to be performed here as a *comedy* either in a bad or in a good translation, we have at last been lucky enough to see represented as an *opera*. It will be seen that we are doing better than the French.
>
> Herr Mozart's music was generally admired by connoisseurs already at the first performance, if I except only those whose egotism and pride will not allow them to find merit in anything not written by themselves.
>
> The *public*, however (and this often happens to the public) did not really know on the first day where it stood. I heard many a *bravo* from unbiassed connoisseurs, but obstreperous louts in the uppermost tier exerted their hired lungs with all their might to deafen singers and audience alike with their *St!* and *Pst!*; and consequently opinions were divided at the end of the piece.
>
> Apart from that, it is true that the first performance did not go as well as possible, owing to the difficulty of the composition.

But now, after several performances, one would be subscribing either to the cabal or to tastelessness if one were to maintain that Herr Mozart's music is anything but a masterpiece of art.

It contains so many beauties, and such a wealth of ideas, as can be drawn only from the source of innate genius.

Some journalists like to report that Herr Mozart's opera did not please at all. It may be guessed what sort of correspondents they must be who recklessly publish such obvious lies. I believe it to be sufficiently well known that it was precisely the third performance of this opera and the frequent demand for encores during it that led to the imperial decree that a few days later publicly announced that in the future it would be forbidden to repeat in an opera any piece written for more than a single voice.[31]

Much of this article is corroborated by other evidence. That mistakes marred the first performance we read also in Niemetschek's account of the first production, quoted below. That Joseph II forbade the repetition of ensembles we know from a letter he wrote to Rosenberg on 9 May 1786, just eight days after the premiere of *Figaro*: "To prevent the excessive duration of the operas, without however prejudicing the fame often sought by opera singers from the repetition of vocal pieces, I deem the enclosed notice to the public (that no piece for more than a single voice is to be repeated) to be the most reasonable expedient. You will therefore cause some posters to this effect to be printed."[32]

Mozart, who considered encores to be a sign of his own success as a composer, probably valued the repetition of ensembles more than the repetition of arias (when applause was more likely meant for the singer than the composer). He probably regarded Joseph's decree – like the attempts fifteen years earlier to reduce the number of encores in *Mitridate* – with a mixture of pleasure and frustration. On the one hand, as the article in the *Wiener Realzeitung* implied, official attempts to stifle applause clearly documented the success of an opera by acknowledging the unusually large number of encores it earned. On the other hand, Mozart must have resented rules that kept his operas – and in particular his ensembles – from receiving as much applause as they could incite.

Niemetschek's account of the reception of *Figaro* in Vienna and Prague needs to be taken with caution, since it is part of a larger narrative in which he, as a Bohemian, sought to emphasize the good will of the musicians of Prague and the good taste of its music lovers. He blamed the weakness of the first performance of *Figaro* not on the difficulty of the music, but on the malice of the Italian singers:

> It was performed in Vienna by the Italian Opera Company. If what is generally stated as the truth is really true (and it is difficult to doubt so many reliable eyewitnesses), that the singers, out of hate, envy, and petty cabals, tried to spoil the opera by making intentional mistakes at the first performance, the reader may gather how much this faction feared the superiority of Mozart's genius . . .
>
> [In Prague] the enthusiasm that it aroused in the public was without precedent; they could not hear it enough. It was soon published in a good keyboard reduction by one of our best masters, Herr Kucharz, and arranged for wind band, as a quintet for chamber music, and as German dances . . . In addition, there was the incomparable orchestra of our Opera, which understood how to execute Mozart's ideas so accurately and diligently . . . The well-known orchestra director Strobach, since deceased, often declared that at each performance he and his colleagues were so excited that they would gladly have started from the beginning again in spite of the hard work.[33]

Niemetschek exaggerated, for rhetorical effect, the differences between the conditions under which *Figaro* was performed in Vienna and Prague. As for the nationality of the singers, the troupe that presented *Figaro* in Prague was more thoroughly Italian than the troupe in Vienna (which included the English Storace and the Irish Kelly). And the rapid dissemination of music from the opera in the form of instrumental arrangements took place in Vienna as well as in Prague. On 3 May, just two days after the premiere in Vienna, the *Wiener Zeitung* carried an announcement by the publisher Christoph Torricella:

> *Le nozze di Figaro, Die Hochzeit des Figaro.*
> Since I am so fortunate as to be able already to supply the highly estimable public with this beautiful as well as ingenious work by the celebrated Herr Kapellmeister Mozart, I did not wish any longer to withhold the news from the respected lovers of music that the score of the whole of this opera is to be had to order from my establishment at the cheapest price.

Acquainted with the hon. public's excellent taste, I have entrusted experienced musicians with the making of a keyboard score as well as of quartets for 2 violins, viola and bass, and amateurs will be able to be served to order with these likewise within a short time; those who wish to possess this opera in one form or another are therefore requested to enter their names in good time, so that they may be most punctiliously served with this opera, which is already much in demand in the neighbouring Imperial & Royal States as well as abroad.[34]

"Perfectly unnatural, and even monstrous": early reactions to Die Zauberflöte

In writing of *Die Zauberflöte*, Zinzendorf had recourse to the dichotomy that he frequently expressed in his judgments of Italian comic operas. He found the music far more attractive than the drama. He wrote on 6 November 1791: "At half past six to the theater of Starhemberg [the nobleman who owned the building in which the Theater auf der Wieden was located] in the suburb of Wieden, the box of M. and Mme. Auersperg, to hear the twenty-fourth performance of *Die Zauberflöte*. The music and the scenery are pretty, the rest is an unbelievable farce. A huge audience."[35] Zinzendorf's opinion was shared by an anonymous critic who, shortly after Mozart's death, interpreted *Die Zauberflöte* as the product of Schikaneder's exploitation of musical genius:

> He employed the clever device of elevating his own inferior products by means of skillful composers and by using their talents so as to win the taste of the public for his farces; this was the case with *Die Zauberflöte*. This ridiculous, senseless and stale product, faced with which understanding must stand still and criticism blush, would but for the composition of the great Mozart be forgotten and scorned, yet through the talents of this genius, which he displayed therein in all their strength, the whole work triumphed, people disregarded the nonsense harangued by a Moor, a bird-catcher, and a witch even as they gave themselves over entirely to the delightful melodies, they laughed at the caricatures and took delight in the magic of the music, regretting only that such great talents had not been put to a more worthy and nobler subject. Not content with grouping together the most far-fetched beings and bringing on a Queen of Night

with her female servants, Zoroaster with his priests, initiates and profane persons, spirits, monsters, and furies, the director has attempted to deceive the eye by means of sixteen different transformations and, in baroque fashion, conjured up the scenes of nature. However ridiculous and absurd the representation of this farce is, so excellent is the music in which the late Mozart showed himself in his greatness; the genius of the musician shows itself in the overture – the chorus of the priests of Zoroaster "In diesen heiligen Maurer" is solemn, the arias "Bei Männern, welche Liebe fühlen" are excellent. The duets and trios, and the recitatives, worthy of a Mozart in their invention, expressiveness and art, whom the genius of humanity mourns. He is no more! This opera, too, has to thank this enchanting harmony for its so often repeated performances and its large receipts. All classes hasten to see *Die Zauberflöte*, and one constantly discerned new musical beauties, the more often one saw it: it must be said in praise of the orchestra that it worthily performed this masterpiece, for its creator himself directed it at its first performance.[36]

John Owen, an English traveler in Vienna in October 1792, agreed with Zinzendorf and this anonymous critic in finding the libretto (which he called "the composition") "monstrous" – but he was able to appreciate and enjoy the spectacle as a whole in a way that helps us understand what made *Die Zauberflöte* such a hit:

> The second theatre to which I was conducted is stiled the Wiedner. This is in the fauxbourgs. It can boast of no great beauty. Its principal excellence arises from the musicians and singers, who support the whimsical performances here exhibited. The pieces presented in this theatre are usually of a metaphorical description and abound in magic and metamorphose. I was much entertained with the representation of the favorite burletta of the Magical Flute. The scenery was varied in a thousand grotesque forms, and the wonderful powers of the magical flute gave birth to many humorous events. The stile of the composition, though perfectly unnatural, and even monstrous, was yet, by the ingenuity of the author, neither uninteresting nor inelegant. The music was simple and characteristic, assorted well with the composition and added to the enchantment of the action the more potent magic of sweet sounds. This species of dramatic entertainment is novel and delicious. Founded upon the fictions of imagination, it sets probability at defiance, and justifies the wildest caprice of genius.[37]

Hard-won success

Two of Mozart's operas that failed to excite enthusiastic applause at their premieres, the Viennese version of *Don Giovanni* and *La clemenza di Tito*, gradually
won over the audience during the course of several performances. Of *Don
Giovanni* in Vienna, Da Ponte wrote in his memoirs:

> The opera went on the stage and . . . need I recall it? . . . *Don Giovanni* did
> not please! Everyone, except Mozart, thought that there was something
> missing. Additions were made; some of the arias were changed; it was
> offered for a second performance. *Don Giovanni* did not please! And what
> did the emperor say? He said: "That opera is divine; I should even venture
> that it is more beautiful than *Figaro*. But such music is not meat for the
> teeth of my Viennese!"
>
> I reported the remark to Mozart, who replied quietly: "Give them time
> to chew on it!" He was not mistaken. On his advice I strove to procure
> frequent repetitions of the opera; at each performance the applause
> increased, and little by little even Vienna of the dull teeth came to enjoy its
> savor and appreciate its beauties, and placed *Don Giovanni* among the most
> beautiful operas that have ever been produced on any stage.[38]

Da Ponte's report is in some respects misleading. Joseph, supervising a military campaign in May 1788, was not present at the premiere (although he
may have performed parts of the opera in his private chamber music sessions before leaving for the field of battle). In responding to Rosenberg's
report of the premiere, Joseph wrote: "Mozart's music is certainly too
difficult for the singers."[39] (Mozart's operas in general or *Don Giovanni* in
particular?)

Rather than a total failure (which would have probably led Rosenberg to
drop the opera entirely), *Don Giovanni* seems to have stirred up a mixed reaction in Vienna. Archduchess Elizabeth Wilhelmina, who did not attend the
premiere, wrote: "In the last few days a new opera by Mozart has been given,
but I was told it did not have much success."[40] Although Zinzendorf found
Mozart's music "agreeable and very varied," a few nights later he reported
the opinion of a friend for whom the music was "learned, little suited to the
voice."[41] The schedule of performances in the Burgtheater corroborates Da
Ponte's account of how he and the management responded to the opera's

initial reception. The twelve performances that *Don Giovanni* received in 1788 far exceeded the number of performances allowed to operas that the management considered flops.

La clemenza di Tito earned its success in a similar way. The premiere, during the coronation of Leopold II in Prague, fell victim to a combination of unfortunate circumstances that included an audience distracted by coronation events and a major delay in the arrival of the royal-imperial family, which brought the rest of the audience and the performers nearly to the point of exhaustion. Zinzendorf left us a description of the occasion:

> At 5 o'clock to the theater in the Old Town, to the spectacle that the Estates are presenting. I was put in a box in the first tier. [There follows mention of some of the dignitaries who shared Zinzendorf's box, and of some of the acquaintances he saw in other boxes.] The court did not arrive until half past seven. We were presented with the most boring spectacle, *La clemenza di Tito*. Rotenhan was in the box with the emperor . . . Marchetti sings very well; the emperor is enthusiastic about her. It was extremely difficult getting out of this theater.[42]

Empress Maria Luisa wrote to her daughter-in-law Maria Theresa the day after the premiere: "In the evening to the theater. The grand opera is not so grand, and the music very bad, so that almost all of us went to sleep. The coronation went marvelously."[43]

The empress's lack of interest in the opera was symptomatic of "a certain prejudice against Mozart's composition" that Count Heinrich Rottenhan, governor of Bohemia, attributed to the imperial court. He did so in a memorandum concerning a request by Guardasoni that he be compensated for losses that he incurred in producing *Tito*:

> It is generally known that by reason of the many court festivities, and the balls and parties given in private houses, both theater managers had very small audiences; and at court there was moreover a certain prejudice against Mozart's composition. Accordingly, as the opera drew scarcely any spectators after the first gala performance, the manager's whole enterprise (apart from the agreed donation from the Estates), which relied on deriving a considerable sum from the sale of tickets, failed completely.[44]

An anonymous assessment of opera in Prague published in 1794, possibly by Niemetschek, offers some further insight into the initial reception of Tito:

> It was given at the time of the coronation as an opera with free admission, and several more times thereafter; but as fate willed it, a pitiful castrato and a prima donna who sang more with her hands than her throat, and whom one had to consider a lunatic, sang the principal parts; since the subject is too simple to be able to interest the mass of people occupied with coronation festivities, balls, and illuminations; and since finally it is – shame on our age – a serious opera, it pleased less, in general, than its truly heavenly music deserved.[45]

But if the first performance of Tito was unsucessful, and some of those that followed sparsely attended, audiences in Prague began to appreciate it quickly. Performances continued until near the end of September, and Mozart wrote to his wife that the final performance was a great success. He reported news he had received from Anton Stadler, who had been playing the clarinet and basset-horn solos in "Parto, ma tu, ben mio," and "Non più di fiori":

> And the strangest thing of all is that on the very evening when my new opera [Die Zauberflöte] was performed for the first time with such success, Tito was given in Prague for the last time with tremendous applause. Bedini sang better than ever. The little duet in A major ["Ah perdona al primo affetto"] that the two girls [Carolina Perini as Annio and Antonia Miklaszewicz as Servilia] sing was repeated; and had not the audience wished to spare Marchetti [as Vitellia], a repetition of the rondò ["Non più di fiori"] would have been very welcome. Cries of "Bravo" were shouted at Stodla [Stadler] from the parterre and even from the orchestra – "What a miracle for Bohemia," he writes, "but indeed I did my very best."[46]

Performances in other cities

Several of Mozart's later operas – from Die Entführung on – were performed frequently, during the composer's lifetime, in cities other than those for which Mozart wrote them, usually in productions over which Mozart had no control and for which he received no payment. Yet he considered these productions another sign of success, boasting to his father on 6 December 1783: "My

German opera *Die Entführung aus dem Serail* has been performed in Prague and Leipzig very well, and with the greatest applause. I have heard both these things from people who saw them there."[47]

Few of those performances probably equalled the first production, with the composer communicating his intentions in person, and with singers in roles written specifically for them. Paisiello's student Ferrari remembered the first production of his teacher's *Nina, ossia La pazza per amore* at Caserta in 1789, "performed to applause of unprecedented enthusiasm. The opera was successfully performed thoughout Europe, but what a difference between hearing an opera staged by the composer who wrote it and sung by the company for whom it was written, and hearing it almost always sacrificed to the caprices of those who direct it and who perform it!"[48] Kelly wrote in similar terms of *Figaro*:

> I have seen it performed at different periods in other countries, and well too, but no more to compare with its original performance than light is to darkness. All the original performers had the advantage of the instruction of the composer, who transfused into their minds his inspired meaning. I shall never forget his little animated countenance, when lighted up with the glowing rays of genius; – it is as impossible to describe it, as it would be to paint sunbeams.[49]

Occasionally Mozart had a chance to put his personal stamp on a production of an opera far from the city for which he wrote it. This happened in Berlin on 19 May 1789, according to an anecdote recorded by Friedrich Rochlitz nine years later:

> When Mozart arrived in Berlin for the last time (after his second visit to Leipzig) it was already evening. Hardly had he alighted when he asked the waiter at the inn . . . who did not recognize him, "Is there any kind of music here this evening?"
> "Oh yes, the German opera has just begun."
> "Really? What are they doing today?"
> "*Die Entführung aus dem Serail*"
> "Charming," exclaimed Mozart, laughing.
> "Yes," the fellow continued, "it is a pretty play. Composed by . . . now what's his name?"

In the meantime Mozart, in his traveling coat, had already left. He stood at the entrance to the parterre, intending to observe unnoticed. But soon he was too delighted with the performance of certain passages, too dissatisfied with some of the tempos, and the singers added too many *Schnörkeleien* [ornamental flourishes], as he called them. In short, his interest became increasingly lively and without realizing what he was doing he pushed closer and closer to the orchestra. Meanwhile he mumbled this and grumbled that, softer or louder, until those standing near him, looking down on this homely little man in a plain overcoat, began to laugh at him – of which he was naturally unaware. Finally the performance reached Pedrillo's aria "Frisch zum Kampfe, frisch zum Streite." Either the management had an inaccurate score or someone had tried to make an improvement and had given the second violins, at the frequently repeated words "nur ein feiger Tropf verzagt," D sharp instead of D natural. Here Mozart could no longer restrain himself. He cried out in plain language: "Damn it! Will you play D!"

Everyone looked around, including many of the players in the orchestra; some of the musicians recognized him, and now the news spread like a wildfire through the orchestra and from there to the stage: Mozart is here! Some of the actors, especially dear Madame [Henriette] B[aranius], who played Blonde, did not want to return to the stage. When this news reached the music director he repeated it, to the embarassment of Mozart, who was now right behind him. In the twinkling of an eye Mozart was behind the wings. "Madame," he said to her, "What is this nonsense? You have sung beautifully, beautifully, and so that you may sing even better I will personally rehearse the role with you."[50]

A picture of this scene (figure 10.1) appeared in a book published in Zurich in 1833. Whether it is based on a drawing by an eyewitness or the product of an artistic imagination fired by Rochlitz's story, the picture quite accurately represents late-eighteenth-century clothing and hairstyles and the interior of a typical eighteenth-century theater. The actors stand on the forestage; behind them six wing flats can be distinguished. The picture has value as a rare depiction of Mozart in the theater, surrounded by the instrumentalists and singers who brought his operas to life and the music lovers who enjoyed them.

A similar incident occurred about a year later, when Mozart, having given a concert in Frankfurt during the imperial coronation of Leopold II, stopped

Fig. 10.1. Mozart at a performance of *Die Entführung aus dem Serail*, Berlin (19 May 1789), from *Biographie von Wolfgang Amadeus Mozart*, Zurich, 1833. Photo by Paul Corneilson

in Mannheim on his way back to Vienna. The actor Wilhelm Backhaus wrote
in his diary on 24 October:

> Kapellmeister Motzard was here on the 23rd and gave numerous tempos
> at the rehearsal of *Figaro*. I embarrassed myself with Motzard. I took him
> for a journeyman tailor. I was standing at the door during the rehearsal.
> He came and asked me if one could listen to the rehearsal. I sent him
> away. "But surely you would let Kapellmeister Mozart listen?" he said.
> Then I was more embarrassed than ever.[51]

Financial rewards for and other benefits of operatic success

The fee, agreed on in advance, that composers normally received for an opera
written to fulfill a scrittura meant its success did not automatically produce
financial success for the composer. Nor did the productions of Mozart's
Viennese operas in other cities enhance his income. Operatic composers
could sometimes use the success of an opera to generate financial rewards,
but Mozart was not particularly good at doing this.

The income from a single performance – a benefit performance – was
sometimes set aside for the composer. Thus Mozart received the proceeds of
the fourth performance of *Don Giovanni* in Prague, in addition to the 100-ducat
fee that, according to Niemetschek, Guardasoni paid him.[52] In such a case
the size of the audience, so often boasted of by Mozart, had an obvious effect
on his earnings.

If he worked quickly a composer could also make money by arranging a
successful opera for wind instruments or as a keyboard-vocal score and selling
the arrangement to a publisher. Mozart intended to make wind arrangements
of *Die Entführung*. "Otherwise" he wrote his father four days after the premiere,
"someone will do it before me and will have the profit instead of me."[53] He
also worked on a keyboard-vocal score, but its publication by the Viennese
firm of Toricella came to a halt when a rival publisher's version came out first.
Leopold wrote bitterly to Nannerl on 16 December 1785:

> What I predicted to my son has now happened. A keyboard arrangement
> of *Die Entführung* has been published in Augsburg by the bookseller
> Stage . . . It has been engraved in Mainz and has been trumpeted forth in

the Augsburg papers with many laudatory remarks about the famous Herr von Mozart. If Toricella has already engraved a large part of it, he will have a considerable loss, and your brother will have wasted his time writing two acts, which were already finished.[54]

Mozart was largely incapable of subjecting himself to the drudgery of arranging his operas for wind instruments or keyboard. After his half-hearted effort to capitalize on the popularity of *Die Entführung* he seems to have given up on such projects. When he visited Prague during Carnival 1787 he heard with delight the arrangements of the opera being played around the city, but expressed no resentment that whatever money being made by these arrangements was not coming to him. At a ball, he wrote, "I looked on with the greatest pleasure while all these people flew about in sheer delight to the music of my *Figaro*, arranged for contradances and German dances. For here they talk about nothing but *Figaro*. Nothing is played, sung, or whistled but *Figaro*. No opera is drawing like *Figaro*. Nothing, nothing but *Figaro*. Certainly a great honor for me."[55]

Although this "great honor" brought Mozart no direct monetary benefit, it did result indirectly in financial rewards. The concert or concerts that Mozart gave in Prague (we do not know the exact number) brought him a good deal of money; Leopold later reported that his son had made 1000 Gulden on his first visit to Prague.[56] And the success of *Figaro* in the Bohemian capital led to the commission of *Don Giovanni*, to a fee of 100 ducats, the proceeds of the fourth performance, and to a payment of 50 ducats when he presented the opera in Vienna a few months later.

The sale of copies of the full score of an opera was not a good source of income for most eighteenth-century composers. At some courts composers were strictly forbidden from allowing their music to circulate. But even where such restrictions did not exist, the circulation of operatic scores usually brought more money to copyists than to composers. Major theaters generally had formal relations with professional copyists whose responsibilities included the preparation of performing scores and parts for the singers and orchestra. With those responsibilities sometimes came the privilege of making and selling extra copies, with no share of the profit going to the composer.[57]

Yet the composer benefitted from this system to the extent that it could document the success of an opera and in doing so bring valuable publicity. During rehearsals for *Mitridate*, favorable reports about the opera pleased the copyist involved in its production, according to Leopold: "The copyist is very happy, which is a good omen in Italy, for if the music is a success, the copyist sometimes makes more money by selling the arias than the composer gets from the composition."[58] The copyist's optimism was justified. Mozart wrote on 12 January 1771, after *Mitridate* had been performed several times to large and enthusiastic crowds: "Yesterday the copyist visited us and said he had just received an order to copy my opera for the court at Lisbon."[59] An order from the Portuguese court was an honor for a composer that might bear fruit later in the form of commissions and fees for other operas (Jommelli earned a substantial amount of money writing operas for Lisbon between 1769 and 1774); but payment for the score of *Mitridate* itself probably went only to the Milanese copyist.

Even when Mozart had a chance to sell an operatic score to one of Europe's most important courts, he found it difficult to fulfill the order. After the early success of *Die Entführung* the Prussian ambassador in Vienna applied directly to Mozart for a copy, so that it could be performed in Berlin. Mozart wrote to his father on 25 September 1782: "The Prussian ambassador Riedesel has written to me that he has been commissioned by the Berlin court to send my opera *Die Entführung aus dem Serail* to Berlin; I am to have it copied, and a reward for the music will soon follow. I promised at once to have it copied."[60]

But Mozart did not have a copy produced immediately, because he had foolishly sent his autograph score to his father in Salzburg. Without the autograph, he had to depend on the court theater's performing score as the source for a copy. But that score seems to have been in almost constant motion between the workshop of Wenzel Sukowaty (the theater's official copyist), the theater, and Emperor Joseph's private music room. Mozart explained to his father:

> Now, since I do not have the opera myself, I would have to borrow it from the copyist, which would be very awkward, for I could not be sure of keeping it for three days in a row, because the emperor often sends for it (which happened only yesterday) and, moreover, it is often performed; indeed since August 16th it has been performed ten times. So my idea

would be to have it copied in Salzburg, where it could be done more secretly and more cheaply! I beg you, therefore, to have it copied out in score right away – and as quickly as possible.[61]

Leopold was understandably reluctant to get involved in his son's business affairs, and may also have feared that Mozart, in selling a score for which he had already been paid by the Viennese court, might endanger his relations with the emperor and his theater. Mozart, hoping to encourage Leopold to have the copy made quickly, pointed out in a subsequent letter that the ambassador could have cut him out of the transaction entirely by applying to Sukowaty: "I am very much indebted to the baron for having ordered the copy from me and not from the copyist, from whom he could have got it at any time by paying cash."[62] That, unfortunately for Mozart and other composers, is how Viennese operas most frequently circulated.

Silent applause

Mozart never tired of applause. It was with obvious pleasure and pride that he reported to Constanze the encores demanded at the last performance of Tito in Prague at the end of September 1791. The crowds that saw, heard, and praised *Die Zauberflöte* in the weeks that followed gave him as much delight as the those that applauded *Ascanio in Alba* two decades earlier. But he also came to value, even more than noisy demands for encores, the silence with which an appreciative audience gave its full attention to the work of art he had created.

Already in *Idomeneo* he discouraged applause, thus reducing the possibility of encores, by orchestral passages at the end of several arias that lead directly into the following recitative. He wrote another applause-inhibiting transition at the end of Vitellia's spectacular rondò in *Tito*. The succession of scenes is exactly analogous to that at the end of act 2 of *Lucio Silla*, where Giunia's bravura aria "Parto, m'affretto" is followed by a change of scene and a chorus of senators and people. But while in 1772 Mozart encouraged the Milanese to applaud Anna de Amicis by bringing her aria to an emphatic close, in 1791 he connected "Non più di fiori" with what follows by means of a majestic passage for full orchestra that ends on an open cadence. The moment of silence that follows – before the great chorus "Che del ciel, che degli dei" – is better than any applause.

Of *Die Zauberflöte* he wrote to Constanze: "As usual the duet 'Mann und Weib' and Papageno's glockenspiel in act 1 had to be repeated and also the trios of the boys in Act 2. But what always gives me most pleasure is the *silent applause!* You can see how this opera is becoming more and more esteemed."[63]

NOTES

1 Mozart in the theater

1 MBA, III, 35–38; Anderson, 675.

2 MBA, III, 138; Anderson, 751.

3 "Oder ich lasse mir mein Klavier stimmen, so gut unser Schulmeister das versteht, und spiele mir selbst eine Sonate von Mozart, oder singe mir eine Arie von Paisiello" (*Menschenhaß und Reue*, Mainz, 1790, 39). Kotzebue's play was given twenty-four times in the Burgtheater during Mozart's lifetime (Franz Hadamowsky, *Die Wiener Hoftheater (Staatstheater)*, part 1, Vienna, 1966, 84).

4 MBA, I, 449; Anderson, 205.

5 MDL, 472; Deutsch, 556. The composer and music director Ignaz von Seyfried was only fifteen years old in 1791; he did not join the staff of Emanuel Schikaneder's Theater auf der Wieden (where *Die Zauberflöte* was first performed) until 1797 (see Peter Branscombe, *W. A. Mozart: Die Zauberflöte*, Cambridge, 1991, 71). The several interesting and highly detailed statements about Mozart's last year and about the composition, rehearsals, and early performances of *Die Zauberflöte* that he made later in life are the testimony not of an eyewitness but of a professional musician in close contact with many of those who knew Mozart personally and took part in the first production of the opera.

6 MBA I, 152; Anderson, 47.

7 Wenzel Swoboda's memories of Mozart as recorded in Wilhelm Kuhe, *My Musical Recollections*, London, 1896, 8.

8 MBA II, 172; Anderson, 410.

9 MDL, 16; Deutsch, 14.

10 MBA, III, 259; Anderson, 842.

11 MBA IV, 160; Anderson, 969.

12 MBA I, 51–52; Anderson, 5.

13 Daniel Heartz, *Haydn, Mozart, and the Viennese School*, New York, 1995, 495.

14 MBA I, 62; Anderson, 12.

15 MBA I, 445; Anderson, 203.

16 MBA III, 261; Anderson, 843.

17 MBA I, 178–179; Anderson, 54–55.

238

18 Ian Woodfield, "New Light on the Mozarts' London Visit: A Private Concert with Manzuoli," *Music & Letters* LXXVI (1995), 195.

19 *MDL*, 89; Deutsch, 98.

20 *MDL, ANF*, 20; Eisen, 4.

21 MBA I, 271; Anderson, 89.

22 Michael Kelly, *Reminiscences of Michael Kelly of the King's Theatre and Theatre Royal Drury Lane*, 2nd edn., 2 vols., London, 1826, I, 3.

23 Kelly, *Reminiscences*, I, 11.

24 Kelly's father followed Rauzzini's advice and sent his son to Naples, where he continued to benefit from the instruction of (among other teachers) male sopranos: "I had the good fortune to be noticed by [that phrase again!] Signor Guarducci, the celebrated soprano, and he gave me a few lessons." He also studied with Giuseppe Aprile (Kelly, *Reminiscences*, 1, 73, 112).

25 Heartz, *Haydn, Mozart, and the Viennese School*, 525, suggests the possibility that the Mozarts attended a performance of *Les Amours de Bastien et Bastienne* (a parody of Rousseau's *Le Devin du village*), which was revived on 28 March 1764. Mozart later set its libretto, translated into German, as *Bastien und Bastienne*.

26 *MBA* I, 142.

27 *MDL*, 54–55; Deutsch, 56.

28 MBA I, 301; Anderson, 105.

29 Giuseppe Afferri. The heroic tenor Giuseppe Tibaldi sang from 1750 to 1778 (Claudio Sartori, *I libretti italiani a stampa dalle origini al 1800*, 7 vols., Cuneo, 1990–94, VII, 637); the Mozarts heard him in Vienna in 1767–68.

30 Carolina Serini.

31 Pasquale Potenza made his operatic debut in 1747 and ended his career in 1777 (Sartori, *I libretti italiani*, VII, 533). If Mozart is correct that he was fifty-five years old in 1770, then he began singing opera at the somewhat unlikely age of thirty-two.

32 Elena Fabris Afferri.

33 Brigida Lolli Anelli, sister of the violinist Antonio Lolli.

34 Giacomo Pannato, a tenor who was indeed making his professional debut in this opera (Sartori, *I libretti italiani*, VII, 493).

35 Karl Rußler, a dancer and choreographer active in Italy during the 1770s. In the libretto for a production of Traetta's *Ifigenia in Tauride* in Mantua during Carnival 1777 he identified himself as "Carlo Rusler Viennese."

36 *MBA*, I, 301–302; Anderson, 105.

37 MBA II, 125; Anderson, 374–375.

38 *MBA*, I, 302; Anderson, 105.

39 The prima donna was Camilla Pasi Sarti (Sartori, *I libretti italiani*, II, 326).

40 The seconda donna was Angiola Maggiori Gallieni, not quite as inexperienced as Mozart believed; she had been singing professionally since 1768 (Sartori, *I libretti italiani*, VII, 386).

41 Vincenzo Caselli.

42 Lorenzo Bertolazzi.

43 Vincenzo Uttini.

44 Giuseppe Pasqualini.

45 The *grottesco* was a dancer who specialized in spectacular leaps and other ath-
letic feats; see *The Grotesque Dancer on the Eighteenth-Century Stage: Gennaro Magri
and His World*, ed. Rebecca Harris-Warrick and Bruce Alan Brown, Madison, WI,
2005.

46 The prima donna, in the role of Vitellia, was Maria Masi Giura (Sartori, *I libretti
italiani*, II, 148).

47 Maddalena Mori della Casa.

48 Giuseppe Cicognani, in the role of Sesto.

49 Carlo Mosca as Annio and Pietro Muschietti as Publio (both in their first known
roles).

50 Salvatore Casetti as Tito.

51 MBA I, 310; Anderson, 110–111.

52 MDL, 96; Deutsch 105.

53 MDL, 97; Deutsch, 107.

54 MBA I, 384; Anderson, 158.

2 Mozart's operas: Function, genres, archetypes

1 Alfred Einstein, *Mozart: His Character, His Work*, New York, 1945.

2 MBA I, 418; Anderson, 181.

3 Piero Weiss, "Opera and Neoclassical Dramatic Criticism in the Seventeenth Century," *Studies in the History of Music* II (1988), 1–30; Robert C. Ketterer, "Why Early
Opera is Roman and not Greek," *Cambridge Opera Journal* XV (2003), 1–14.

4 MBA I, 466; Anderson, 219.

5 MBA III, 132; Anderson, 746.

6 MDL, 476; Deutsch, 561.

7 MBA I, 289.

8 On eighteenth-century opera as Carnival entertainment and embodiment of the
carnivalesque see Martha Feldman, "Magic Mirrors and the *Seria* Stage: Thoughts
toward a Ritual View," *Journal of the American Musicological Society* XLVIII (1995),
478–483, and Mary Hunter, *The Culture of Opera Buffa in Mozart's Vienna: A Poetics of
Entertainment*, Princeton, NJ, 1999, 71–79.

9 MBA I, 302; Anderson, 105.

10 Kathleen Hansell, *Opera and Ballet at the Regio Ducal Teatro of Milan, 1771–1776:
A Musical and Social History*, PhD dissertation, University of California, Berkeley,
1980, 52.

11 Hansell, *Opera and Ballet*, 82.

12 The engraving (reproduced in full in the article on "Milan" in the *New Grove Dictionary of Opera*) contains a sonnet dedicated "to the incomparable merit of Signora Violante Vestri who to applause and universal pleasure represented in the drama entitled *Il Tigrane* the character of Apamia in the theater of Milan" and a portrait of the singer. Violante Vestri created the role of Apamia in Carcani's *Tigrane* at the Regio Ducal Teatro of Milan during Carnival 1750.

13 Daniel Heartz, *Mozart's Operas*, ed. Thomas Bauman, Berkeley, CA, 1990, 138. The opera's final words sound like an invitation to a Carnival ball: "Sposi, amici, al ballo, al gioco. /Alle mine date foco, /Ed al suon di lieta marcia/Corriam tutti a festeggiar."

14 MDL, 264–265; Deutsch, 300.

15 Mozart, who sometimes signed his name "Trazom," probably enjoyed this quasi-anagrammatic play as much as librettists did.

16 For a perceptive and persuasive analysis of the opera, see Jessica Waldoff, *Recognition in Mozart's Operas*, New York, 2006, 104–164.

17 Heartz, *Haydn, Mozart, and the Viennese School*, 597.

18 Northrop Frye, "The Mythos of Spring: Comedy," in his *Anatomy of Criticism*, Princeton, NJ, 1957, 163–186.

19 Jessica Waldoff, "Don Giovanni: Recognition Denied," in *Opera Buffa in Mozart's Vienna*, ed. Mary Hunter and James Webster, Cambridge, 1997, 292; Waldoff has explored her thesis in greater depth in *Recognition in Mozart's Operas*.

20 Hunter, *The Culture of Opera Buffa*, 3.

21 Hunter, *The Culture of Opera Buffa*, 40.

22 Hunter, *The Culture of Opera Buffa*, 41.

23 Heartz, *Haydn, Mozart, and the Viennese School*, 552, points to similarities between Lucio Silla and Pasha Selim: "Like the Pasha in *Die Entführung*, Silla's amorous fire is stoked by resistance."

24 "Guilelmo" is the spelling that Da Ponte used in the first edition of the libretto and that Mozart used through most of the autograph score, making it preferable to the "Guglielmo" that became standard because of its use by Breitkopf & Härtel in the first published score (Leipzig, 1810).

25 On the operatic "conversation" between *La grotta di Trofonio* and *Così fan tutte* see Hunter, *The Culture of Opera Buffa*, 257–272.

3 Commissions, fees, and the origins of Mozart's operas

1 MDL, ANF, 59, 61; Eisen, 55–56.

2 MBA III, 393; Anderson, 890. On this letter, see Daniel Heartz, "Mozart and Anton Klein," *Newsletter of the Mozart Society of America* X (2006), no. 1, 7–10.

3 Giacomo Gotifredo Ferrari, *Aneddoti piacevoli e interessanti*, ed. Mariasilvia Tatti, Bergamo, 1998, 211.

4 Ignaz von Mosel, *Ueber das Leben und die Werke des Anton Salieri*, Vienna, 1827, 29.

5 "Zwei Selbstbiographien von Joseph Weigl (1766–1846)," ed. Rudolph Angermüller, *Deutsches Jahrbuch der Musikwissenschaft* XVI (1971), 46–85 (54).

6 For example, Niccolò Jommelli's contract with the court of Portugal granted him an annual pension of 400 zecchini in exchange for one serious opera, one comic opera, and an unspecified quantity of church music per year (Marita McClymonds, *Niccolò Jommelli: The Last Years, 1769–1774*, Ann Arbor, MI, 1980, 548, 593, 500).

7 John A. Rice, *Antonio Salieri and Viennese Opera*, Chicago, 1998, 536.

8 MDL, AC, 67–68; Eisen, 67–68. For a diplomatic transcription and useful commentary, see Sergio Durante, "The Chronology of Mozart's 'La clemenza di Tito' Reconsidered," *Music & Letters* LXXX (1999), 562–564, 591.

9 Rice, *Salieri*, 505–507.

10 For a dramatic example of the priority given by impresarios to the engagement of the musico (over such matters as the choice of libretto and composer), see Mario Armellini, "*L'olimpiade* del Metastasio ristretta in due atti: Luigi Gatti, Domenico Cimarosa ed il dramma per musica a fine Settecento," in *Domenico Cimarosa: Un "napoletano" in Europa*, ed. Paologiovanni Maione and Marta Columbro, 2 vols., Lucca, 2004, 29–158.

11 The contract is published in Margaret Butler, *Operatic Reform at Turin's Teatro Regio: Aspects of Production and Stylistic Change in the 1760s*, Lucca, 2001, 306.

12 MBA I, 325; Anderson, 120. "Signora Gabrielli and her sister" were Caterina and Francesca Gabrielli; "Signor Ettore" was the tenor Guglielmo d'Ettore.

13 MBA I, 339–340; Anderson, 130–131.

14 MBA II, 44; Anderson, 303.

15 MBA I, 377; Anderson, 153.

16 William C. Holmes, *Opera Observed: Views of a Florentine Impresario in the Early Eighteenth Century*, Chicago, 1993, 40.

17 Armellini, "*L'olimpiade* del *Metastasio*," 39–40.

18 Rice, *Salieri*, 234.

19 Rice, *Salieri*, 234–235.

20 MBA I, 340; Anderson, 131. On this concert, see Anthony Pryor, "Mozart's Operatic Audition, the Milan Concert, 12 March 1770: A Reappraisal and Revision," *Eighteenth-Century Music* I (2004), 265–288.

21 MBA I, 320; Anderson, 118.

22 MBA I, 325; Anderson, 119.

23 Letter from Carlo Flaminio Raiberti to Antonio Greppi dated Turin, 26 January 1771, published with facsimile and translation in Harrison James Wignall, *Mozart, Guglielmo d'Ettore and the Composition of Mitridate (K. 87/74a)*, PhD dissertation, Brandeis University, 1995, 99–100, 101, 524.

24 MDL, 119; Deutsch, 133.

25 MBA I, 456; Anderson, 209.

26 In 1777–78 Leopold wrote twice to Michele dell'Agata, the Venetian impresario with whom he had earlier concluded and then broken a scrittura, asking about the possibility of Mozart writing an opera for Venice. He got no response (MBA II, 276; Anderson, 477).

27 An unusual instance of a composer agreeing, in his contract, to write an opera on a specific subject is Ferdinando Bertoni's contract for the Turin Carnival of 1762. Signed very late, on 15 August 1761, the contract states: "Signor Ferdinando Bertoni . . . agrees to compose with completely new and never before heard music the second opera, entitled Ifigenia in Aulide" (Butler, Operatic Reform, 305).

28 Holmes, Opera Observed, 41.

29 Antonietta Cerocchi, "Il Teatro Alibert o 'delle dame' nella seconda metà del Settecento: struttura e organizzazione," Mozart, Padova e La Betulia liberata, ed. Paolo Pinamonti, Florence, 1991, 395–405; see especially the documents quoted on p. 401.

30 MBA I, 339; Anderson, 131.

31 Saverio Mattei, "Elogio del Jommelli, o sia Il progresso della poesia, e musica teatrale," in Memorie per servire alla vita del Metastasio, Colle, 1785, 59–136, 90.

32 Armellini, "L'olimpiade del Metastasio," 32.

33 Wignall, Mozart, Guglielmo d'Ettore and the Composition of Mitridate, 8–9.

34 No libretto was apparently printed for the performance of Mozart's Il re pastore on 23 April 1775. Although Mozart biographers are almost unanimous in assigning Consoli to the role of Aminta in Mozart's Il re pastore, I know of no evidence that he created that role or that he even sang in Mozart's opera. In Munich Consoli portrayed Elisa, not Aminta, in Guglielmi's Il re pastore. In Salzburg all we know for sure is that he was engaged to sing in Domenico Fischietti's Gli orti esperidi, performed the day before Mozart's opera.

35 In An Extract from the Life of Lorenzo Da Ponte, New York, 1819, 17–18, the poet asked: "Why did Mozart refuse to set to music the Don Giovanni (of evil memory) by Bertati, and offered to him by one Guardasoni . . . ? Why did he insist upon having a book written by Da Ponte on the same subject . . . ?"

36 Karl Böhmer, W. A. Mozarts Idomeneo und die Tradition der Karnevalsopern in München, Tutzing, 1999, 64–68, 342–344, summarized in Karl Böhmer, "Zum Wandel des Münchner Operngeschmacks vor Idomeneo: Die Karnevalsopern am Cuvilliés-Theater 1753–1780," in Mozarts Idomeneo und die Musik in München zur Zeit Karl Theodors, ed. Theodor Göllner and Stephan Hörner, Munich, 2001, 13.

37 On the composition and first production of La finta giardiniera, see Robert Münster, "ich würde München gewis Ehre machen": Mozart und der Kurfürstliche Hof zu München, Weissenhorn, 2002, 40–60.

38 Böhmer, W. A. Mozarts Idomeneo, 344.

39 MBA I, 513; Anderson, 255.

40 My thanks to Karl Böhmer for this point.

41 MBA I, 504; Anderson, 249.

42 MBA I, 505; Anderson, 249. The structure of Leopold's last sentence caused Emily Anderson to believe that "for the first time" refers to the performance on 29 December. My thanks to Michael Lorenz for suggesting that "for the first time" refers instead to the performance "before Christmas," and that 29 December was to be the date of the second performance.

43 Böhmer, *W. A. Mozarts* Idomeneo, 342–344.

44 By way of comparison, the Burgtheater in Vienna had only seven comic operas in the repertory in May 1786 and January 1790, when *Figaro* and *Così fan tutte* were first performed.

45 MBA I, 513; Anderson, 255–256.

46 MBA I, 516; Anderson, 258.

47 Böhmer, "Zum Wandel des Münchner Operngeschmacks," 37.

48 Heartz, *Haydn, Mozart, and the Viennese School*, 512–516.

49 MBA I, 279–283; Deutsch, 80–83; Heartz, *Haydn, Mozart, and the Viennese School*, 733–736.

50 MBA I, 257; Anderson, 82.

51 MBA I, 270–272; Anderson, 88–89.

52 Mosel, *Salieri*, 30–31.

53 Mosel, *Salieri*, 33–34.

54 During the seven years from 1783 to 1789 Salieri wrote seven operas for the court theaters, one of which, *Cublai, gran kan de' tartari*, was not performed.

55 That Joseph commissioned *Il re Teodoro* is stated by Kelly, *Reminiscences*, I, 235; that he commissioned *Il burbero di buon core* is implied by Lorenzo Da Ponte, *Memorie*, ed. Cesare Pagnini, Milan, 1960, 103, who quotes the emperor as saying: "Perché non fate un'opera per quello spagnuolo?" Da Ponte, *Memorie*, 103, tells us that *Il finto cieco* resulted from "ordine de' direttori teatrali di scrivere un dramma per Gazzaniga."

56 MBA II, 235–237; Deutsch, 170.

57 MBA II, 254; Anderson, 462.

58 Mosel, *Salieri*, 72.

59 Mosel, *Salieri*, 73.

60 MBA III, 109; Anderson, 726.

61 MBA III, 127; Anderson, 742.

62 MBA III, 132; Anderson, 746.

63 MBA III, 143; Anderson, 754–755.

64 MBA III, 143; Anderson, 755.

65 Da Ponte, *Memorie*, 105.

66 Da Ponte, *Memorie*, 108.

67 Da Ponte, *Memorie*, 96.

68 On the origins of *Figaro*, see Heartz, *Mozart's Operas*, 133–138; and Dexter Edge, *Mozart's Viennese Copyists*, PhD dissertation, University of Southern California, 2001, 1416–1446.

69 Da Ponte, *Memorie*, 108–109.

70 For a full discussion of the fees received by operatic composers in Vienna from 1778 to 1792 see Dexter Edge, "Mozart's Fee for *Così fan tutte*," *Journal of the Royal Musical Association* CXVI (1991), 211–235.

71 Mozart may have been irked by Salieri's having received for his Singspiel *Der Rauchfangkehrer* the same 100-ducat fee. The Burgtheater's practice of giving the authors of new spoken plays (but not the composers of new operas) the proceeds of the third performance probably also contributed to Mozart's sense of being unfairly treated.

72 *MBA* III, 236; Anderson, 826.

73 *MBA* III, 255; Anderson, 839.

74 *MBA* II, 332; Anderson, 522.

75 *MBA* II, 473–474; Anderson, 613.

76 *MBA* III, 221; Anderson, 815.

77 *MDL*, 332; Deutsch, 377–378. See Judith Milhous, Gabriella Dideriksen, and Robert Hume, *Italian Opera in Late Eighteenth-Century London, Volume 2: The Pantheon Opera and Its Aftermath, 1789–1795*, Oxford, 2001, 51–54.

4 Mozart and his librettists

1 Heartz, *Mozart's Operas*, 89–105. Some theaters that lacked a house poet had a permanent stage director on staff. For example, the Pergola Theater in Florence employed Giuseppe Borgini as its *macchinista e direttore del palcoscenico* from 1774 until some time after 1800; see Robert Lamar Weaver and Norma Wright Weaver, *A Chronology of Music in the Florentine Theater, 1751–1800*, Warren, MI, 1993, 879.

2 For the original see Rice, *Salieri*, 46.

3 The complete poem is in Lorenzo Da Ponte, *Lettere, epistole in versi, dedicatorie e lettere dei fratelli*, ed. Giampaolo Zagonel, Vittorio Veneto, 1995, 94–100; for an excerpt (with English translation) see Heartz, *Mozart's Operas*, 99–101.

4 When Da Ponte wrote more librettos than his contract required he was paid extra; see *MDL*, 240, and Edge, *Mozart's Viennese Copyists*, 1461.

5 Sergio Durante, "Considerations on Mozart's Changing Approach to Recitatives and on Other Choices of Dramaturgical Significance," *Mozart-Jahrbuch* 2001, 233–238.

6 Mosel, *Salieri*, 31.

7 Mosel, *Salieri*, 33.

8 Maynard Solomon, *Mozart: A Life*, New York, 1995, 30.

9 MBA I, 513; Anderson, 256.

10 MBA III, 67–68; Anderson, 694–695.

11 Durante, "Considerations on Mozart's Changing Approach to Recitatives," 238–239.

12 "Poesia del signor De Gamera, adattata al comodo del compositor della musica" (Sartori, I libretti italiani, IV, 40).

13 MBA III, 13; Anderson, 659–660.

14 MBA III, 17–18; Anderson, 663.

15 MBA III, 34–35, Anderson, 674.

16 MBA III, 20; Anderson, 664.

17 MBA III, 34; Anderson, 674.

18 MBA III, 73; Anderson, 699.

19 Emanuel Schikaneder, preface to his libretto Der Spiegel von Arkadien, Vienna, 1995, quoted in Branscombe, W. A. Mozart: Die Zauberflöte, 89.

20 On the transformation of Bretzner's libretto by Stephanie and Mozart see Thomas Bauman, W. A. Mozart: Die Entführung aus dem Serail, Cambridge, 1987, 12–61.

21 MBA III, 143; Anderson, 755.

22 MBA III, 162; Anderson, 768.

23 MBA III, 163–164; Anderson, 770.

24 Helga Lühning, "Zur Entstehungsgeschichte von Mozarts Titus," Musikforschung XXVII (1974), 309; Helga Lühning, Titus-Vertonungen im 18. Jahrhundert: Untersuchungen zur Tradition der Opera seria von Hasse bis Mozart, Laaber, 1983, 102–104.

25 Armellini, "L'olimpiade del Metastasio," 46.

26 MBA III, 162; Anderson, 768. The translation of the last sentence is Thomas Bauman's; he discusses this passage in "Coming of Age in Vienna: Die Entführung aus dem Serail," in Heartz, Mozart's Operas, 79–80.

27 MBA II, 13; Anderson, 660. My thanks to Daniel Heartz for this point.

28 MBA III, 163; Anderson, 769.

29 MBA III, 167; Anderson, 772–773.

30 MBA III, 167–168 Anderson, 773.

31 MDL, 191–192 Deutsch, 215–217.

32 MBA III, 268; Anderson, 848.

33 MBA III, 268; Anderson, 848.

34 MBA III, 275; Anderson, 853.

35 For a discussion of this aborted project, see Rice, Salieri, 465–468.

36 MBA III, 300; Anderson, 866.

37 Da Ponte, Memorie, 97.

38 MBA III, 443–444; Anderson, 893.

39 Lorenzo da Ponte, Libretti viennesi, ed. Lorenzo della Chà, 2 vols., Parma, 1999, I, 235.

40 John W. Francis, *Old New York, or, Reminiscences of the Past Sixty Years*, New York, 1865, 265–266, quoted in Heartz, *Mozart's Operas*, 174.

41 Bruce Alan Brown and John A. Rice, "Salieri's *Così fan tutte*," *Cambridge Opera Journal* VIII (1996), 17–43.

5 Composition

1 *MBA* II, 265; Anderson, 468.

2 *Joseph Haydn: Gesammelte Briefe und Aufzeichnungen*, ed. Dénes Bartha, Kassel, 1965, 185.

3 McClymonds, *Jommelli*, 535.

4 McClymonds, *Jommelli*, 746.

5 Franz Xaver Niemetschek, *Lebensbeschreibung des K. K. Kapellmeisters Wolfgang Amadeus Mozart*, 2nd edn., Prague, 1808, facsimile edn., Laaber, 2005, 82.

6 *MBA* II, 330; Anderson, 520.

7 *MBA* III, 144; Anderson, 756.

8 Ulrich Konrad, *Mozarts Schaffensweise: Studien zu den Werkautographen, Skizzen und Entwürfen*, Göttingen, 1992.

9 Margaret Butler, "Vicente Martín y Soler's Operas for Turin's Teatro Regio: Elements of Production and Ensemble Writing in *Andromeda* (1780) and *Vologeso* (1783)," forthcoming in the proceedings of the conference "The Many Worlds of Vicente Martín y Soler," Valencia, 14–18 November 2006.

10 Galuppi's contract is transcribed in Butler, *Operatic Reform*, 313. Other contracts transcribed by Butler document similar compositional schedules for Tommaso Traetta (p. 294) and Ferdinando Bertoni (p. 305).

11 *MBA* I, 325; Anderson, 119–120.

12 *MBA* I, 365–366; Anderson, 146.

13 *MBA* I, 460; Anderson, 215–216.

14 *MBA* I, 397; Anderson, 166.

15 Berlin *Musikalisches Wochenblatt*, in *MDL*, 380; Deutsch, 432.

16 Durante, "Considerations on Mozart's Changing Approach to Recitatives", 236–237.

17 Mosel, *Salieri*, 31–33.

18 Heartz, *Mozart's Operas*, 139.

19 *MBA* III, 143; Anderson, 755.

20 *MBA* I, 405; Anderson, 171.

21 *MBA* I, 406; Anderson, 172.

22 *MBA* I, 466; Anderson, 219.

23 *MBA* I, 462; Anderson, 216.

24 *MBA* I, 464; Anderson, 218.

25 *MBA* I, 466; Anderson, 220.

26 MBA I, 437; Anderson, 197.

27 MBA II, 162; Anderson, 769.

28 MBA II, 162–163; Anderson, 769.

29 MBA I, 432; Anderson, 194. This kind of housing for musicians may have been common in eighteenth-century Italy. All participants in the operas presented at the Teatro Alibert in Rome (including singers and orchestra) were housed for free in a building opposite the theater known as the *abitazione dei musici* (Cerocchi, "Il Teatro Alibert," 404).

30 MDL, 472; Deutsch, 556.

31 Bruce Alan Brown, *W. A. Mozart: Così fan tutte*, Cambridge, 1995, 23. For directing me to the portrait of Ferrarese (until recently unknown to Mozart specialists) I am most grateful to Catherine Sprague and Michael Lorenz.

32 MBA III, 121; Anderson, 736–737.

33 MBA III, 443, Anderson, 893.

34 MBA III, 163; Anderson, 770.

35 MDL, 533–534; Deutsch, 571.

36 Niemetschek, *Mozart*, 84–85.

37 MBA I, 212–213.

38 The following comments appeared in a somewhat different format in my introduction to a facsimile of the autograph of *Così fan tutte* (Los Altos, CA, 2007).

39 Alan Tyson, *Mozart: Studies of the Autograph Scores*, Cambridge, MA, 1987, 177–221.

40 On the surviving sketches for *Così fan tutte*, see Konrad, *Mozarts Schaffensweise*, 190–92.

41 Wenzel Sukowaty, the court theaters' chief music copyist from 1778 to 1796, employed several copyists to do work under his name; see Edge, *Mozart's Viennese Copyists*, 1294–1997.

42 Ian Woodfield, "Lovers Crossed or Uncrossed?," Inaugural Lecture, Queen's University Belfast, 6 May 2000 (unpublished); *Mozart's Così fan tutte: A Compositional History*, Woodbridge, Suffolk, 2008.

43 Daniel Heartz, "When Mozart Revises: The Case of Guglielmo in *Così fan tutte*," in *Wolfgang Amadé Mozart: Essays on His Life and His Music*, ed. Stanley Sadie, Oxford, 1996, 355–361.

6 Mozart and his singers

1 MBA II, 29–30; Anderson, 290–291.

2 MBA I, 324; Anderson, 121–122.

3 MBA I, 326; Anderson, 120.

4 MBA III, 18; Anderson, 663.

5 Folchino Schizzi, *Elogio storico di Wolfgango Amedeo Mozart*, Cremona, 1817, quoted in MDL, ANF, 87; Eisen, 23–24.

6 MBA II, 304; Anderson, 496–497.

7 MBA III, 13–14; Anderson, 660.

8 Kelly, *Reminiscences*, I, 239–240.

9 MBA I, 402; Anderson, 169–170.

10 MBA III, 14; Anderson, 660.

11 MBA III, 20; Anderson, 664.

12 MBA III, 19; Anderson, 664.

13 MBA III, 28; Anderson, 669.

14 MBA III, 40; Anderson, 677.

15 Dorothea Link, *The National Court Theatre in Mozart's Vienna: Sources and Documents, 1783–1792*, Oxford, 1998, 245.

16 Link, *The National Court Theatre*, 263.

17 MBA IV, 100; Anderson, 935.

18 McClymonds, *Jommelli*, 506, 510, 512, 518.

19 MBA III, 28; Anderson, 669.

20 Mosel, *Salieri*, 38.

21 *Poesie di Antonio Carpaccio fra gli Arcadi Carippo Megalense*, Warsaw, 1790, 116. My thanks to Daniel Brandenburg for telling me of this poem and sending me a copy of it.

22 *Theaterkalender auf das Jahr 1793*, Gotha, 1792.

23 MDL, AC, 81.

24 The critic's remarks on Guardasoni's production of *Die Zauberflöte* in Italian translation (MDL, AC, 81) likewise carefully avoid mentioning Tamino, from which we might suspect that Baglioni portrayed Tamino. But *Il flauto magico* was first performed in Prague on 22 January 1794, when Baglioni was in Venice (*Prager Neue Zeitung*, 24 January 1794, quoted in Jiří Berkovec, *Musicalia v pražském periodickém tisku 18. století*, Prague, 1989, 86–87); so the tenor who created the role of Tamino in *Il flauto magico* must have been someone other than Baglioni.

25 MDL, AC, 70.

26 MBA IV, 157; Anderson, 967. On the identification of the singer who portrayed Servilia, see Walther Brauneis, "Wer war Mozarts 'Sig[no]ra Antonini' in der Prager Uraufführung von 'La clemenza di Tito'? Zur Identifizierung der Antonina Miklaszewicz als Interpretin der Servilia in der Krönungsoper am 6. September 1791," *Mitteilungen der Internationalen Stiftung Mozarteum* XLVII (1999), 32–40.

27 Stanley Sadie, "Some Operas of 1787," *Musical Times* CXXII (1981), 474–477; Heartz, *Mozart's Operas*, 160.

28 Nino Pirotta, *Don Giovanni's Progress: A Rake Goes to the Opera*, New York, 1994, 90, 188; Michel Noiray, "La Construction de Don Giovanni," in *L'Avant-scène Opéra: Don Giovanni*, Paris, 1996, 126–133.

29 For example, in Padua, 1788 and Forlì, 1789; see Sartori, *I libretti italiani*, II, 67–68.

30 My thanks to Michel Noiray for sending me a photocopy of "S'io rimiro quel visetto" from the Paris manuscript.

31 "Wenzel Johann Tomaschek, geboren zu Skutsch am 17. April 1774. Selbstbiographie," part 1, Libussa: Jahrbuch für 1845, Prague, [1845], 371.

32 Alina Żórawska-Witkowska, Muzyka na dworze i w teatrze Stanisława Augusta, Warsaw, 1995, 337.

33 Kelly, Reminiscences, I, 223.

34 Kelly, Reminiscences, I, 273–274.

35 Letter from Ignaz von Seyfried to Georg Friedrich Treitschke, probably written in Vienna in 1840, quoted in MDL, 471; Deutsch, 555.

36 From the diary of Wilhelm Backhaus, in David J. Buch, "Three Posthumous Reports Concerning Mozart in His Late Viennese Years," Eighteenth-Century Music II (2005), 125.

37 MDL, 532; Deutsch, 514.

38 Mary Novello interviewed Aloysia in 1829: "She told me Mozart always loved her until the day of his death" (Vincent and Mary Novello, A Mozart Pilgrimage, Being the Travel Diaries of Vincent and Mary Novello in the Year 1829, ed. Rosemary Hughes, London, 1955).

39 MBA II, 226–227; Anderson, 447–448. The aria in question was one of Giunia's in Lucio Silla, probably "Ah se il crudel periglio" or "Parto m'affretto."

40 MBA II, 251; Anderson, 460.

41 MBA II, 254; Anderson, 462.

42 MBA II, 266; Anderson, 469–470.

43 MBA I, 466; Anderson, 220.

44 MBA II, 304–305; Anderson, 497.

45 That Mozart and Storace performed the scena together we know from Thomas Attwood, Mozart's student and Storace's friend, who wrote: "The last time I heard him, He played his concerto in D Minor & 'Non temere' at Storace's Benefit for whom he composed that Cantata with the Pianoforte solo" (MDL, ANF, 90; Eisen, 39).

46 Heartz, Haydn, Mozart, and the Viennese School, 612.

APPENDIX

1 This designation from Indice de' teatrali spettacoli (hereafter ITS), 1786–87, 13.

2 This designation from ITS, 1786–87, 225.

3 This designation from ITS, 1786–87, 226.

4 Baglioni's appearances in Parma as primo mezzo carattere are documented in ITS, 1787–88, 133.

5 Roberto defined as primo mezzo carattere in libretto printed for premiere (Venice, 1784).

6 Baglioni's appearances in Bologna as *primo mezzo carattere nelle due prime opere* is documented in ITS, 1787–88, 17, according to which the summer season continued with two more operas in which Baglioni did not sing.

7 Cav. Balena is described as the *primo mezzo carattere* role in librettos printed for productions in Udine (1783) and Pavia (1784).

8 Repertory for Fall 1787 and Carnival 1788 from ITS, 1787–88, 147, which lists Baglioni among the *signori attori*.

9 ITS, 1788–89, 90: "Lipsia, Estate 1788. Si rappresentarono in quel Teatro varie Opere buffe in Musica dagli stessi Signori Attori addetti al Teatro Nazionale di Praga per Autunno [1788] e Carnevale [1789], colà descritti."

10 Repertory for Fall 1788 and Carnival 1789 from ITS, 1788–89, 177, which lists Baglioni as one of two *tenori mezzi-caratteri*.

11 Repertory for 1789 and Carnival 1790 from ITS, 1789–90, 231–232, where Baglioni is listed as one of two *primi mezzi caratteri*.

12 The opera entitled *L'impresario innamorato* is probably fictive – the name of its composer "Guardasino" is obviously a play on the name of the impresario Guardasoni.

13 Repertory for Fall 1790 and Carnival 1791 from ITS, 1790–91, which lists Antonio Baglioni as one of two *primi mezzi caratteri* during these seasons.

14 Repertory for Lent and Spring, 1791 from ITS, 1791–92, which lists Baglioni among the *signori cantanti*.

15 According to ITS, 1791–92, 147, a troupe that included Baglioni performed *Don Giovanni* and *Axur* in Prague "in tutto l'anno" 1791.

16 Repertory from ITS, 1792–93, 77, which names Baglioni as *primo mezzo carattere*.

17 Librettos assign this role and that of Barbadoro to Giuseppe Baglioni (otherwise unknown), evidently a mistake resulting from confusion between two *primi mezzi caratteri* (as designated in ITS, 1793–94, 168): Giuseppe Viganoni and Antonio Baglioni.

18 MDL, AC, 81.

19 *Prager Neue Zeitung*, 7 September 1795, quoted in Jiří Berkovec, *Musicalia v pražském periodickém tisku 18. století*, Prague, 1989, 93.

20 All information on Baglioni's roles in Vienna is from *Theaterzettel* (playbills) preserved in the library of the Österreichisches Theatermuseum, Vienna.

21 This was Baglioni's last performance in Vienna.

7 Rehearsal, revision, and promotion

1 The schedule is transcribed in Margaret Butler, "Vicente Martín y Soler's Operas for Turin's Teatro Regio," forthcoming.

2 MBA I, 407; Anderson, 173.

3 Quoted in Gerardo Guccini, "Directing Opera," in *Opera on Stage*, ed. Lorenzo Bianconi and Giorgio Pestelli, trans. Kate Singleton (used here, with some changes), Chicago, 2002.

4 Da Ponte, *Memorie*, 130. Salieri's *Axur re d'Ormus* was indeed performed in celebration of the archducal wedding, but that wedding did not take place until 6 January 1788 (with the premiere of *Axur* on 8 January). Salieri evidently wanted Da Ponte in Vienna so that they could work together on the libretto for *Axur*, for which rehearsals probably did not begin until early December 1787.

5 Paul Nettl, *Mozart in Böhmen*, Prague, 1938, 184.

6 MBA III, 72–73; Anderson, 698–699.

7 MBA III, 74; Anderson, 700.

8 Kelly, *Reminiscences*, I, 256–258.

9 MBA I, 408; Anderson, 174.

10 MBA III, 39; Anderson, 677.

11 MBA III, 64–65; Anderson, 692.

12 MBA I, 409–410; Anderson, 175.

13 MBA IV, 102; Anderson, 935.

14 Undated letter, probably written in 1768; English translation (used here, slightly altered) in *The Collected Correspondence and London Notebooks of Joseph Haydn*, ed. H. C. Robbins Landon, Fair Lawn, NJ, 1959, 9.

15 *Allgemeine musikalische Zeitung* 1799–1800, col. 522; translation (used here) in Thomas Forrest Kelly, *First Nights at the Opera*, New Haven, CT, 2004, 90.

16 [Johann Ferdinand von Schönfeld], *Jahrbuch der Tonkunst von Wien und Prag*, facsimile, with afterword and index by Otto Biba, Munich, 1976, 96, cited in Dexter Edge, "Mozart's Viennese Orchestras," *Early Music* XX (1992), 78.

17 MBA I, 408; Anderson, 174.

18 Charles Burney, *Music, Men, and Manners in France and Italy, 1770*, ed. H. Edmund Poole, London, 1974, 46.

19 This paragraph is based on Edge, "Mozart's Viennese Orchestras". The theatrical year in Vienna extended, with minor variations, from the day after Easter to Shrove Tuesday – the end of Carnival – of the following calendar year.

20 Johann Kaspar Riesbeck, *Briefe eines reisenden Franzosen über Deutschland an seinen Bruder zu Paris*, ed. Wolfgang Gerlach, Stuttgart, 1967; quoted in English translation (from which I have borrowed some turns of phrase) in H. C. Robbins Landon, *Haydn: Chronicle and Works*, 5 vols., London, 1976–80, II, 214, and Neal Zaslaw, *Mozart's Symphonies: Context, Performance Practice, Reception*, Oxford, 1989, 100.

21 MBA III, 71; Anderson, 698.

22 MBA I, 408; Anderson, 174.

23 MBA III, 536; Anderson, 897.

24 MBA I, 444; Anderson, 202.

25 MBA IV, 100; Anderson, 935.

26 MBA I, 280; English translation (used here, with minor changes) in Heartz, *Haydn, Mozart, and the Viennese School*, 734.

27 MBA I, 408; Anderson, 174.

28 MBA III, 39–40; Anderson, 677.

29 MBA III, 64; Anderson, 692.

30 MBA III, 71–72; Anderson, 698.

31 MBA III, 69; Anderson, 698.

32 MBA I, 469; Anderson, 221.

33 MBA III, 70; Anderson, 696–697.

34 Tomislav Volek, "Prague Operatic Traditions and Mozart's *Don Giovanni*," in *Mozart's Don Giovanni in Prague*, ed. Jan Kristek, Prague, 1987, 77.

35 Niemetschek, *Mozart*, 87–88.

36 Volek, "Prague Operatic Traditions," 76–78; Heartz, *Mozart's Operas*, 169.

37 Kelly, *Reminiscences*, I, 255–256.

38 Da Ponte, *Memorie*, 116–117.

39 MBA III, 66; Anderson, 693.

40 Daniel Heartz, "Raaff's Last Aria: A Mozartian Idyll in the Spirit of Hasse," *Musical Quarterly* LX (1974), 517–543.

41 Tyson, *Mozart* , 177–221.

42 Edge, *Mozart's Viennese Copyists*, 1922–1961.

43 MDL, 480–481; Deutsch, 568.

44 MBA I, 510; Anderson, 253–254.

45 Heartz, *Haydn, Mozart, and the Viennese School*, 605.

46 MBA III, 536; Anderson, 897.

47 MBA IV, 54–55; Anderson, 911.

48 MBA IV, 55; Anderson, 911–912.

49 Quoted in Frederick C. Petty, *Italian Opera in London, 1760–1800*, Ann Arbor, MI, 1980, 258.

50 MDL, AC, 99–100. My thanks to Michael Lorenz for telling me of this anecdote.

51 MBA III, 20; Anderson, 664.

52 Quoted in Kelly, *First Nights at the Opera*, 108.

53 Georg Nikolaus von Nissen, *Biographie W. A. Mozarts*, Leipzig, 1828, 519–520. Štěpánek, born in 1783, could not have witnessed this incident himself. His source was probably the double bassist Wenzel Swoboda, whom Wilhelm Kuhe, retelling the story much later, cited as his source. According to Kuhe the incident took place at the dress rehearsal. In response to Zerlina's cry Mozart said: "Admirable! Mind you scream like that tonight!" (Kuhe, *My Musical Recollections*, 9–10).

54 MDL, 266; Deutsch, 302.

55 Mosel, *Salieri*, 35.

8 Theaters and stage design

1 The earliest testimony associating the commission and performance of *Bastien und Bastienne* with Mesmer is Nissen, *Biographie W. A. Mozart's*, 127.

2 That no libretto for the first production of *La finta giardiniera* exists may mean that none was printed; that would have been in keeping with a performance in the court ballroom, where comic operas were sometimes performed during Carnival balls. Mozart's statements, in a letter to his mother reporting the successful premiere of *La finta giardiniera* (MBA I, 516), that the opera was performed "on stage" ("in scena"), and that "the whole theater was so packed that a great many people were turned away" have been cited as evidence that the premiere took place in the Salvatortheater. But the presence of a stage ("Theater" in eighteenth-century German) at one end of the Redoutensaal leaves open the possibility that *La finta giardiniera* was first performed there.

3 Hansell, *Opera and Ballet*, 135–158.

4 Hildegard Steinmetz and Johann Lachner, *Das Alte Residenztheater zu München: "Cuvilliéstheater,"* Starnberg, c. 1959; Herbert Brunner, *Das Altes Residenztheater in Munich (Cuvilliés-Theater)*, Munich, 1972.

5 Konrad Zobel and Frederick E. Warner, "The Old Burgtheater: A Structural History, 1741–1888," *Theatre Studies* no. 19 (1972–73), 19–53; Otto G. Schindler, "Der Zuschauerraum des Burgtheaters im 18. Jahrhundert," *Maske und Kothurn* XXII (1976), 20–53; Daniel Heartz, "Nicolas Jadot and the Building of the Burgtheater," *Musical Quarterly* XLVIII (1982), 1–31.

6 On the Nostitz Theater, see Jiří Hilmera, "The Theatre of Mozart's *Don Giovanni*," in *Mozart's Don Giovanni in Prague*, ed. Jan Kristek, Prague, 1987, 12–20. On the Theater auf der Wieden, see Otto Erich Deutsch, *Das Freihaustheater auf der Wieden 1787–1801*, Vienna, 1937; Else Spiesberger, *Das Freihaus*, Vienna, 1980, 39–60; Evan Baker, "Theaters in Vienna during Mozart's Lifetime," *Mozart Jahrbuch 1991*, 984–990; and Michael Lorenz, "New Archival Documentation on the Theater auf der Wieden and Emanuel Schikaneder," forthcoming in the proceedings of the conference "*Die Zauberflöte*: Sources, Interpretations," Brussels, 1–2 December 2006.

7 These measurements are from the plans reproduced here, with *braccia milanesi*, *pieds de France*, and *Wiener Klafter* converted to meters at the following approximate rates: 1 *braccio* = 0.59 m, 1 *pied* = 0.32 m, and 1 *Klafter* = 1.9 m.

8 Hansell, *Opera and Ballet*, 110–111.

9 Burney, *Music, Men, and Manners*, 45.

10 These figures are derived from subscription lists for the theatrical season 1786–87 in Link, *The National Court Theatre*, 463–466. Whether there were also boxes in the third tier is uncertain, since subscriptions in the third tier were for individual seats rather than boxes.

11 According to a description of the soon-to-be-opened Nostitz Theater in the *Theaterkalender auf das Jahr 1783*, Gotha, 1782, 274–276, quoted in Věra Ptáčková, "Scenography of Mozart's *Don Giovanni* in Prague," in *Mozart's Don Giovanni in Prague*, ed. Jan Kristek, Prague, 1987, 96.

12 I use the terminology of Iain Mackintosh, "Scenic Stage, Acting Stage, Orchestra Pit and Auditorium: A Review of 20th Century Research and Practice on how these Areas connect in European 18th Century Theatres," in *The World of Baroque Theatre*, ed. Jarmila Musilová, Český Krumlov, 2003, 9–23. The distinction between forestage and scenic stage is clear in eighteenth-century discussions of theatrical design, for example in a printed notice dating from around the time of the construction of the Regio Ducal Teatro in Milan and preserved in the Archivio di Stato, Milan. It divides the theater into three parts: the *uditorio*, the *proscenio* for the action and the *scena* for the scenery (*la rappresentazione*; Hansell, *Opera and Ballet*, 139). Note that this three-fold division makes no provision for an orchestral area separate from the auditorium.

13 According to Antonio Planelli, *Dell'opera in musica*, Naples, 1772, ed. Francesco Degrada, Fiesole, 1981, 98, the three qualities most essential to a successful stage design were "vastità, novità e verisimiglianza."

14 Five banks of grooves are indicated on the plan reproduced here; but another version of the plan shows six banks of grooves; see Baker, "Theaters in Vienna during Mozart's Lifetime."

15 Mercedes Viale Ferrero, *La scenografia del '700 e i fratelli Galliari*, Turin, 1963; and Mercedes Viale Ferrero, "Gli allestimenti scenici delle opere in musica composte da Mozart o viste da Mozart in Italia," in *Atti del XIV congresso internazionale della Società Internazionale di Musicologia: trasmissione e recezione delle forme di cultura musicale*, ed. Angelo Pompilio *et al.*, 3 vols., 1990, III, 293–306; Hansell, *Opera and Ballet*, 230–244.

16 Sketches for some of the sets designed by the Galliari for Gasparini's *Mitridate* are reproduced in Viale Ferrero, *La scenografia del '700*, 168, 169, 227. On the Galliari's reuse of existing scenery see Hansell, *Opera and Ballet*, 233–235.

17 Mercedes Viale Ferrero, "Le scene per il 'Lucio Silla' di Mozart al Regio Ducal Teatro di Milano," in *Milano e la Lombardia al tempo dei soggiorni milanesi di Mozart*, exhibition catalogue, Como, 1991, 31–38.

18 My thanks to Dorothea Link for sending me photocopies of payment records "für die Decoration Illumin: und das Feuer" for the theatrical year 1786–87 (Haus-, Hof- und Staatsarchiv, Generalintendenz der Hoftheater, Rechnungsbücher), in which no permanent scenic painter is listed.

19 Otto Michtner, *Das alte Burgtheater als Opernbühne von der Einführung des deutschen Singspiels (1778) bis zum Tod Kaiser Leopolds II. (1792)*, Vienna, 1970, 280.

20 Michtner, *Das alte Burgtheater*, 280.

21 Memorandum from Rosenberg to Emperor Franz, 10 October 1792, transcribed in
    Elisabeth Großegger, *Das Burgtheater und sein Publikum*, vol. 2: *Pächter und Publikum*,
    1794–1817, Vienna, 1989, 65–66.
22 Mosel, quoted in Rice, *Salieri*, 149.
23 *Historisch-Kritische Theaterchronik* 11 (29 October 1774), 166–167; quoted in
    Angermüller, *Leben* II, 41, and, in English translation, in Rice, *Salieri*, 216.
24 Rice, *Salieri*, 471–474.
25 Facsimile of the libretto published for the first production of Mozart's *La clemenza
    di Tito*, Prague, 2006.
26 Sergio Durante, "Le scenografie di Pietro Travaglia per 'La clemenza di Tito,'
    (Praga, 1791): problemi di identificazione ed implicazioni," *Mozart-Jahrbuch* 1994,
    157–169.
27 Fabrizio Galliari, in his sketches for Salieri's *Europa riconosciuta* (Milan, 1778)
    differentiated between *cortissima* and *corta* in two successive sets: "V. Carcere
    oscuro [scena] cortissima . . . VI. Gabinetto nella Reggia. [Scena] corta." See
    Mercedes Viale Ferrero, "I 'pensieri' di Fabrizio Galliari per *Europa riconosciuta*,"
    program book for the production of Salieri's *Europa riconosciuta* at La Scala, Milan,
    2004, 120.
28 Viale Ferrero, *La scenografia del '700*, 178, 226, 246; Heartz, *Haydn, Mozart, and the
    Viennese School*, 551.
29 Durante, "The Chronology of Mozart's 'La clemenza di Tito' Reconsidered," 570–
    571.
30 Christof Bitter, *Wandlungen in den Inszenierungsformen des "Don Giovanni" von 1787
    bis 1928*, Regensburg, 1961, 34. Julian Rushton, *W. A. Mozart: Don Giovanni*,
    Cambridge, 1981, 8–26, follows Bitter's distribution of long and short sets, using
    the phrases "full stage" and "half stage."
31 Michel Noiray, "Interrogations sur le *rondò* de Donna Anna," in *D'un opéra l'autre:
    hommage à Jean Mongrédien*, ed. Jean Gribenski et al., Paris, 1996, 253–261.
32 Kelly, *First Nights at the Opera*, 107.
33 Ptáčková, "Scenography of Mozart's *Don Giovanni* in Prague," 96–113.
34 Ptáčková, "Scenography of Mozart's *Don Giovanni* in Prague," 98–99, 111.
35 David J. Buch, "Mozart and the Theater auf der Wieden: New Attributions and
    Perspectives," *Cambridge Opera Journal* IX (1997), 195–232; and David J. Buch, "*Der
    Stein der Weisen*, Mozart, and Collaborative Singspiels at Emanuel Schikaneder's
    Theater auf der Wieden," *Mozart-Jahrbuch* 2000, 91–126.
36 Emanuel Schikaneder, *Der Stein der Weisen* (critical edn. of the libretto), ed. David J.
    Buch and Manuela Jahrmärker, Göttingen, 2002; *Der Stein der Weisen* (critical edn.
    of the opera), ed. David J. Buch, Middleton, WI, 2007.
37 This engraving is reproduced and discussed in Buch, "*Der Stein der Weisen*,
    Mozart, and Collaborative Singspiels," 114, and in David J. Buch, "Newly

Identified Engravings of Scenes from Emanuel Schikaneder's Theater auf der Wieden 1789–1790 in the *Allmanach für Theaterfreunde* (1791)," *Theater am Hof und für das Volk: Beiträge zur vergleichenden Theater- und Kulturgeschichte (Festschrift für Otto G. Schindler zum 60. Geburtstag)*, ed. Brigitte Marschall, Vienna, 2002, 343–369.

38 Baker, "Theaters in Vienna during Mozart's Lifetime," interprets the picture somewhat differently, seeing Lubano's house as constituting the first of four wing flats.

9 The audience

1 [Ange Goudar], *Supplement au supplement sur les remarques de la musique et de la danse ou Lettres de Mr. G . . . a Milord Pembroke*, n. p., 1774, 106.

2 Quoted in translation (used here, with some changes) in Hansell, *Opera and Ballet*, 117.

3 John Rosselli, *The Opera Industry in Italy from Cimarosa to Verdi: The Role of the Impresario*, Cambridge, 1984, 42–43.

4 Quoted in English translation (used here) in Ernest Eugene Helm, *Music at the Court of Frederick the Great*, Norman, OK, 1960, 94, from Louis Schneider, *Geschichte der Oper und des königlichen Opernhauses in Berlin*, Berlin, 1852, 21, who cites "Briefe zur Erinnerung an merkwürdige Zeiten und rühmliche Personen aus dem Zeitlaufe von 1740 bis 1778."

5 Quoted in translation (used here, with minor changes) in Hansell, *Opera and Ballet*, 100.

6 Charles Burney, *The Present State of Music in Germany, the Netherlands, and United Provinces*, 2nd edn., London, 1775.

7 Letter from Kaunitz to Joseph, 22 July 1781, in *Joseph II. Leopold II. und Kaunitz: Ihr Briefwechsel*, ed. Adolf Beer, Vienna, 1873, 92. The dancers mentioned were Auguste Vestris and Anne Heinel.

8 Joseph to Kaunitz, Versailles, 31 July 1781, in *Joseph II., Leopold II. und Kaunitz: Ihr Briefwechsel*, 101.

9 Francesco Albergati Capacelli and Francesco Zacchiroli, *Lettere capricciose*, Venice, 1780–81, quoted in John A. Rice, "Sense, Sensibility, and Opera Seria: An Epistolary Debate," *Studi musicali* XV (1986), 101–138.

10 MBA IV, 10; Anderson, 904.

11 MBA I, 414; Anderson, 178–179.

12 MBA I, 414; Anderson, 179.

13 MBA IV, 160; Anderson, 969.

14 Kelly, *Reminiscences*, I, 64–65.

15 Ferrari, *Aneddoti*, 189.

16 Ferrari, *Aneddoti*, 185.

17 Ferrari, *Aneddoti*, 209. A *duetto da piazza* is perhaps a duet of the kind street musicians might sing.

18 Quoted in Rice, "Sense, Sensibility, and Opera Seria," 114–115.

19 Burney, *Music, Men and Manners*, 46.

20 Quoted in translation (used here) in Rice, *Salieri*, 250.

21 Zinzendorf's remarks on Viennese theater from 1783 to 1792 have been transcribed (in the original French) and annotated in Link, *The National Court Theatre*, 204–398. In the discussion that follows, all quotations from Zinzendorf's diary during the period 1783–92 use Link's edition; other quotations are based on my own transcriptions from the original manuscript.

22 "M. Keith, a coté duquel je me trouvois, me rendit tres attentif a la musique de la *Secchia rapita* petit opera Italien, ou le sérieux est merveilleusement allié avec le Comique. La musique est de Salieri, la fin du Ier acte admirable."

23 "On donna *Alceste*... c'est un opera de Calzabigi tres lugubre... Les choeurs n'ont rien de saillant, la piece est éternellement triste."

24 "*La fiera di venezia* m'ennuya, il n'y a rien qu'une tres belle musique." Quoted in Rice, *Salieri*, 193.

25 "Sot opera, les hommes en femmes, les femmes en hommes. Belle musique." Quoted in Rice, *Salieri*, 545.

26 MBA III, 153; Anderson, 762.

27 "Mandini et la Sessi faisent les notes que fesoit autre fois Benucci et la Storace, mais quelle difference!" Zinzendorf, 5 July 1795.

28 Link, *The National Court Theatre*, 205.

10 Performance and reception

1 MBA III, 212; Anderson, 807.

2 MBA I, 472; Anderson, 223.

3 Mosel, *Salieri*, 35.

4 MBA I, 409; Anderson, 174.

5 MBA I, 411; Anderson, 175–176.

6 MDL, 267; Deutsch, 303–304.

7 MDL, 380–381; Deutsch, 432–433.

8 MDL, 241; Deutsch, 276.

9 Ignaz Seyfried, "Commentar zur Erzählung: Johan Schenk, von J. P. Leyser," *Neue Zeitschrift für Musik* XII (1840), 184, quoted in Buch, "Three Posthumous Reports Concerning Mozart in His Late Viennese Years," 129.

10 Niemetschek, *Mozart*, 88.

11 Novello, *A Mozart Pilgrimage*, 113.

12 MBA, III, 212; Anderson, 807–808.

13 MDL, 244; Deutsch, 278.

14 MDL, 246; Deutsch, 281.

15 As quoted in Kuhe, *My Musical Recollections*, 9.

16 MDL, 267; Deutsch, 303.

17 MBA I, 471–472; Anderson, 223.

18 MBA I, 516–517; Anderson, 259.

19 Heartz, *Haydn, Mozart, and the Viennese School*, 605.

20 All data on the number of performances in this and the following paragraphs are from Hadamowsky, *Die Wiener Hoftheater*, part 1.

21 The quotations from Zinzendorf's diary in this paragraph are derived from transcriptions in Link, *The National Court Theatre*.

22 Link, *The National Court Theatre*, 350.

23 MBA I, 516; Anderson, 259.

24 Heartz, *Haydn, Mozart, and the Viennese School*, 605.

25 MBA I, 411; Anderson, 176.

26 MDL, 117; Deutsch, 130–131.

27 MBA I, 416; Anderson, 180.

28 MBA III, 212; Anderson, 808.

29 MBA III, 215; Anderson, 810.

30 MDL, 180; Deutsch, 203.

31 MDL, 243–244; Deutsch, 278–279.

32 MDL, 241; Deutsch, 275.

33 Niemetschek, *Mozart*, 37–39.

34 MDL, 240–241; Deutsch, 275.

35 Link, *The National Court Theatre*, 386; Deutsch, 412.

36 *Vertraute Briefe zur Charakteristik von Wien*, 2 vols., Görlitz, 1793, II, 50–53, quoted in English translation (used here, with minor changes), in Branscombe, *W. A. Mozart: Die Zauberflöte*, 158–159.

37 Letter dated Vienna, 13 October 1792, in John Owen, *Travels into different Parts of Europe in the Years 1791 and 1792*, quoted in Eisen, 76–77.

38 Da Ponte, *Memorie*, 131–132.

39 MDL, 277; Deutsch, 315.

40 MDL, 276; Deutsch, 314.

41 Link, *The National Court Theatre*, 315.

42 Link, *The National Court Theatre*, 382.

43 MDL, ANF, 71.

44 MDL, AC; Deutsch, 411. Guardasoni's contract, as quoted and discussed in chapter 3, made no provision for the compensation he sought.

45 MDL, AC, 81; translation (used here, with some changes) in Landon, *1791: Mozart's Last Year*, New York, 1988, 117.

46 MBA IV, 157; Anderson, 967.

47 MBA III, 295; Anderson, 862.

48 Ferrari, *Aneddoti*, 222.

49 Kelly, *Reminiscences*, I, 255.

50 *Allgemeine musikalische Zeitung* I (1798–99), cols. 20–22. Solomon, *Mozart*, 447, doubts the veracity of Rochlitz's anecdote.

51 MDL, ANF, 66.

52 MBA IV, 58; Niemetschek, *Mozart*, 96.

53 MBA III, 213; Anderson, 808.

54 MBA III, 471; Anderson, 895.

55 MBA IV, 10; Anderson, 903.

56 MBA IV, 28; Anderson, 906.

57 Contracts under which copyists for the Teatro Regio in Turin operated specified the amount of time they could keep a composer's original score. A contract dated 1765 allowed the copyists Francesco Antonio and Giuseppe Antonio Le Messier to keep the autograph score for "three months after every Carnival, with permission granted to them to make copies of everything they please" (transcribed in Butler, *Operatic Reform*, 237).

58 MBA I, 408; Anderson, 174.

59 MBA I, 416; Anderson, 180.

60 MBA III, 231; Anderson, 822.

61 MBA III, 231–232; Anderson, 822.

62 MBA III, 236; Anderson, 826.

63 MBA IV, 157; Anderson, 967.

A complete bibliography of the scholarly and critical literature on Mozart's operas would fill several volumes. This list is limited mostly to books and articles cited in this book and does not include the books already cited in the list of abbreviations.

Abert, Hermann, W. A. Mozart, 3rd edn., 2 vols., Leipzig, 1955–56

Adrian, Irene, "Rolle und Bedeutung der Kastraten in Leben und Werk Wolfgang Amadeus Mozarts," in Mozart: gli orientamenti della critica moderna, ed. Giacomo Fornari, Lucca, 1994

Allanbrook, Wye Jamison, Rhythmic Gesture in Mozart: Le nozze di Figaro and Don Giovanni, Chicago, 1983

Angermüller, Rudolph, Antonio Salieri: Seine Leben und seine weltlichen Werke unter besonderer Berücksichtigung seiner "großen" Opern, 3 vols., Munich, 1974
Mozart's Operas, New York, 1988

Armbruster, Richard, "Salieri, Mozart und die Wiener Fassung des Giulio Sabino von Giuseppe Sarti: Opera seria und 'Rondò-Mode' an der italienischen Oper Josephs II," Studien zur Musikwissenschaft XLV (1996), 133–166

Armellini, Mario, "L'olimpiade del Metastasio ristretta in due atti: Luigi Gatti, Domenico Cimarosa ed il dramma per musica a fine Settecento" in Domenico Cimarosa: Un 'napoletano' in Europa, ed. Paologiovanni Maione and Marta Columbro, 2 vols., Lucca, 2004, 1, 29–158

Baker, Evan, "Theaters in Vienna during Mozart's Lifetime," Mozart-Jahrbuch 1991, 984–990

Bauman, Thomas, W. A. Mozart: Die Entführung aus dem Serail, Cambridge, 1987
"Coming of Age in Vienna: Die Entführung aus dem Serail," in Daniel Heartz, Mozart's Operas, ed. Thomas Bauman, Berkeley, CA, 1990, 64–87
"Mozart's Belmonte," Early Music XIX (1991), 557–563
"Salieri, Da Ponte, and Mozart: The Renewal of Viennese Opera Buffa in the 1780s," in Internationaler Musikwissenschaftlicher Kongress zum Mozartjahr 1991 Baden-Wien: Bericht, ed. Ingrid Fuchs, Tutzing, 1993, 65–70

Berkovec, Jiří, Musicalia v pražkém periodickém tisku 18. století, Prague, 1989

Bitter, Christof, *Wandlungen in den Inszenierungsformen des "Don Giovanni" von 1787 bis 1928*, Regensburg, 1961

Böhmer, Karl, *W. A. Mozarts* Idomeneo *und die Tradition der Karnevalsopern in München*, Tutzing, 1999

"Zum Wandel des Münchner Operngeschmacks vor *Idomeneo*: Die Karnevalsopern am Cuvilliés-Theater, 1753–1780," in *Mozarts* Idomeneo *und die Musik in München zur Zeit Karl Theodors*, ed. Theodor Göllner and Stephan Hörner, Munich, 2001, 9–37

Branscombe, Peter, *W. A. Mozart*: Die Zauberflöte, Cambridge, 1991

Brauneis, Walther, "Wer war Mozarts 'Sig[no]ra Antonini' in der Prager Uraufführung von 'La clemenza di Tito'? Zur Identifizierung der Antonina Miklaszewicz als Interpretin der Servilia in der Krönungsoper am 6. September 1791," *Mitteilungen der Internationalen Stiftung Mozarteum*, XLVII (1999), 32–40

Brophy, Brigid, *Mozart the Dramatist*, New York, 1964

Brown, Bruce Alan, *W. A. Mozart*: Così fan tutte, Cambridge, 1995

Brown, Bruce Alan and John A. Rice, "Salieri's *Così fan tutte*," *Cambridge Opera Journal* VIII (1996), 17–43

Brown-Montesano, Kristi, *Understanding the Women of Mozart's Operas*, Berkeley, CA, 2007

Brunner, Herbert, *Altes Residenztheater in Munich (Cuvilliés-Theater)*, Munich, 1972

Buch, David J., "Mozart and the Theater auf der Wieden: New Attributions and Perspectives," *Cambridge Opera Journal* IX (1997), 195–232

"*Der Stein der Weisen*, Mozart, and Collaborative Singspiels at Emanuel Schikaneder's Theater auf der Wieden," *Mozart-Jahrbuch* 2000, 91–126

"Newly Identified Engravings of Scenes from Emanuel Schikaneder's Theater auf der Wieden 1789–1790 in the *Allmanach für Theaterfreunde* (1791)," *Theater am Hof und für das Volk: Beiträge zur vergleichenden Theater- und Kulturgeschichte (Festschrift für Otto G. Schindler zum 60. Geburtstag)*, ed. Brigitte Marschall, Vienna, 2002, 343–369

"Three Posthumous Reports Concerning Mozart in His Late Viennese Years," *Eighteenth-Century Music* II (2005), 125–129

Burney, Charles, *The Present State of Music in Germany, the Netherlands, and United Provinces*, 2nd edn., London, 1775

Music, Men, and Manners in France and Italy, 1770, ed. H. Edmund Poole, London, 1974

Butler, Margaret, *Operatic Reform at Turin's Teatro Regio: Aspects of Production and Stylistic Change in the 1760s*, Lucca, 2001

"Vicente Martín y Soler's Operas for Turin's Teatro Regio: Elements of
    Production and Ensemble Writing in *Andromeda* (1780) and *Vologeso* (1783),"
    forthcoming in the proceedings of the conference "The Many Worlds of
    Vicente Martín Vicente y Soler," Valencia, 14–18 November 2006
Cairns, David, *Mozart and His Operas*, Berkeley, CA, 2006
Campana, Alessandra, "Mozart's Italian Buffo Singers," *Early Music* XIX (1991),
    580–583
Carter, Tim, *W. A. Mozart: Le nozze di Figaro*, Cambridge, 1987
Cerocchi, Antonietta, "Il Teatro Alibert o 'delle dame' nella seconda metà del
    Settecento: struttura e organizzazione," in *Mozart, Padova e La Betulia
    liberata*, ed. Paolo Pinamonti, Florence, 1991, 395–405
Cole, Malcolm S., "Mozart and Two Theaters in Josephinian Vienna," in *Opera in
    Context: Essays on Historical Staging from the Late Renaissance to the Time of Puccini*,
    ed. Mark A. Radice, Portland, OR, 1998, 111–145
Corneilson, Paul, "Mozart's Ilia and Elettra: New Perspectives on *Idomeneo*," in
    Mozarts Idomeneo und die Musik in München zur Zeit Karl Theodors, ed. Theodor
    Göllner and Stephan Hörner, Munich, 2000, 97–113
Da Ponte, Lorenzo, *Memorie*, ed. Cesare Pagnini, Milan, 1960
    Lettere, epistole in versi, dedicatorie e lettere dei fratelli, ed. Giampaolo Zagonel,
        Vittorio Veneto, 1995
    Libretti viennesi, ed. Lorenzo della Chà, 2 vols., Parma, 1999
    An Extract from the Life of Lorenzo da Ponte, New York, 1819; ed. Lorenzo della Chà,
        Milan, 1999
Dent, Edward J., *Mozart's Operas: A Critical Study*, 2nd edn., Oxford, 1947
Deutsch, Otto Erich, *Das Freihaustheater auf der Wieden 1787–1801*, Vienna, 1937
Durante, Sergio, "Le scenografie di Pietro Travaglia per 'La clemenza di Tito'
    (Praga, 1791): problemi di identificazione ed implicazioni," *Mozart-Jahrbuch*
    1994, 157–169
    "The Chronology of Mozart's 'La clemenza di Tito' Reconsidered," *Music &
        Letters* LXXX (1999), 560–594
    "Considerations on Mozart's Changing Approach to Recitatives and on Other
        Choices of Dramaturgical Significance," *Mozart-Jahrbuch* 2001, 233–
        238
Edge, Dexter, "Mozart's Fee for *Così fan tutte*," *Journal of the Royal Musical
    Association* CXVI (1991), 211–235
    "Mozart's Viennese Orchestras," *Early Music* XX (1992), 64–88
    "Mozart's Reception in Vienna, 1787–1791," in *Wolfgang Amadé Mozart: Essays
        on His Life and His Music*, ed. Stanley Sadie, Oxford, 1996, 66–117

Mozart's Viennese Copyists, PhD dissertation, University of Southern California, 2001

Einstein, Alfred, _Mozart: His Character, His Work_, New York, 1945

Feldman, Martha, "Magic Mirrors and the _Seria_ Stage: Thoughts toward a Ritual View," _Journal of the American Musicological Society_ XLVIII (1995), 423–484

Ferrari, Giacomo Gotifredo, _Aneddoti piacevoli e interessanti_, ed. Mariasilvia Tatti, Bergamo, 1998

Frye, Northrop, _Anatomy of Criticism_, Princeton, NJ, 1957

Gianturco, Carolyn, _Mozart's Early Operas_, London, 1981

Gidwitz, Patricia Lewy, "Ich bin die erste Sängerin: Vocal Profiles of Two Mozart Sopranos," _Early Music_ XIX (1991), 565–579

"Mozart's Fiordiligi: Adriana Ferrarese del Bene," _Cambridge Opera Journal_ VIII (1996), 199–214

Goehring, Edmund J., _Three Modes of Perception in Mozart: The Philosophical, Pastoral and Comic in Così fan tutte_, Cambridge, 2004

Großegger, Elisabeth, _Pächter und Publikum, 1794–1817 (Das Burgtheater und sein Publikum, vol. 2)_, Vienna, 1989

The Grotesque Dancer on the Eighteenth-Century Stage: Gennaro Magri and His World, ed. Rebecca Harris-Warrick and Bruce Alan Brown, Madison, WI, 2005

Guccini, Gerardo, "Directing Opera," in _Opera on Stage_, ed. Lorenzo Bianconi and Giorgio Pestelli, trans. Kate Singleton, Chicago, 2002

Gutman, Robert W. _Mozart: A Cultural Biography_, New York, 1999

Hadamowsky, Franz, _Die Wiener Hoftheater (Staatstheater)_, part 1, Vienna, 1966

Hansell, Kathleen, _Opera and Ballet at the Regio Ducal Teatro of Milan, 1771–1776: A Musical and Social History_, PhD dissertation, University of California, Berkeley, 1980

Haydn, Joseph, _Gesammelte Briefe und Aufzeichnungen_, ed. Dénes Bartha, Kassel, 1965

Heartz, Daniel, "Raaff's Last Aria: A Mozartian Idyll in the Spirit of Hasse," _Musical Quarterly_ LX (1974), 517–543

"Nicolas Jadot and the Building of the Burgtheater," _Musical Quarterly_ XLVIII (1982), 1–31

Mozart's Operas, ed. Thomas Bauman, Berkeley, CA, 1990

Haydn, Mozart, and the Viennese School, New York, 1995

"When Mozart Revises: The Case of Guglielmo in _Così fan tutte_," in _Wolfgang Amadé Mozart: Essays on His Life and His Music_, ed. Stanley Sadie, Oxford, 1996, 355–361

"Mozart and Anton Klein," _Newsletter of the Mozart Society of America_ X (2006), no. 1, 7–10

Helm, Ernest Eugene, *Music at the Court of Frederick the Great*, Norman, OK, 1960

Henze-Döhring, Sabine, *Opera seria, opera buffa und Mozarts "Don Giovanni": Zur Gattungskonvergenz in der italienischen Oper des 18. Jahrhunderts*, Laaber, 1986

Hilmera, Jiří, "The Theatre of Mozart's Don Giovanni," in Mozart's Don Giovanni in Prague, ed. Jan Kristek, Prague, 1987, 12–20

Holmes, William C., *Opera Observed: Views of a Florentine Impresario in the Early Eighteenth Century*, Chicago, 1993

Hunter, Mary, "Landscapes, Gardens, and Gothic Settings in the *Opere Buffe* of Mozart and his Italian Contemporaries," *Current Musicology* LI (1993), 94–104

The Culture of Opera Buffa in Mozart's Vienna: A Poetics of Entertainment, Princeton, NJ, 1999

Indice de' teatrali spettacoli, ed. Roberto Verti, 2 vols., Pesaro, 1996

Kelly, Michael, *Reminiscences of Michael Kelly of the King's Theatre and Theatre Royal Drury Lane*, 2nd edn., 2 vols., London, 1826

Kelly, Thomas Forrest, *First Nights at the Opera*, New Haven, CT, 2004

Ketterer, Robert C., "Why Early Opera is Roman and not Greek," *Cambridge Opera Journal* XV (2003), 1–14

Konrad, Ulrich, *Mozarts Schaffensweise: Studien zu den Werkautographen, Skizzen und Entwürfen*, Göttingen, 1992

Kuhe, Wilhelm, *My Musical Recollections*, London, 1896

Kunze, Stefan, *Mozarts Opern*, Stuttgart, 1984

Landon, H. C. Robbins, *Haydn: Chronicle and Works*, 5 vols., London, 1976–80

1791: Mozart's Last Year, New York, 1988

Mozart: The Golden Years, New York, 1989

Lert, Ernst, *Mozart auf dem Theater*, Berlin, 1918

Liebner, János, *Mozart on the Stage*, London, 1972

Link, Dorothea, *The National Court Theatre in Mozart's Vienna: Sources and Documents, 1783–1792*, Oxford, 1998

Lorenz, Michael, "New Archival Documentation on the Theater auf der Wieden and Emanuel Schikaneder," forthcoming in the proceedings of the conference "Die Zauberflöte. Sources, Interpretations," Brussels, 1–2 December 2006

Lühning, Helga, "Zur Entstehungsgeschichte von Mozarts Titus," *Musikforschung* XXVII (1974), 300–318

Titus-Vertonungen im 18. Jahrhundert: Untersuchungen zur Tradition der Opera seria von Hasse bis Mozart, Laaber, 1983

Mackintosh, Iain, "Scenic Stage, Acting Stage, Orchestra Pit and Auditorium: A
    Review of 20th Century Research and Practice on how these Areas Connect
    in European 18th Century Theatres," in *The World of Baroque Theatre*,
    ed. Jarmila Musilová, Český Krumlov, 2003, 9–23
Mann, William, *The Operas of Mozart*, New York, 1977
Mattei, Saverio, "Elogio del Jommelli, o sia Il progresso della poesia, e musica
    teatrale," in *Memorie per servire alla vita del Metastasio*, Colle, 1785, 59–136
McClymonds, Marita, *Niccolò Jommelli: The Last Years, 1769–1774*, Ann Arbor, MI,
    1980
    "Opera seria? Opera buffa? Genre and Style as Sign," in *Opera Buffa in Mozart's
    Vienna*, ed. Mary Hunter and James Webster, Cambridge, 1997, 197–231
Melamed, Daniel R., "Evidence on the Genesis of *Die Entführung aus dem Serail*
    from Mozart's Autograph Score," *Mozart-Jahrbuch* 2003–2004, 25–42.
Michtner, Otto, *Das alte Burgtheater als Opernbühne von der Einführung des deutschen
    Singspiels (1778) bis zum Tod Kaiser Leopolds II. (1792)*, Vienna, 1970
Milhous, Judith, Gabriella Dideriksen, and Robert Hume, *Italian Opera in Late
    Eighteenth-Century London, Volume 2: The Pantheon Opera and Its Aftermath,
    1789–1795*, Oxford, 2001
Mosel, Ignaz von, *Ueber das Leben und die Werke des Anton Salieri*, Vienna, 1827
Mozart and His Operas, ed. Stanley Sadie, London, 2000
Mozart, Padova e La Betulia liberata, ed. Paolo Pinamonti, Florence, 1991
Mozart's Don Giovanni in Prague, ed. Jan Kristek, Prague, 1987
Mozarts Idomeneo und die Musik in München zur Zeit Karl Theodors, ed. Theodor
    Göllner and Stephan Hörner, Munich, 2001
Mozartův Don Giovanni, exhibition catalogue, ed. Tomislav Volek and Jitřenka
    Pešková, Prague, 1987
Münster, Robert, "ich würde München gewis Ehre machen": *Mozart und der Kurfürstliche
    Hof zu München*, Weißenhorn, 2002
Nettl, Paul, *Mozart in Böhmen*, Prague, 1938
Niemetschek, Franz Xaver, *Lebensbeschreibung des K. K. Kapellmeisters Wolfgang
    Amadeus Mozart*, 2nd edn., Prague, 1808; facsimile edn., Laaber, 2005
Nissen, Georg Nikolaus von, *Biographie W. A. Mozart's*, Leipzig, 1828
Noiray, Michel, "Interrogations sur le rondò de Donna Anna," in *D'un opéra l'autre:
    hommage à Jean Mongrédien*, ed. Jean Gribenski et al., Paris, 1996, 253–261
    "La Construction de Don Giovanni," in *L'Avant-scène Opéra: Don Giovanni*, Paris,
    1996
Novello, Vincent and Mary, *A Mozart Pilgrimage, Being the Travel Diaries of Vincent
    and Mary Novello in the Year 1829*, ed. Rosemary Hughes, London, 1955

Opera Buffa in Mozart's Vienna, ed. Mary Hunter and James Webster, Cambridge, 1997

Osborne, Charles, *The Complete Operas of Mozart: A Critical Guide*, New York, 1983

Osthoff, Wolfgang, "Die Opera buffa," *Gattungen der Musik in Einzeldarstellungen: Gedenkschrift Leo Schrade*, ed. Wulf Arlt et al., Bern, 1973, 678–743

Petrobelli, Pierluigi, "The Italian Years of Anton Raaff," *Mozart-Jahrbuch* 1973–74, 233–273

Petty, Frederick C., *Italian Opera in London, 1760–1800*, Ann Arbor, MI, 1980

Pirani, Federico, "L'opera buffa tra Roma e Vienna al tempo di Giuseppe II: Cantanti e repertori," in *Mozart, Padova e La Betulia liberata*, ed. Paolo Pinamonti, Florence, 1991, 407–416

Pirotta, Nino, *Don Giovanni's Progress: A Rake Goes to the Opera*, New York, 1994

Planelli, Antonio, *Dell'opera in musica*, Naples, 1772, ed. Francesco Degrada, Fiesole, 1981

Platoff, John, "Musical and Dramatic Structure in the Opera Buffa Finale," *Journal of Musicology* VII (1989), 191–230

"The Buffa Aria in Mozart's Vienna," *Cambridge Opera Journal* II (1990), 99–120

"Catalogue Arias and the 'Catalogue Aria,'" in *Wolfgang Amadè Mozart: Essays on His Life and His Music*, ed. Stanley Sadie, Oxford, 1996, 296–311

Polzonetti, Pierpaolo, "Mesmerizing Adultery: *Così fan tutte* and the Kornman Scandal," *Cambridge Opera Journal* XIV (2002), 263–296

Pryor, Anthony, "Mozart's Operatic Audition, the Milanese Concert, 12 March 1770: A Reappraisal and Revision," *Eighteenth-Century Music* I (2004), 265–288

Ptáčková, Věra, "Scenography of Mozart's Don Giovanni in Prague," in *Mozart's Don Giovanni in Prague*, ed. Jan Kristek, Prague, 1987, 94–159

Quétin, Laurine, *L'opéra seria de Johann Christian Bach à Mozart*, Geneva, 2003

Rabin, Ronald J., *Mozart, Da Ponte, and the Dramaturgy of Opera Buffa: Italian Comic Opera in Vienna, 1783–1791*, PhD dissertation, Cornell University, 1996

Rice, John A., "Sense, Sensibility, and Opera Seria: An Epistolary Debate," *Studi musicali* XV (1986), 101–138

Emperor and Impresario: Leopold II and the Transformation of Viennese Musical Theater, 1790–1792, PhD dissertation, University of California, Berkeley, 1987

W. A. Mozart: La clemenza di Tito, Cambridge, 1991

"Mozart and His Singers: The Case of Maria Marchetti Fantozzi, the First Vitellia," *Opera Quarterly* XI (1995), 31–52

Antonio Salieri and Viennese Opera, Chicago, 1998

Robinson, Michael F., *Giovanni Paisiello: A Thematic Catalogue of His Works*, vol. 1,
    Stuyvesant, NY, 1991
Rosselli, John, *The Opera Industry in Italy from Cimarosa to Verdi: The Role of the
    Impresario*, Cambridge, 1984
Rushton, Julian, *W. A. Mozart: Don Giovanni*, Cambridge, 1981
    W. A. Mozart: Idomeneo, Cambridge, 1993
    Mozart, Oxford, 2006
    The New Grove Guide to Mozart and His Operas, New York, 2007
Sadie, Stanley, "Some Operas of 1787," *Musical Times* CXXII (1981), 474–477
    Mozart: The Early Years, 1756–1781, New York, 2006
Sartori, Claudio, *I libretti italiani a stampa dalle origini al 1800*, 7 vols., Cuneo,
    1990–94
Schindler, Otto G., "Das Publikum des Burgtheaters in der Josephinischen Ära,"
    in *Das Burgtheater und sein Publikum*, ed. Margret Dietrich, Vienna, 1976,
    11–95
    "Der Zuschauerraum des Burgtheaters im 18. Jahrhundert," *Maske und Kothurn*
    XXII (1976), 20–53
Solomon, Maynard, *Mozart: A Life*, New York, 1995
Spaethling, Robert, *Mozart's Letters, Mozart's Life*, New York, 2000
Spiesberger, Else, *Das Freihaus*, Vienna, 1980
Steinmetz, Hildegard and Johann Lachner, *Das Alte Residenztheater zu München:
    "Cuvilliéstheater,"* Starnberg, c. 1959
Steptoe, Andrew, *The Mozart–Da Ponte Operas: The Cultural and Musical Background to
    Le nozze di Figaro, Don Giovanni and Così fan tutte*, Oxford, 1988
Stiffoni, Gian Giacomo, *"Non son cattivo comico": Caratteri di "riforma" nei drammi
    giocosi di Da Ponte per Vienna*, Turin, 1998
The Collected Correspondence and London Notebooks of Joseph Haydn, ed. H.C. Robbins
    Landon, Fair Lawn, NJ, 1959
Till, Nicholas, *Mozart and the Enlightenment: Truth, Virtue and Beauty in Mozart's
    Operas*, New York, 1993
Tomaschek, Wenzel Johann, "Wenzel Johann Tomaschek, geboren zu Skutsch
    am 17. April 1774: Selbstbiographie," part 1, *Libussa: Jahrbuch für 1845*,
    349–398
Tyson, Alan, *Mozart: Studies of the Autograph Scores*, Cambridge, MA, 1987
Vertraute Briefe zur Charakteristik von Wien, 2 vols., Görlitz, 1793
Viale Ferrero, Mercedes, *La scenografia del '700 e i fratelli Galliari*, Turin, 1963
    "Gli allestimenti scenici delle opere in musica composte da Mozart o viste da
    Mozart in Italia," in *Atti del XIV congresso internazionale della Società*

Internazionale di Musicologia: trasmissione e recezione delle forme di cultura musicale, eds. Angelo Pompilio et al., 3 vols., 1990, III, 293–306

"Le scene per il 'Lucio Silla' di Mozart al Regio Ducal Teatro di Milano," in Milano e la Lombardia al tempo dei soggiorni milanesi di Mozart, exhibition catalogue, Como, 1991, 31–38

"I 'pensieri' di Fabrizio Galliari per Europa riconosciuta," program book for the production of Salieri's Europa riconosciuta at La Scala, Milan, 2004, 118–188

Volek, Tomislav, "Über den Ursprung von Mozarts Oper 'La clemenza di Tito,'" Mozart-Jahrbuch 1959, 274–286

"Prague Operatic Traditions and Mozart's Don Giovanni," in Mozart's Don Giovanni in Prague, ed. Jan Kristek, Prague, 1987, 22–91

Waldoff, Jessica, "Don Giovanni: Recognition Denied," in Opera Buffa in Mozart's Vienna, ed. Mary Hunter and James Webster, Cambridge, 1997, 286–307

Recognition in Mozart's Operas, New York, 2006

Weaver, Robert Lamar and Norma Wright Weaver, A Chronology of Music in the Florentine Theater, 1751–1800, Warren, MI, 1993

Webster, James, "The Analysis of Mozart's Arias," Mozart Studies I, ed. Cliff Eisen, Oxford, 1991, 101–199

Weigl, Joseph, "Zwei Selbstbiographien von Joseph Weigl (1766–1846)," ed. Rudolph Angermüller, Deutsches Jahrbuch der Musikwissenschaft XVI (1971), 46–85

Weiss, Piero, "Opera and Neoclassical Dramatic Criticism in the Seventeenth Century," Studies in the History of Music II (1988), 1–30

Wignall, Harrison James, Mozart, Guglielmo d'Ettore and the Composition of Mitridate (K. 87/74a), PhD dissertation, Brandeis University, 1995

Wolfgang Amadé Mozart: Essays on His Life and His Music, ed. Stanley Sadie, Oxford, 1996

Woodfield, Ian, "New Light on the Mozarts' London Visit: A Private Concert with Manzuoli," Music & Letters LXXVI (1995), 187–208

"Lovers Crossed or Uncrossed?", Inaugural Lecture, Queens University Belfast, 6 May 2000 (unpublished)

Mozart's Così fan tutte: A Compositional History, Woodbridge, Suffolk, 2008

Zaslaw, Neal, Mozart's Symphonies: Context, Performance Practice, Reception, Oxford, 1989

Zobel, Konrad and Frederick E. Warner, "The Old Burgtheater: A Structural History, 1741–1888," Theatre Studies no. 19 (1972–73), 19–53

Żórawska-Witkowska, Alina, Muzyka na dworze i w teatrze Stanisława Augusta, Warsaw, 1995

INDEX